# THE ORACLES OF GOD

# CONCORDIA ACADEMIC PRESS

# THE ORACLES OF GOD

## The Old Testament Canon

Andrew E. Steinmann

CONCORDIA PUBLISHING HOUSE · SAINT LOUIS

ACADEMIC PRESS

**Library of Congress Cataloging-in-Publication Data.**

Steinmann, Andrew.
    The oracles of God : the Old Testament canon / Andrew E. Steinmann.
        p.    cm.
    Includes biographical references and index.
    ISBN 0-570-04282-8
    1. Bible.  O.T.—Canon.  I. Title.
BS1135.S67    1999
221.1'2—dc21                                    99-30819

2  3  4  5  6  7  8  9  10  11      14  13  12  11  10  09  08  07  06  05

# Contents

# Tables

# Figures

# Pictured Manuscripts

# Abbreviations

| | |
|---|---|
| AB | Anchor Bible |
| *ABD* | *Anchor Bible Dictionary* |
| *AUSS* | *Andrews University Seminary Studies* |
| *BA* | *Biblical Archaeologist* |
| *BASOR* | *Bulletin of the American Schools of Oriental Research* |
| *BBR* | *Bulletin for Biblical Research* |
| *BETS* | *Bulletin of the Evangelical Theological Society* |
| *BJRL* | *Bulletin of the John Rylands University Library of Manchester* |
| *BRev* | *Bible Review* |
| *BSac* | *Bibliotheca Sacra* |
| *BZ* | *Biblische Zeitschrift* |
| BZAW | Beihefte zur *ZAW* |
| *CBQ* | *Catholic Biblical Quarterly* |
| CRINT | Compendia rerum iudaicarum ad novum testamentum |
| *CurTM* | *Currents in Theology and Mission* |
| DJD | Discoveries in the Judaean Desert |
| *EDNT* | Horst Balz and Gerhard Schneider, eds. *Exegetical Dictionary of the New Testament* |
| *EvQ* | *Evangelical Quarterly* |
| HSS | Harvard Semitic Studies |
| *HTR* | *Harvard Theological Review* |
| *HUCA* | *Hebrew Union College Annual* |
| *IB* | *Interpreter's Bible* |
| *IBHS* | Bruce K. Waltke and M. O'Connor, *An Introduction to Biblical Hebrew Syntax.* (Winona Lake, IN: Eisenbrauns, 1990). |
| *Int* | *Interpretation* |
| *JBL* | *Journal of Biblical Literature* |
| *JBR* | *Journal of Bible and Religion* |
| *JETS* | *Journal of the Evangelical Theological Society* |
| *JJS* | *Journal of Jewish Studies* |

| JSNTSup | Journal for the Study of the New Testament — Supplement Series |
| JSOTSup | Journal for the Study of the Old Testament — Supplement Series |
| *JTS* | *Journal of Theological Studies* |
| LSJ | Liddell-Scott-Jones, *Greek-English Lexicon* [http://www.perseus.tufts.edu/cgi-bin/resolveform] |
| NRSV | New Revised Standard Version |
| *OTP* | J. H. Charlesworth, ed. *Old Testament Pseudepigrapha* |
| *OTS* | *Oudtestamentische Studiën* |
| *PG* | J. Migne, *Patrologia graeca* |
| *PL* | J. Migne, *Patrologia latina* |
| *RevQ* | *Revue de Qumran* |
| *RHPR* | *Revue d'histoire et de philosophie religieuses* |
| *SR* | *Studies in Religion/Sciences religieuses* |
| *ST* | *Studia Theologica* |
| STDJ | Studies on the Texts of the Desert of Judah |
| *TDNT* | G. Kittel and G. Friedrich (eds.) *Theological Dictionary of the New Testament* |
| *TynBul* | *Tyndale Bulletin* |
| *VT* | *Vetus Testamentum* |
| *WTJ* | *Westminster Theological Journal* |
| *ZAW* | *Zeitschrift für die alttestamentliche Wissenschaft* |
| *ZNW* | *Zeitschrift für die neutestamentliche Wissenschaft* |

*The Great Isaiah Scroll* (1QIsᵃ), the Albright Institute of Archaeological Research and the Shrine of the Book. Jerusalem, 1972. William Cloves and Sons, Limited, London.

# 1

# Introduction

Modern discussions of the Old Testament canon date to Luther's rejection of the apocrypha in 1519. In a debate with Johannes Eck at Leipzig, Luther admitted that Eck had correctly quoted 2 Maccabees 12:46 and did not dispute that it encouraged prayers for the dead. Luther did, however, deny the canonical status of 2 Maccabees. Yet, Luther was not the first. Questions of the extent of the canon have been a subject among Christians since the second century. Originally the question was largely a debate over whether certain books belonged in the Bible (with a few exceptions such as Esther, this involved the apocryphal/deuterocanonical books). However, for Christians from various traditions today the question of the extent of the OT canon has been settled for their particular tradition.[1] Roman Catholics accept a wider canon that includes books not found in the Jewish canon. Protestants reject these additional books, although they differ on their usefulness.[2]

---

[1] The only possible exceptions are the ambiguous approach of the Eastern Orthodox churches, the wider canon of the Ethiopic church, and the Eastern Syriac canon. See Elias Oikonomos, "The Significance of the Deuterocanonical Writing in the Orthodox Church," in *The Apocrypha in Ecumenical Perspective*, ed. Siegfried Meurer. UBS Monograph Series 6 (Reading, UK: United Bible Societies, 1992), 16–32; Hans Peter Rüger, "The Extent of the Old Testament Canon," in *The Apocrypha in Ecumenical Perspective*, 151–60.

[2] Traditionally Lutherans and Anglicans have retained the apocrypha and placed them between the Testaments as useful reading (see Luther's German Bible or the original arrangement of books in the King James Version). Both have at times included these books as part of the lectionary readings. However, due to the influence of Reformed and, later, evangelical Christians, especially in the United States and Canada, many

For Protestants this rejection of the apocrypha stems from a historical question of the extent of the canon used by Jesus and his apostles. The Reformers answered this question when they accepted the Hebrew OT. They asserted that this was the canon in use by Jews in Jesus' day. Protestants, therefore, have rejected the apocrypha. For the Roman Catholic Church the question of Christian tradition is of primary importance (which itself implies a historical question). The Council of Trent affirmed the canonical status of the wider OT canon. Therefore, Catholics prefer to call the books labeled *apocrypha* by Protestants *deuterocanonical* books.

This study addresses the historical question of the OT canon. Simply put, this question is: Was the canon formed and accepted among Jews by the time of Jesus and the apostles, or was it still to be formed? This question is of primary importance for deciding between the competing claims on the canon. If the canon was not formed in Jesus' day, then the church would have nowhere to look except to its own traditions to determine the extent of the canon. However, if a generally accepted canon did exist in Jesus' day, then later tradition may not be valid, especially for those Christians who reject tradition as determinative of doctrine.

To answer this question, I will examine the historical evidence for the OT canon from the second century BC through the third century AD, with some references to the fourth century as appropriate. This chapter will deal with preliminary questions: definition of *canon*, modern theories on the formation of the canon, and the method of investigation into the question of the canon. Subsequent chapters will examine the evidence for the canon from the second century BC through the fourth century AD. The final chapter will summarize the evidence and the conclusions about the OT canon.

## A Definition of Canon

The English word *canon* was derived from the Greek word κανών which means *reed* or *measuring stick*. An additional meaning—*rule*—was derived from this basic meaning. The New Testament (Gal. 6:16) and the early church fathers used the word with this additional meaning. Later, the word came to be used to describe a collection of books viewed

---

Episcopalians and nearly all Lutherans in North America use Bibles without the apocrypha.

as sacred and authoritative for Christian faith and life.[3] Thus, the word
*canon* when applied to scripture primarily denotes a list of books viewed
as authoritative. It secondarily implies (connotes) the concept of their
divine origin (inspiration) which leads to their authoritative nature. Its
synonym *scripture* denotes sacred written revelation of divine origin.
Therefore, while the concept of canon cannot be totally separated from
the question of inspiration, the primary focus of canon is on the *collection* of books. James Barr notes, "The word 'canon' meant simply
'list', i.e. the list of books that counted as holy scripture." He adds, "This
is, and has always been, the normal meaning of the word in English
when applied to scripture."[4] Eugene Ulrich states, "A strict definition of
canon will also include these latter concepts: conscious decision [to
include or exclude certain books], unique status [divine origin],
necessarily binding [authoritative]."[5]

While this seems straightforward enough, a number of scholars have
taken issue with this definition. Brevard Childs notes that some writers
distinguish sharply between *canon* and *scripture*.[6] They argue that
*scripture* denotes a body of authoritative writings whereas *canon* adds
the denotation of restriction, implying that some books have been
excluded from the collection. For these writers *canon* implies a closed
collection to which no more books may be added. Therefore, while some
scholars may speak of a period when the canon was open (i.e., the
theoretical possibility existed that more books could be added), these
scholars would argue that the term *canon* implies a closed list of books
which cannot be supplemented by further authoritative writings.

The problem with this approach to *canon* is that it implies an all-or-
nothing view of the concept of canonicity. That is, it denies the
possibility some books were already disqualified as scripture while
others were already considered scripture before the canon became the
complete, closed collection we have today. It would seem to imply that
*no* books were generally accepted authoritative until *the entire collection*

---

[3] Hermann Wolfgang Beyer, κανών *TDNT*, 3.596–602.

[4] James Barr, *Holy Scripture: Canon, Authority, Criticism.* (Philadelphia: Westminster,
1983), 49.

[5] Eugene Ulrich, "The Canonical Process and Textual Criticism," in *Sha'arei Talmon:
Studies in the Bible, Qumran, and the Ancient Near East Presented to Shemaryahu
Talmon.* ed. Michael Fishbane and Emanuel Tov (Winona Lake, IN: Eisenbrauns,
1992), 270.

[6] Brevard S. Childs, *Introduction to the Old Testament as Scripture.* (Philadelphia:
Fortress, 1979), 50.

was generally accepted. Considering the several centuries over which the OT books were written, this seems to be highly unlikely.

Sid Leiman offers another definition of canon. Based on his study of rabbinic literature he concludes that two categories of canonical books were recognized by Jewish authorities: inspired canonical literature and uninspired canonical literature.[7] Inspired canonical literature is co-terminous with the OT. Uninspired canonical literature includes all other books seen as authoritative for Jews (Mishnah in its oral form and Megillath Taanith in written form).

Leiman's definition would seem to combine a *scriptural* canon with a collection of other books held to be authoritative, but not of divine origin (i.e., a canon of religious literature, but not a canon of scripture). That religious communities oftentimes accept other collections of books as authoritative but not on the level of scripture does not mean that they have one canon divided into two categories. Instead, it implies that they recognize two collections: a collection of Scripture and a collection of other books that, though useful, are not recognized as both authoritative and inspired. Thus, Lutheranism could be said to recognize a scriptural canon of the Old and New Testaments, but also to recognize as author-itative the works that are collected in the Book of Concord (a canon in the sense that it is a collection of authoritative books, but not a scriptural canon). However, these are really two distinct collections. Lutherans do not view the Book of Concord as part of a larger canon containing both Scriptures and their confessional documents.

In the same way the rabbis cannot be said to have recognized one canon with two categories of literature in it. Rather they recognized two distinct, but related, collections. A canon of scripture (the OT) and a collection of other documents that came to be regarded as authoritative (the Talmud).

Lee McDonald, following the definition of canon proposed by Gerald Sheppard, makes a similar distinction in the definition of canon.[8] This definition of canon defines canon in two senses. *Canon 1* designates

---

[7] Sid Z. Leiman, *The Canonization of Hebrew Scripture: The Talmudic and Midrashic Evidence*. Transactions of the Connecticut Academy of Arts and Sciences 47. 2nd ed. (New Haven: Connecticut Academy of Arts and Sciences, 1991), 14–15.

[8] Lee M. McDonald, *The Formation of the Christian Biblical Canon*. (rev. and expanded ed. Peabody, MA: Hendrickson, 1995), 20–21; also "The Integrity of the Biblical Canon in Light of Its Historical Development," *BBR* 6 (1996), 101–3; Gerald T. Sheppard, "Canon" in *The Encyclopedia of Religion*. ed. Mircea Eliade. (New York: Macmillian, 1987), 3.62–69.

any authoritative voice, whether written or oral. *Canon 2* designates writings in a temporary (open canon) or permanent standardization (closed canon). This, according to McDonald, explains why some writings that were once considered inspired and authoritative within the Christian community (canon 1) were later excluded from the author- itative collection of literature for the church (canon 2).

The problem with McDonald's approach to canon is that it purposely confuses two different meanings of *canon* in the definition of *canon 1* for ideological reasons. The meaning of canon as *rule* or *norm* is combined with the meaning of *a generally recognized authoritative collection of inspired books* in order to argue that the canon was not closed until a relatively late date. McDonald argues that since some in the church accepted certain books as authoritative or argued about the sacredness of certain books, the church had no OT canon (canon 2) until the fourth or fifth centuries, and the Jews had no scriptural canon during the first century.[9]

The flaw in McDonald's approach is that he equates any question raised within the church about whether or not a book belonged in the canon with an indication that the canon was not yet closed (no canon 2 yet existed). However, that the rabbis debated the merits of books like Ezekiel and Ecclesiastes or that some Christians considered Sirach or Wisdom inspired does not necessarily indicate that the canon had not been closed. It only indicates that some within a religious group may from time to time express doubts about the extent of a canon that may well have been considered closed for some time.[10]

In this regard, Luther's comments on certain books of the New Testament, notably James, are significant. No one would argue that the New Testament canon had not long been a closed collection in Luther's day. Luther's objections to James did not change that, and, in fact, it has had little influence even on Lutherans, the vast majority of whom have always accepted the canonicity of James.

---

[9] Though he does admit that the Hebrew canon was recognized as authoritative by most Jews from the first century on. See McDonald, *Formation,* 21.

[10] Noteworthy here is the observation by Roger Beckwith that "the failure to distinguish between the canon which a community recognized and used and the eccentric view of individuals about the canon" is one of the fallacies that has vitiated much of the writing about the canon. See Roger T. Beckwith, *The Old Testament Canon of the New Testament Church.* (Grand Rapids, MI: Eerdmans, 1986), 8.

Therefore, McDonald's redefinition of canon is motivated by his conclusions about the canon, especially his conclusion that the canon was closed at a late date. However, the mixing of two definitions of *canon* is less than helpful in the debate about the close of the canon. Certainly *canon* can mean *rule*. It can also mean *authoritative collection of books*. But this does not imply that one can use one sense of this term against another sense of this term in order to aid in proving an argument about the date of the closing of the canon. That would be like using the word *diamond* in the sense of a field on which baseball is played to argue that the gem known as *diamond* was not recognized until the nineteenth century.

Most recently Philip R. Davies has suggested a looser definition of canon.[11] Though he never offers a rigorous definition, he seems to operate with a definition of canon that would include any collection of works deemed to be classics. Thus, Davies can state, "A work becomes canonized (a) by being preserved by copying until its status as a classic is ensured; and (b) by being classified as belonging to a collection of some kind."[12] The problem with this minimal definition is that it does not distinguish between collections of books that are revered as good literature (i.e., a definitive collection of the works of Shakespeare) and books that are considered divinely inspired and authoritative (i.e., a *scriptural* canon) for a religious community. The discussion of the canon of Scripture turns precisely on the notion of religious authority, something that Davies' view does not seem to recognize or appreciate.

How then should we define *canon* when it is used to describe Scripture? In this study, the term *canon* will mean *a collection of authoritative and divinely inspired books accepted as such by an overwhelming majority in a religious community.*

This definition implies several corollaries:

The acceptance of books as authoritative means that they exercise an authority not only for the present generation, but also (in some sense) for all generations.[13]

---

[11] Philip R. Davies, *Scribes and Schools: The Canonization of the Hebrew Scriptures.* (Louisville: Westminster/John Knox, 1998).

[12] Davies, Scribes and Schools, 9.

[13] For example, Christians still accept Leviticus as authoritative, though not in the sense that it was authoritative for ancient Israel. For ancient Israel it was not only an authoritative guide to God's law and an authoritative presentation of the Gospel in the forgiveness offered in the sacrificial system, but it also authoritatively dictated specific worship practices. Though Christians do not view it as authoritative in dictating

The acceptance of some books as authoritative and inspired immediately implies that other works are excluded because they are viewed by the community as either not authoritative or not inspired (or both).

The canon may be open. That is, the community can recognize that additional books may yet be written and will be added to the canon as authoritative and inspired without denying that it has already chosen to include some books and exclude others. However, by accepting some books as canonical it is asserting that none of these books can be later excluded. (To do so would deny that such books are authoritative.)

The canon may be closed. That is, the community can recognize that it will no longer allow any other books, already written or yet to be written, to be added to the canon.

The peculiar views of individuals or groups within the community about the addition or deletion of a book or books does not necessarily imply that no canon exists or that it is still in formation. It may imply that some individual or group is challenging an accepted canon's contents.

### *Modern Theories on the Formation of the Canon*

### The Triple Canon Theory

From the end of the nineteenth century to the middle of the twentieth century a generally held theory about the formation of the OT canon prevailed among scholars. This theory held that the OT canon formed in three stages corresponding to the three divisions of the canon found in Jewish Bibles. The Torah was the original section of the canon, and it was recognized by 400 BC. The Prophets were accepted by 200 BC. The Writings rounded out the canon and were officially recognized no later than AD 90 by a rabbinic council held at Jamnia. This council was responsible not only for adopting the Writings but also for closing the canon.

This consensus among scholars was challenged by some but remained the working hypothesis of most scholars for over fifty years. H. E. Ryle in his book *The Canon of the Old Testament* put forth the classic summary of this theory.[14]

---

worship practices and other aspects of God's law, other authoritative functions (its moral underpinnings and its Gospel presentation) are still functional for Christians.

[14] Herbert Edward Ryle, *The Canon of the Old Testament: An Essay on the Gradual*

This theory was supported by an earlier theory, Alexandrian Canon Hypothesis. Since the closing of the canon occurred after the beginning of the Christian church, Christians struggled on their own with the extent of the canon. Some eventually adopted the Hebrew scriptures of the rabbis. Christians in the West eventually adopted a wider canon. In order to explain this wider canon, the Alexandrian Canon Hypothesis was proposed.

The Alexandrian Canon Hypothesis held that Diaspora Judaism, especially in Alexandria, honored a larger set of books as sacred. These books were preserved in Greek, the language of the Diaspora, and were eventually adopted by the early church, whose language was also Greek.

It was noted that the codices of the Septuagint do not group the books of the OT into the Hebrew Bible's threefold division. They do group the books of Moses together, but the books of the Prophets and the Writings are not grouped the same way as in the Hebrew Bible. This was seen as an indication that the Jews in Alexandria were developing their own view of the canon before 200 BC when the Prophets were adopted into the Hebrew canon. This development continued in that a number of books not included in the Hebrew canon were adopted as Scripture by Alexandrian Jews. When the rabbis were closing the Hebrew canon at Jamnia, Christians had already begun to adopt the Greek Scriptures of Diaspora Judaism as their own. Later, Christians in the East fell under the influence of the rabbinical canon of Jamnia, and many of them eventually rejected the wider canon. Christians farther away continued to use the wider canon of Alexandria. Eventually, this wider canon became the one adopted by the Roman Catholic Church at the Council of Trent, while the Hebrew canon was endorsed by Protestants on the notion that it predated Jesus and was the canon he used.

The consensus for the Triple Canon Theory was built around four major assumptions:

1.  The threefold division of the Hebrew Scriptures into Torah, Prophets, and Writings is an indication of the history of the canon, and not a later arrangement imposed upon the canon.
2.  Many of the books contained in the Writings were completed too late to be considered canonical in Jesus' day. In particular Psalms, Ecclesiastes, Job, and Daniel were held to have been

---

*Growth and Formation of the Hebrew Canon of Scripture.* 2nd ed. London: Macmillan, 1892.

written in the Maccabean period, allowing little time for their recognition as Scripture.

3.  The meeting of rabbis at Jamnia about AD 90 functioned like a church council in adopting a list of books that ever after defined the canon.

4.  The OT books as preserved in the great Septuagint codices exemplify the Alexandrian Canon: Codex Alexandrinus, Codex Vatincanus, and Codex Sinaiticus, as well as others.

Although the Triple Canon Theory seemed to explain the formation of the canon and the source for different canons among Christians, it increasingly came under attack in the latter half of the twentieth century. While it still survives in modified form and has its defenders (e.g., McDonald[15]), each of its four major assumptions has been shown to be erroneous at least in part, if not entirely. It is the evidence that discredits these assumptions to which we now turn.

## The Collapse of the Triple Canon Theory

The collapse of the Triple Canon Theory that was formulated in the late nineteenth century came about during the last half of the twentieth century. The details of the evidence discussed below that discredit the old consensus will be explored in subsequent chapters. Here I will offer only a summary of the evidence that undermines each of these assumptions.

The first of the four assumptions listed above depends on the traditional arrangement of the books of the Hebrew OT into three sections. While this arrangement is an ancient one, the first firm evidence for it is references in the Talmud. The oldest of these passages that can be confidently dated come from the early second century and are attributed to Elisha ben Abuyah (110–135), Gamaliel (80–110) and Ben Azzai (110–135).[16] Considering that the statements attributed to these men

---

[15] McDonald, *Formation*, 30 "Ryle's only unreasonable proposal is his dating of the threefold development of the Hebrew Bible" and 49 "H. E. Ryle's theory that the three-tiered OT canon gained recognition by the time when the so-called council of Jamnia met to discuss such matters has been challenged by a number of scholars. A three-stage development of the Jewish biblical canon, however, is not as unlikely as some have supposed, *even though it has little direct evidence*." (emphasis mine)

[16] Leiman, *Canonization*, 66–67. Note: Luke 24:44 is often assumed to refer to the tradtional three sections of the Hebrew OT. However, it most likely does not. See the analysis of Luke 24:44 beginning on page 90.

were not recorded in their own day, were collected and edited around AD 200, and may not have been reduced to writing until as late as the fourth century, this evidence can only be a provisional indication that the canon was divided into the three traditional sections even as early as the second century. Scholars who hold that the threefold division of the canon predates the early second century usually buttress their contention by referring to statements in the Greek prologue to Ben Sira (c. 132 BC), Philo's *The Contemplative Life* (early first century), Luke 24:44 and Josephus' *Against Apion* (late first century). However, none of these contains the threefold division of the OT corresponding to the latter Jewish divisions.

The Prologue to Ben Sira explicitly mentions the Law and the Prophets, but the supposed third division is variously referred to as "those who followed them," "the others books of our fathers," or "the rest of the books." One cannot be certain that these are even references to canonical books.

Both Philo and Luke mention only one book—Psalms—apart from the Law and the Prophets.

Josephus, on the other hand, divides the canon into three parts: Five books of Moses, the Prophets (thirteen books), and hymns to God and precepts for human life (four books). Josephus' arrangement of twenty-two books in three divisions is different from the traditional threefold arrangement of 24 books. Only the first division containing the five books of Moses is identical in both Josephus and the traditional threefold division of the OT canon.

Each of these pieces of evidence will be examined in more detail in later chapters. However, given the fact that no unambiguous evidence exists for the traditional threefold division of the canon before the second century AD, and that the most common way of dividing the OT canon in the NT is a twofold one (the Law and the Prophets), some scholars have challenged the notion that the threefold division of the canon has any relevance to the history of the canon's formation.[17]

The second major assumption behind the Triple Canon—that certain books contained in the third section of the canon were of Maccabean origin and, therefore, too young to be included in a canon by Jesus'

---

[17] Barr, *Holy Scripture*, 54–56; R. Laird Harris, "Was the Law and the Prophets Two-thirds of the Old Testament Canon?" *BETS* 9 (1966), 163–71. An early challenge to the threefold division of the canon as indicative of the development of the OT was Willis J. Beecher, "The Alleged Triple Canon of the Old Testament," *JBL* 15 (1896), 118–28.

day—has been abandoned because of evidence from both the Cairo Geniza manuscripts of Ben Sira and the manuscripts from Qumran and Masada. The Cairo Geniza manuscripts of Ben Sira in Hebrew, discovered in the late nineteenth century, were first published by Solomon Schechter. Schechter's examination of the Hebrew text revealed many passages in which Ben Sira employed phrases, expressions, and even entire verses from nearly every OT book. From this evidence Schechter concluded, "in the case of *all* the canonical books, with the doubtful exception of the Book of Daniel, these books must as a whole have been familiar to B.S., and must therefore be much anterior to him in date."[18]

Since Ben Sira wrote his book sometime between 200 and 180 BC, this evidence ruled out the Maccabean dating of Psalms, Ecclesiastes and other books. However, some scholars challenged Schechter's conclusion, maintaining that the medieval Geniza Ben Sira manuscripts were actually a retroversion into Hebrew from either Syriac or Greek versions. With the discovery of the scrolls at Qumran and Masada this argument proved false on three counts:

1.  The first century AD Ben Sira manuscripts discovered at Masada show remarkable agreement with the Geniza manuscripts.
2.  Non-biblical manuscripts from Qumran clearly demonstrate that the Hebrew of the Hasmonean era is different from that of the Psalms, Ecclesiastes, and other books.
3.  The existence of Qumran manuscripts of Psalms, Ecclesiastes, Job, and other books, (some as early as the mid-second century BC) make it highly unlikely that these books could have been Maccabean compositions.

No one currently holds to a Maccabean date for any book of the OT, with the exception of Daniel, which many scholars still date to about 164 BC.

The third assumption, that the rabbis closed the canon about AD 90 at Jamnia, was discredited by Jack Lewis in 1964.[19] The Council of Jamnia assertion was built on a passage in the Mishnah indicating that the rabbis at Jamnia debated the status of two books, Ecclesiastes and

---

[18] S. Schechter. and C. Taylor, *The Wisdom of Ben Sira: Portions of the Book of Ecclesiasticus from Hebrew Manuscripts in the Cairo Genizah Collection Presented to the University of Cambridge by the Editors.* (Cambridge: Cambridge, 1899), 35.

[19] Jack P. Lewis, "What Do We Mean by Jabneh?" *JBR* 32 (1964), 125–32.

Song of Songs—not about the Writings in general.[20] Nothing in this passage indicates that the rabbis were deciding the contents of the canon or seeking to close either the third division of the OT or the canon as a whole. In fact, the debate over some books of the canon continued for some time, as other passages in the Mishnah indicate. Leiman offers this conclusion about the supposed Council of Jamnia:[21]

> In summary, all that can safely be said is that at a session of the academy at Jamnia that convened sometime between 75–117 C.E., it was decided that Ecclesiastes and the Songs of Songs defile the hands. (According to R. Akiba, a decision was necessary and made only with regard to Ecclesiastes.) These decisions were still being questioned 100 years later. The widespread view that the Council of Jamnia closed the biblical canon, or that it canonized any books at all, is not supported by the evidence and need no longer be seriously maintained.

Consequently, few, if any, scholars today maintain that a council at Jamnia closed the canon around AD 90.

The final assumption, that of the Alexandrian Canon Hypothesis, was thoroughly discredited by A. C. Sundberg in 1964, the same year that Lewis discredited the Council of Jamnia.[22] Sundberg assumed that the Jewish canon was closed at Jamnia. Despite this flaw, his proof that no separate canon existed among Jews of the Diaspora remains valid.

The heart of Sundberg's analysis was a comparison of the lists of canonical books found in the church fathers to the contents of the great Septuagint codices. He demonstrated that little agreement could be found either in their contents or order, indicating that the church did not simply adopt a canon from Diaspora Judaism. Since the codices were only an indication of later *Christian* usage, they fail to prove the existence of a distinct canon that was used by *Jews* in pre-Christian Alexandria or anywhere else. As a result of Sundberg's work the Alexandrian Canon Theory has been completely abandoned.

---

[20] The debate was about whether these books "defile the hands." Many scholars understand the rabbinical concept of books defiling hands as a mark of sacredness and canonicity.

[21] Leiman, *Canonization*, 124.

[22] Albert C. Sundberg, Jr., *The Old Testament of the Early Church.* Harvard Theological Studies 20. Cambridge: Harvard., 1964.

## Newer Theories about the Closing of the Canon

With the destruction of the foundation upon which the Triple Canon Theory rested, newer theories about the formation of the canon began to be proposed. These fall into two categories: theories that place the closing of the canon in the late first century or even later and theories that place the closing of the canon sometime before Jesus.

### Late Date Theories for the Closing of the Canon

Many scholars continue to date the closing of the canon at the end of the first century AD, even though scholars acknowledge that it was not fixed by a council of rabbis at Jamnia. Instead, for many scholars the witness of Josephus to a canon of 22 books, the witness of the book of 4 Ezra (written late first century or early second century) to a canon of 24 books, and the appearance of lists of canonical books after that time would seem to make this the latest possible date for the closing of the canon. The primary argument against dating the canon earlier than the late first century is that no lists of books belonging to the canon can be dated earlier than the second century AD and no enumeration of the books can be dated prior to Josephus. Scholars who take this view include Eugene Ulrich[23] and Joseph Blenkinsopp.[24] Moreover, this view is commonly found in Bible dictionaries and encyclopedias.[25]

John J. Collins offers a more detailed view of this theory.[26] Collins argues that the canon was closed for all Jews around the end of the first century, but that the canon chosen was a canon that took shape among one sect of Jews (presumably certain Pharisees) before the fall of Jerusalem in AD 70. This theory is a possible way of bridging the gap between the late date theory and the early date theories yet to be examined. Its weakness is that it can point to no date for the closing of

---

[23] Eugene Ulrich, "The Canonical Process, Textual Criticism, and Latter Stages in the Composition of the Bible" in *"Sha'arei Talmon": Studies in the Bible, Qumran and the Ancient Near East Presented to Shemaryahu Talmon*, (Winona Lake, IN: Eisenbrauns, 1992), 267–91.

[24] Joseph Blenkinsopp, *Prophecy and Canon: A Contribution to the Study of Jewish Origins*. (Notre Dame, IN: Notre Dame, 1977), 126.

[25] E.g., "Canon" in *ABD*, 1.840.

[26] John J. Collins, "Before the Canon: Scriptures in Second Temple Judaism," in James Luther Mays, David L. Petersen and Kent Harold Richards, eds. *Old Testament Interpretation: Past, Present, and Future. Essays in Honor of Gene M. Tucker.* (Nashville: Abingdon, 1995), 225–41.

this canon. Moreover, it assumes that there were differences among various Jewish sects in the first century BC and first century AD despite a strange silence in the sources concerning any friction between this one sect of late Second Temple Judaism and other sects that may have wanted to include or exclude other books.

The strength of this late date theory is that it places the closing of the canon at the time when enumerations and lists of canonical books were appearing. However, the weakness of this theory is that it fails to explain earlier evidence for the canon that appears to arrange the canon into a twofold (Law and Prophets) or threefold arrangement. Authors before the late first century seem to assume a fixed content.[27]

In a more radical approach, Lee M. McDonald argues that the canon was not closed until much later.[28] He argues that in Jesus' day the Jews recognized an amorphous collection of books as sacred. This collection apparently had a core of books accepted by nearly everyone, but also contained other books on the fringes that were accepted by some but viewed suspiciously by others. For Jews, the closing of the canon began with the rabbis responsible for shaping the Mishnah around AD 200 and within 100 years resulted in the Hebrew OT we have today. For Christians the process took longer. Christians accepted some of the books eliminated in the process followed by the rabbis. Eventually church councils accepted the larger canon in the fifth century.

In this way McDonald can explain the two divergent canons. He also believes that his theory better accounts for the evidence. Chief among these are the continuing discussions about the status of some books of the OT by the rabbis as recorded in the Talmud and the reference to noncanonical books in the NT.

On the other hand, McDonald has to discount some evidence as unreliable in order to push the date of the canon's closing as back as far as he does. Most notable is the evidence from Josephus. According to McDonald the canon put forth by Josephus is partly exaggeration for apologetic purposes and partly Josephus' idiosyncratic view. Against

---

[27] One could claim that the New Testament's reference to "the Law and the Prophets" does not necessarily refer to a closed and well-defined collection of books, but that it is a general way of referring to a sort of proto-canon that had yet to be strictly defined. However, the Law was already a strictly defined collection of the five books of Moses. It would be a strange collocation if "the Law and the Prophets" meant "five prophetic books from Moses and an undetermined number of books from an undetermined number of prophets."

[28] McDonald, *Formation* and "Integrity."

Josephus, McDonald asserts that Jews generally accepted some books later deleted from the canon as of divine origin and possessing authority in Josephus' day.[29]

Finally, we should note that other scholars have argued that the pluriform nature of Judaism in the first century (BC or AD) argue against any early date for a canon among Jews.[30] However, if pluriformity is an indication of lack of canonical formation, then modern Protestantism has no canon!

## Early Date Theories for the Closing of the Canon

On the other side of the debate on the closing of the canon are scholars who believe the canon was closed before Jesus' day. Among these are David Noel Freedman. Freedman argues that, with the exception of Daniel, the canon was formed and closed in the time of Ezra.[31] Fundamental to Freedman's approach is his view that the composition of each of the OT books is to be dated close to the last recorded episodes in it. Therefore, the last books of the canon were Chronicles and Ezra-Nehemiah (not counting Daniel). Freedman's theory would appear to agree with tradition that dates back at least to Josephus that the canon was closed during the Persian period.[32] Indeed, modern scholars, in contrast to scholars in the nineteenth century, have tended to date all of the books of the OT except Daniel to the Persian period. Thus, Freedman's theory that the canon formed near this time is attractive, since there is no intrinsic need to date it later.

Freedman's argument for the closing of the canon is based on symmetry that he discerns in the books of the Bible themselves and in their arrangement in the canon. To achieve this symmetry Freedman divides the Prophets into two sections. The Former Prophets (Joshua, Judges, Samuel and Kings) are grouped with the Pentateuch to form what Freedman labels the Primary History. The Latter Prophets (Isaiah,

---

[29] McDonald, *Formation*, 53–58; "Integrity," 108–11.

[30] David M. Carr, "Canonization in the Context of Community: An Outline of the Formation of the Tanakh and the Christian Bible," *A Gift of God in Due Season: Essays on Scripture and Community in Honor of James A. Sanders.* (JSOTSup 225, Sheffield: Sheffield, 1996), 22–64. Carr is following the approach laid out by James Sanders.

[31] David Noel Freedman, *The Unity of the Hebrew Bible.* Distinguished senior faculty lecture series. (Ann Arbor: University of Michigan, 1991); also "The Symmetry of the Hebrew Bible," *ST* 46 (1992) 83–108.

[32] However, Freedman himself does not mention this tradition.

Jeremiah, Ezekiel and the Twelve) are grouped with the Writings.[33]
These two groupings are approximately the same size. The Primary
History contains 149,641 words, whereas the remaining books (minus
Daniel) contain 149,940 words.[34] This and other patterns in the OT
convince Freedman that the canon was a conscious arrangement of books
at the time of the composition of the last of them. That is, this symmetry
could only be achieved once all of the canonical books were written and
assembled in a collection for the first time. Therefore, twenty-three of the
twenty-four books of the OT were canonized in the days of Ezra. Daniel,
which Freedman dates to the Maccabean era, was added shortly after it
was composed. Therefore, according to Freedman the canon was
essentially formed by about 400 BC and took its final shape around 160
BC.

However, his thesis could be criticized for two weaknesses. First, his
theory depends entirely on internal biblical evidence. He does not cite
any evidence external to the biblical text for dividing the OT canon as he
does. His evidence depends on his detection of certain patterns within the
OT itself, but he offers little proof that his observations of these patterns
are indeed what the editors/compilers of the canon had in mind.[35]

Second, part of his evidence is the traditional arrangement of the
Hebrew OT. I have already discussed the lack of hard evidence for this
arrangement of the books before the early second century AD and will
examine this in detail in the following chapters. Therefore, Freedman's
theory remains debatable in its details.

Nevertheless, based on the historical arguments he adduces elsewhere as well as in his book on the canon, Freedman certainly has made
a strong case for the OT canon as formed early.[36] His theory that the
entire canon was formed early not only is supported by historical
evidence, but also by the currently scholarly consensus on the date of the

---

[33] Freedman, *Unity*, 5.

[34] Freedman, *Unity*, 79.

[35] For a more detailed critique of Freedman's thesis see my review of *The Unity of the Hebrew Bible* in *The Michigan Academician*, 54 (1993), 108–9.

[36] David Noel Freedman, "Canon of the Bible," in G. Wigoder, W. M. Paul, B. T. Viviano, O.P. and E. Stern, eds., *Illustrated Dictionary and Concordance of the Bible* (New York: Macmillan, 1986), 211–16; "The Formation of the Canon of the Old Testament: The Selection and Identification of the Torah as the Supreme Authority of the Post-Exilic Community," in E. B. Firmage, B. G. Weiss and J. W. Welch, eds. *Religion and Law: Biblical-Judaic and Islamic Perspective* (Winona Lake, IN: Eisenbrauns, 1990), 315–33.

composition or final editing of all of the OT books (with the exception of Daniel).

Several other scholars date the closing of the canon to Maccabean times. Sid Leiman marshals an impressive array of evidence from the Talmud and Midrash that point in this direction.[37] Roger Beckwith assembles Jewish and Christian evidence from the second century BC through the fifth century AD to argue, like Leiman, that the canon was closed by Judas Maccabeus around 160 BC.[38] E. Earle Ellis also believes the canon was closed before Jesus' day.[39]

In all three cases these scholars rely on external witnesses to the canon, beginning with the second century BC. This evidence will be examined in the following chapters. However, all three of these scholars still rely on the assumption that the canon was accepted in the traditional threefold arrangement from early times. Therefore, as we examine the evidence on the canon we will need to carefully investigate the possible references to the divisions of the canon.

These early date theories have the opposite problem of the late date theory: They explain why the canon can be referenced by its main divisions as early as the second century. However, the supporters of this theory have yet to explain why the enumeration and listing of the books of the OT canon do not begin to appear until 250 years or more after the canon has been closed.

### Toward a New Theory of the Canon

Since it is obvious that no theory takes into account or explains all the evidence, a new theory is needed. Such a theory should be able to

---

[37] Leiman, *Canonization*; also "Inspiration and Canonicity: Reflections on the Formation of the Biblical Canon." in *Jewish and Christian Self-Definition*. 2nd ed. E. P. Sanders, A. I. Baumgarten and Alan Mendelson, eds. (Philadelphia: Fortress, 1981), 2.56–63.

[38] Roger Beckwith, *The Old Testament Canon of the New Testament Church.* (Grand Rapids, MI: Eerdmans, 1986); also "Canon of the Hebrew Bible and the Old Testament." in *The Oxford Companion to the Bible.* Bruce M. Metzger and M. D. Coogan, eds. New York: Oxford, 1993, 102–4; "Formation of the Hebrew Bible" in *Mikra: Text, Translation, Reading and Interpretation of the Hebrew Bible in Ancient Judaism and Early Christianity.* CRINT. M. J. Mulder, ed. Minneapolis: Fortress, 1990, 39–86; "A Modern Theory of the Old Testament Canon," *VT* 41 (1991), 385–95.

[39] E. Earle Ellis, *The Old Testament in Early Christianity: Canon and Interpretation in the Light of Modern Research.* Grand Rapids: Baker, 1991; also "The Old Testament Canon in the Early Church," in *Mikra: Text, Translation, Reading and Interpretation of the Hebrew Bible in Ancient Judaism and Early Christianity* CRINT. M. J. Mulder and H. Sysling, eds. Minneapolis: Fortress, 1990, 653–90.

offer a reasonable explanation for evidence before the late first century when references seem to indicate a canon and an explanation for references from the late first century forward that not only begin to enumerate and list the books of the canon, but also at times incorporate books not found in the present Hebrew OT. In order to do this, we will have to examine the data in chronological order. Chapter two of this study will examine the references to the canon before Jesus' time. Chapter three will investigate the evidence from the first century after the time of Jesus. Chapter four will look at the evidence after the first century. Along the way I will build a theory to explain the evidence. Chapter five will summarize the evidence and present a united theory on the OT canon.

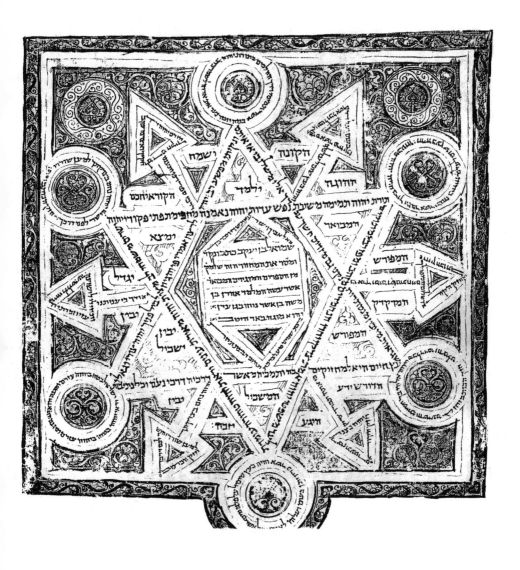

Carpet page, The Leningrad Codex. Grand Rapids: Wm. B. Eerdmannns
Publishing Co., 1998.

# 2

# The BC Canon

Since scholars have found evidence relating to the existence of the OT canon as early as the second century BC, our examination must begin with this oldest evidence. In this chapter we will examine writings from the second century BC through the early first century AD. The relevant sources can be grouped into seven categories: The book of Ben Sira (Sirach, Ecclesiasticus; especially the surviving Hebrew manuscripts); the Greek prologue to Sirach; 1 and 2 Maccabees; evidence from Qumran; the Samaritans; Philo Judaeus and evidence from 4 Maccabees.

### Ben Sira

The book of Ben Sira, known in Greek as Sirach and in Latin as Ecclesiasticus, is the work of a certain Jesus, son of Sirach. His book is preserved in Hebrew manuscript fragments from the Cairo Geniza, Qumran, and Masada. An ancient Greek translation made by his grandson as well as Syriac and Latin translations also survive from antiquity.

The date of composition for Ben Sira is relatively easy to fix. Ben Sira has a long section in praise of his ancestors (44:1–50:21). The last one mentioned is the high priest Simeon, son of Jochanan (Onias in some Greek manuscripts). This is commonly assumed to be Simeon II who served as high priest from 219 to 196 BC, making 196 BC the earliest possible date for Ben Sira. Ben Sira shows no knowledge of the trouble brought on the Jewish people by the Seleucid king Antiochus IV Epiphanies, who reigned from 175 to 164 BC. Therefore, Ben Sira had to be written between 196 and 175 BC. This is confirmed by the Prologue to the Greek translation of Ben Sira produced by Ben Sira's grandson. In this prologue the translator dates his work as beginning in the thirty-eighth year of the Egyptian king Ptolemy VII Physkon Euergetes II. Since Ptolemy's reign began in 170 BC, the grandson began his translation in 132 BC. If we assume that the grandson was an adult when he began his work, his grandfather's work can be dated roughly fifty years earlier, about 180 BC.

In the late nineteenth century Hebrew manuscripts of Ben Sira became available to scholars with the discovery of medieval manuscript fragments of Ben Sira among the manuscript finds in the Cairo Synagogue's Geniza. Additionally, manuscript finds at Qumran and Masada have confirmed the antiquity of the text of the Geniza manuscript fragments.[40] Alexander Di Lella, however, believes that 5:4–6; 10:31; 15:14, 15, 20; 16:3 and 32:16 in the Geniza manuscripts are retroversions from the Syriac into Hebrew.[41] Israel Lévi held that most of the text of 51:13–30 in Geniza manuscript B was a retroversion from Syriac.[42] In addition, J. Ziegler has proposed that 11:2b; 20:13a; and 37:20b are retroversions from the Greek.[43] Hans Peter Rüger, on the other hand, argues that these are not retroversions, but stem from two different recensions of the Hebrew text.[44] Whether these portions of Ben Sira were original or retroversions is of no consequence for this study, however. None of these passages will play a role in determining the possible extent of Ben Sira's canon.

While none of the Hebrew manuscripts of Ben Sira that have survived is complete, a large portion of the book is extant in Hebrew. Skehan and Di Lella note:[45]

> About 68 percent of the book is now extant in Hebrew:
> about 2,200 cola of the 3,221 that are found in the
> complete book according to the Greek text of Codex
> Vaticanus. Of these 2,200 cola, about 530 are extant in
> whole or in part (many of the Masada cola are,

---

[40] Patrick W. Skehan and Alexander A. Di Lella, *The Wisdom of Ben Sira.* AB 39. (New York: Doubleday, 1987), 54.

[41] Alexander A. Di Lella, *The Hebrew Text of Sirach: A Text-Critical and Historical Study.* (The Hague: Mouton, 1966), 106–47.

[42] Israel Lévi, *The Hebrew Text of the Book of Ecclesiasticus.* Semitic Study Series 3. (Leiden: Brill, 1904; reprinted 1951).

[43] J. Ziegler, "Zwei Beiträge zu Sirach," *BZ* N.F. 8 (1964), 277–84.

[44] Hans Peter Rüger, *Text und Textform in hebräischen Sirach.* (BZAW 112, 1970).

[45] Patrick W Skehan and Alexander A. Di Lella, *The Wisdom of Ben Sira.* AB 39. (New York: Doubleday, 1987), 53.

unfortunately, fragmentary) in two MSS at the same time,
and 36 are found in three MSS.

Consulting the Hebrew text is important, because the Greek text at
times reveals that the translator did not understand his *Vorlage* or
misread it. For instance, until the discovery of Hebrew Ben Sira the
mention of Job in 49:9 was lost because the translator apparently misread
the Hebrew text, reading איוב (Job) as איב (enemy). The Greek text
reads:

καὶ γὰρ ἐμνήσθη τῶν ἐχθρῶν ἐν ὄμβρῳ

For he certainly remembered his enemies in a storm.

Whereas the Hebrew text reads:

וגם הזכיר את איוב נ[ב] יא[46]

He also mentioned the pro[ph]et Job.

This should not be surprising to anyone, considering the translator's
own admission that things originally expressed in Hebrew "do not
convey exactly the same sense when translated into another language"
(οὐ γὰρ ἰσοδυναμεῖ αὐτὰ ἐν ἑαυτοις Ἑβραϊστὶ λογόμενα καὶ
μεταχθῇ εἰς ἑτέραν γλῶσσαν), and even the books that his grandfather
studied are different (perhaps different base texts?) in their original
language (οὐ μικρὰν ἔχει τὴν διαφορὰν ἐν ἑαυτοῖς λεγόμενα).

Ben Sira's book is a book designed to teach wisdom. As such, we
should not be surprised that it relies heavily on the book of Proverbs.
Skehan and Di Lella conclude "Ben Sira, though, did not consider the
authors of the several collections in Proverbs simply as colleagues in a
long line of Wisdom writers but rather as inspired writers whose work
was already viewed as sacred and virtually canonical."[47]

When teaching wisdom Ben Sira often equates God's law with
wisdom, especially the תורה. In his study of law and wisdom in Ben

---

[46] Underlined letters are partially extant in the manuscript. Letters in brackets are not
extant in the manuscript and are supplied.

[47] Skehan and Di Lella, *Ben Sira*, 44–45. Skehan and Di Lella use the phrase "virtually
canonical" because they subscribe to the theory that the canon was not officially
defined until the end of the first century AD (see p. 45, n. 3).

Sira, Schnabel concludes that this is the five books of the Pentateuch, stating "of the 12 occurrences of תורה in Sirach, 11 refer to the Torah, the *lex revelata*, the constitutional and spiritual basis of Israel's life."[48] Therefore, the Pentateuch as a collection was extant in Ben Sira's day. However, Ben Sira does not seem to make any distinction between the Torah and other books of the OT in his use of them.

As far as separate groupings of Prophets and Writings as in the present Hebrew OT, Ben Sira shows no evidence that he recognized these divisions. In 39:1–3 he mentions several types of literature that one who studies God's law reads including prophecies, sayings of famous people, parables, and proverbs. However, Ben Sira is hardly setting out the canon and its divisions here. Rather, he is urging anyone who would like to learn wisdom to study various kinds of sacred literature.

### Ben Sira's Praise of His Ancestors

Ben Sira 44:1–50:21 is dedicated to praising the Jewish people's ancestors. It begins:[49]

שבח אבות עולם
אהללה נא אנשי חסד [את] אבותינו בדורותם

Praise of Ancient Ancestors
Let us now praise faithful men, our ancestors according to
their generations. (44:1)

This section then proceeds to record praise of various prominent men in the OT. The sequence, along with the biblical book giving the account on which Ben Sira is drawing is summarized in Table 1.

---

[48] Eckhard J. Schnabel, *Law and Wisdom from Ben Sira to Paul: A Tradition Historical Enquiry in to the Relation of Law, Wisdom and Ethics* (Tübingen: J.C.B. Mohr, 1985), 33.

[49] Throughout this study the Hebrew text of Ben Sira is taken from Z. Ben-Hayyim, ed. *The Book of Ben Sira: Text, Concordance and an Analysis of the Vocabulary.* Jerusalem: Academy of the Hebrew Language and the Shrine of the Book, 1973.

## Table 1
## Ancestors Praised by Ben Sira and His Biblical Sources

| Reference | Ancestor | OT Book |
|---|---|---|
| 44:16 | Enoch | |
| 44:17–18 | Noah | |
| 44:19–21 | Abraham | Genesis |
| 44:22a | Isaac | |
| 44:22b–23a | Israel (Jacob) | |
| 44:23b–45:5 | Moses | Exodus– |
| 45:6–22 | Aaron | Deuteronomy |
| 45:23–26 | Phinehas | Numbers |
| 46:1–8 | Joshua | Joshua/Numbers |
| 46:7–10 | Caleb | |
| 46:11–12 | The Judges | Judges |
| 46:13–20 | Samuel | Samuel |
| 47:1 | Nathan | Samuel/Chronicles |
| 47:2–11 | David | Samuel/Chronicles[50] |
| 47:12–22 | Solomon | Kings/Chronicles |
| 47:21–25 | Rehoboam & Jeroboam | Kings/Chronicles |
| 48:1–11 | Elijah | Kings |
| 48:12–16 | Elisha | Kings |
| 48:17–22 | Hezekiah | Kings/Chronicles |
| 48:23–25 | Isaiah | Kings/Chronicles & |
| 49:1–3 | Josiah | Isaiah[51] |
| 49:6–7 | Jeremiah | Kings/Chronicles |
| | | Kings/Chronicles & |
| | | Jeremiah[52] |
| 49:8 | Ezekiel | Ezekiel |
| 49:9 | Job | Ezekiel/Job[53] |

---

[50] Though many scholars understand the section on the kings as referencing only the books of Samuel and Kings, the parallels in Chronicles cannot be ruled out. 47:9 mentions David appointing singers for the temple, a fact attested only in Chronicles.

[51] It is likely that both Kings and Isaiah are referred to here. The language seems to reflect both books.

[52] It is likely that both 2 Kings and Jeremiah is referred to here. The language of 49:6 and 7 echoes Jeremiah 1:5,10. However the passage is set in the context of the sins of the kings of Judah (except David, Hezekiah, and Josiah), a theme from Kings.

[53] Though the language is reminiscent of Ezekiel 14:14, Job is called a prophet (the most likely reconstruction of the partial word on the mss). Since Ezekiel does not use this

| 49:10 | The Twelve Prophets | Hosea–Malachi |
|---|---|---|
| 49:11–12 | Zerubbabel & Jeshua | Haggai & Ezra[54] |
| 49:13 | Nehemiah | Nehemiah |
| 49:14 | Enoch | |
| 49:15 | Joseph | Genesis |
| 49:16a | Shem, Seth, Enosh | |
| 49:16b | Adam | |
| 50:1–21 | Simeon son of Jochanan | |

This list of illustrious ancestors draws from every book of the Hebrew OT except Ruth, Esther, Psalms, Proverbs, Ecclesiastes, Song of Songs, Lamentations and Daniel. Little in Psalms, Proverbs, Ecclesiastes, Song of Songs and Lamentations commend them as sources for the history of the ancestors. That Boaz (in Ruth), Mordecai (in Esther) and Daniel are not mentioned is not necessarily significant. Ben Sira's list is selective. He mentions Jeshua, Shem, Enosh, and Seth—men that would probably not be regarded by most as among the greatest in the OT. He mentions none of the judges by name, nor does he mention Ezra, though he probably refers to his book. In sum, he appears to be selectively drawing on the OT in a form very similar, if not identical, to the Hebrew canon. He makes special use of books that present historical narratives or prophetic oracles.

Another claim about the OT canon is often made on the basis of this section of Ben Sira: That Ben Sira knew the prophetic books in canonical order (of the Hebrew OT).[55] However, that is not quite the case. Instead, he appears to be arranging his list in chronological order. He does follow the order Joshua (with a digression to Numbers) – Judges – Samuel – Kings – Isaiah. But then he digresses to Kings, then Jeremiah (which ends the treatment of Kings), then Ezekiel (with a reference to Job) and then the Twelve.

---

designation for Job, the reference is probably to Job's words as recorded in the book of Job.

[54] Zerubbabel and Jeshua are mentioned together as instrumental in building the house of the Lord. In Ezra, Nehemiah, and Haggai are they mentioned together. The reference in Ben Sira 49:11–12 is to Zerubbabel as a signet ring (Hag 2:23; Ben Sira 49:11) and to Jeshua and Zerubbabel having built the temple. While Haggai urges the building of the temple, it is Ezra that reports its completion (Ezra 6:14; Ben Sira 49:12)

[55] E.g., see Leiman, *Canonization*, 27 and Brevard Childs, *Introduction to the Old Testament as Scripture*. (Philadelphia: Fortress, 1979), 64.

The inclusion of the Twelve probably left Ben Sira with a dilemma. The earliest predate Isaiah, whereas the latest post-date Ezekiel. Most probably Ben Sira chose to include the Twelve on the basis of their latest books and as a transition to his mention of the post-exilic figures of Zerubbabel, Jeshua, and Nehemiah. These last three men are his treatment of the books of Ezra and Nehemiah, books not counted among the Prophets in the Hebrew OT.

Therefore, Ben Sira *roughly* follows the order of the Hebrew OT section known as the Prophets, but his main concern is chronological. If we argue that he is following the canonical order of the Prophets as he knew it, then he may have included Ezra and Nehemiah among the prophets, not the writings.

On the other hand, Ben Sira's mention of the Twelve demonstrates that this subgroup of the canon was already in place in the early second century. It implies that some notion of canon was already operative. Authoritative prophecies were being collected and organized.

Moreover, he clearly distinguishes biblical history as drawn from the books of the OT from contemporary history. This is seen in his summary at the end of his treatment of biblical history (49:14–16). Here Ben Sira reverts to Genesis to close his praise of biblical figures before he moves on to praise a nonbiblical figure, Simeon, son of Jochanan. Thus, Ben Sira consciously differentiates between the history of one of his older contemporaries and biblical history. Biblical history for Ben Sira ends in the Persian period with Nehemiah.

## Ben Sira's Use of Language from the OT

In addition to Ben Sira's reliance on all but a few books of the OT to construct his praise to his ancestors, Ben Sira also includes in his book phrases, expressions, and sentences drawn from various OT books. Schechter identified 340 phrases, idioms, expressions and entire verses from the OT in Hebrew Ben Sira.[56] Eberharter found 327 allusions and 275 references to the OT in Ben Sira.[57] Middendorp found nearly 330 allusions to the OT in Ben Sira.[58]

---

[56] Solomon Schechter and C. Taylor, *The Wisdom of Ben Sira: Portions of the Book of Ecclesiasticus from Hebrew Manuscripts in the Cairo Genizah Collection Presented to the University of Cambridge by the Editors.* (Cambridge: Cambridge, 1899), 13–25.

[57] A. Eberharter, *Der Kanon des Alten Testaments zur Zeit des Ben Sira auf Grund der Beziehungen des Sirachbuches zu den Scriften des Alten Testaments dargestellt.*

From his study of Hebrew Ben Sira Schechter drew the following conclusions:[59]

> This list [of OT passages used by Ben Sira] speaks for itself; it extends almost over the whole Canon of the O.T., and, what is of special importance, it covers all the books or groups of the Psalms. In fact the impression produced by the perusal of B.S.'s original on the student who is at all familiar with the Hebrew Scriptures is that of reading the work of a post-canonical author, who already knew his Bible and was constantly quoting it....
> The results at which we thus arrive with regard to B.S. are the following: (1) that he was a conscious imitator; (2) that the classical portions in his work are due to his skilful (sic) manipulating of Biblical passages and patching them together; (3) that his composition shows already such traces of an artificial way of interpreting and using the contents of the Scriptures as are only to be found in post-Biblical writers...
> From these results two conclusions appear to follow:
> (1) that when the same phrase occurs in one of the canonical writers and in B.S., the balance of probability is strongly in favour of the supposition that B.S. was the imitator of the canonical writer and not *vice versa*.
> (2) that as clear examples of such imitation by B.S. can be found in the case of *all* the canonical books, with the doubtful exception of the Book of Daniel, these books must as a whole have been familiar to B.S., and must therefore be much anterior to him in date.

An examination of Schechter's list reveals that his last statement should be modified. He lists no references to Ruth or Ezra, but does list three references to Daniel. His "doubtful exception" of Daniel is related to the critical dating of Daniel to about 164 BC, some two decades after the composition of Ben Sira. (The book itself claims to be the work of Daniel in the late sixth century BC.)

---

(Münster: Aschendorff, 1911), 6–52. An allusion was defined as a correspondence, but not strong enough to rule out independent formulation. A reference was defined as a correspondence close enough clearly to indicate dependence on an OT text. The statistics were compiled by Schnabel, *Law and Wisdom*, 61.

[58] T. Middendorp, *Die Stellung Jesu Ben Siras zwischen Judentum und Hellenismus.* (Leiden: Brill, 1973), 49–91. Statistics are from Schnabel, *Law and Wisdom*, 62.

[59] Schechter and Taylor, *Ben Sira*, 25–26, 34, 35.

Skehan and Di Lella characterize Ben Sira's use of the OT by stating:[60]

> Ben Sira's procedure is to adapt the older Scriptures in order to popularize them and make them relevant to the new Hellenistic age in which he lived. Though he often quotes or refers to a sacred text, he does not hesitate to alter it or change the wording so that there is a new emphasis or a different meaning....
>
> In his exposition of wisdom motifs, Ben Sira cites or alludes to the Torah or Pentateuch (Genesis, Exodus, Leviticus, Numbers, Deuteronomy), Joshua, 1–2 Samuel, 1–2 Kings, 1–2 Chronicles, Nehemiah, Psalms, Job, Isaiah, Jeremiah, Ezekiel, Haggai, and Malachi. He mentions in passing the Judges (46:11–12), the Twelve Minor Prophets as a group (49:10), the Psalms as compositions of David (47:9), and Proverbs as the work of Solomon (47:14–17), but he does not refer at all to Ruth, Ezra, Tobit, Judith, Esther, Daniel, or Baruch. Thus Ben Sira occupies a position between the OT on the one hand and intertestamental literature on the other. This alone makes Ben Sira a figure of great importance in the history of Israel, for he opens the way for the later rabbis.

Unlike Schechter, Skehan and Di Lella claim that Daniel is not referenced in Ben Sira, and they note the absence of Ruth and Ezra, which Schechter did not list in his references. Though Esther is listed in one reference in Schechter, Skehan and Di Lella apparently discount this identification. The other books they mention (Tobit, Judith, and Baruch) are the only books of the Apocrypha that could possibly be older than Ben Sira, though this is likely only in the case of Tobit. Since the disagreement between Schechter and Skehan and Di Lella involves Esther and Daniel, we will need to look closely at the supposed references to those two books. As we have seen earlier, Ben Sira does refer to the book of Ezra in his praise of his ancestors (compare Ezra 3:8; 4:3; 5:2; 6:14 with Ben Sira 49:12 and see the discussion above, especially page 38).

However, before we proceed to the examination of the possible references to Esther and Daniel, we should note that Ben Sira did

---

[60] Skehan and Di Lella, *The Wisdom of Ben Sira,* 40–41.

occasionally also include language modeled on some Gentile literature.[61]
Skehan and Di Lella note:[62]

> The dependence of Ben Sira on several non-Jewish
> writings seems beyond question. As mentioned above, he
> probably even read, in whole or in part, the works of
> Theognis and Phibis, and incorporated into his own book
> some of their insights and ideas as well as others that
> were circulating at the time. But we must keep in mind
> that Ben Sira utilized certain Gentile expressions and
> aphorisms only because he considered these to be true and
> hence, in his mind, conformable to Jewish tradition and
> doctrine. In effect, what Ben Sira does with the non-
> Jewish material is to make it as Jewish as possible...he
> felt he had to show others how the best of Gentile thought
> is no danger to the faith but could even be incorporated
> into an authentically Jewish work, the purpose of which
> was to encourage fidelity to their ancestral practices.

Thus, Ben Sira's use of the OT as a source and other works as
sources is different in quality as well as quantity.

### Esther and Ben Sira

The only phrase in Ben Sira identified as possibly coming from
Esther is the phrase לא זע in Esther 5:9 and Ben Sira 48:12. The root זוע
occurs only three times in the OT (Esth 5:9, Eccl 12:3, Hab 2:7). Only in
Esther 5:9 is it negated with לא. Esther 5:9 reads:

ההוא שמח וטוב לב וכראות המן את־מרדכי בשער המלך
ולא־קם ולא־זע ממנו וימלא המן על־מרדכי חמה:

Haman was happy and in good spirits that day. But when
Haman saw Mordecai in the king's gate, and when
Mordecai neither rose *nor trembled* in front of him,
Haman was infuriated with Mordecai.

Ben Sira 48:12b reads

מימיו לא זע מכל ולא משל ברוחו כל בשר

---

[61] For a thorough discussion of this phenomenon in Ben Sira and a summary of studies on
it see Skehan and Di Lella, *Ben Sira*, 46–50.

[62] Skehan and Di Lella, *Ben Sira*, 49–50.

In his days he [Elisha] *never trembled* before anyone;
he was not intimidated by any person.

In both contexts the thrust of the phrase is that the subject (Mordecai, Elisha) did not cower before others in fear. However, in Esther Mordecai failed to cower before a person of high rank—one of the king's officials. In Ben Sira Elisha was said not to cower before anyone. While this surely assumes that such cowering would be in front of powerful people, it is much more broadly stated in Ben Sira than in Esther.

Yet one piece of evidence suggests that in ancient times Ben Sira was indeed adopting language from Esther. This is in the Greek translation of Ben Sira, which reads:

καὶ ἐν ἡμέραις αὐτοῦ οὐκ ἐσαλεύθη ὑπὸ ἄρχοντος
καὶ οὐ κατεδυνάστευσεν αὐτὸν οὐδείς

In his days he did not tremble *in front of any ruler;*
nor could anyone ever intimidate him.

The addition of the phrase ὑπὸ ἄρχοντος in the Greek translation suggests that the translator (Ben Sira's grandson) understood לא זע to be a reference to Esther so that he drew the parallel more precisely for his readers. He made an explicit reference to trembling in front of rulers to help the reader connect this reference to Mordecai's failure to tremble in front of Haman.

Therefore, it is very likely, though not certain, that Ben Sira was borrowing and adapting a phrase from Esther. His changing its referent from Mordecai to Elisha is in keeping with his procedure. Skehan and Di Lella note this procedure when they state, "Though he often quotes or refers to a sacred text, he does not hesitate to alter it or change the wording so that there is a new emphasis or a different meaning."[63] We cannot be absolutely certain that Ben Sira knew and used Esther, because this is the only parallel in his book and its application of the Hebrew text is broader than in the proposed source. Nevertheless, since Ben Sira was a conscious imitator and adapter of biblical phrases, the probabilities weigh in favor of the conclusion that Esther was among the books of the OT known and used by Ben Sira.

---

[63] Skehan and Di Lella, *Ben Sira*, 40.

## Daniel and Ben Sira

Ben Sira's use of Daniel is more controversial than his use of Esther. The reason for this is that most critical scholars date Daniel to about 164 BC, which would have made it impossible for Ben Sira to quote Daniel. However, many evangelical scholars defend the more traditional sixth century date for the book. It is not possible to delve into the debate about the date of Daniel here. The only line of evidence pursued here will be the correspondences between Ben Sira and Daniel.

Schechter proposed three possible adaptations of Daniel: Ben Sira 3:30 (Dan 4:24); Ben Sira 36:10 (Dan 8:19; 11:27, 35); Ben Sira 36:22 (Dan 9:17).[64]

### Ben Sira 3:30 (Daniel 4:24)

Schechter proposed that the words צדקה תכפר חמאת were adapted from Daniel 4:24 (4:27 in English versions). The problem of comparing Ben Sira to Daniel is that Daniel 4:24 is Aramaic, while Ben Sira is Hebrew. Therefore, we must also determine whether the words in Ben Sira appear to be a Hebrew representation of this Aramaic text.

Daniel 4:24 reads:

$$\text{להן מלכא מלכי ישפר עליך } \textit{וחטיך בצדקה פרק} \text{ ועויתך}$$
$$\text{במחן ענין הן תהוא ארכה לשלותך:}$$

Therefore, Your Majesty, may my advice be acceptable to you: *tear away from your sins with righteousness* and your iniquities with mercy to the oppressed. Perhaps your prosperity may be prolonged.

Ben Sira 3:30 reads:

$$\text{אש לוהטת יכבו מים כן צדקה } \textit{תכפר חטאת}$$

As water extinguishes a blazing fire, so *righteousness atones for sin.*

---

[64] Schechter and Taylor, *Ben Sira*, 13, 17, 18. The versification followed here will be that of the NRSV. Schechter follows a slightly different versification so that 36:10 is 36:8 in his list and 36:22 is 36:17 in his list. Ben-Hayyim lists 36:10 and 36:22 as 33:10 and 36:22 respectively. Ben-Hayyim's versification is a result of attempting to reconstruct the text by assuming that in the Greek mss there has been a disruption and rearrangement of material in Ben Sira 30:24–36:16. Ben Hayyim, *Ben Sira*, xii.

The question of whether the language of this passage in Ben Sira is drawn from Daniel revolves around the equivalence of Daniel's Aramaic verb פְּרַק (tear away) and Ben Sira's Hebrew verb כפר (atone). Admittedly, פְּרַק is difficult to understand in this context. However, we should note that both the Old Greek and Theodotion translate this verb in Daniel 4:24 in a way that is similar to Ben Sira. Both use the verb λυτρόω, which normally means *redeem*, but in this verse by context can only mean *atone by your actions* (i.e., your actions will pay the price to redeem you and, therefore, atone for your sins).

The Old Greek of Daniel 4:24 is

πάσας τὰς ἀδικίας σου ἐν ἐλεημοσύναις λύτρωσαι

Atone for all your unrighteousness with donations to the poor.

Theodotion reads:

τὰς ἁμαρτίας σου ἐν ἐλεημοσύναις λύτρωσαι

Atone for your sins with donations to the poor.

Interestingly, both of these translations understand the righteousness (צְדָקָה) of the Aramaic text as charitable giving (probably from the mention of showing mercy to the oppressed later in the verse). This same connection is made by Ben Sira's grandson in his translation of Ben Sira 3:30, confirming the identification of Ben Sira's language with Daniel 4:24:

πῦρ φλογιζόμενον ἀποσβέσει ὕδωρ καὶ ἐλεημοσύνη
ἐξιλάσεται ἁμαρτίας

As water extinguishes a blazing fire, so donations to the
poor atone for sin.

All of this evidence points in the direction of Ben Sira being dependent on Daniel, not the reverse. One can explain how Ben Sira, the Greek translation of Ben Sira and the two Greek translations of Daniel are dependent on the Aramaic text of Daniel. It is highly improbable that twenty years after Ben Sira was written Daniel borrowed this thought and transformed its vocabulary in Aramaic. Then thirty years later Ben Sira's grandson interpreted the older Ben Sira 3:30 in light of a younger book of Daniel and that at about the same time Daniel was being translated in the Old Greek with the same understanding.[65] It is much more probable that Daniel is prior to Ben Sira, its Greek translation, and the Old Greek translation of Daniel. Therefore, we have ancient confirmation that Ben Sira 3:30 does reflect the language of Daniel 4:24.

### Ben Sira 36:10 (Daniel 8:19; 11:27, 35)

The parallel between Daniel 8:19, 11:27, 35 and Ben Sira 36:10 has been recognized not only by Schechter but also by Torrey[66] and Fox.[67] All have noted the same thing. The collocation of the Hebrew words קץ (end) and מועד (appointed time) occurs in the OT only at Daniel 8:19; 11:27, 35.

The three passages are:

...כי למועד קץ

...because it refers to the appointed time of the end. (8:19)

:כי־עוד קץ למועד...

...because the end must wait until the appointed time (11:27)

:וללבן עד־עת קץ כי־עוד למועד...

...and make them white until the time of the end because it is still for the appointed time. (11:35)

This same collocation of קץ and מועד is found at Ben Sira 36:10:

...החיש קץ ופקוד מועד

---

[65] The Old Greek Daniel dates to the late second or early first century BC. See John J. Collins, *Daniel: A Commentary on the Book of Daniel.* Hermenia. (Minneapolis: Fortress, 1993), 8.

[66] C. C. Torrey, "The Hebrew of the Geniza Sirah" in Saul Liebermann, ed. *The Alexander Marx Jubilee Volume.* (New York: Jewish Theological Seminary of America, 1950), 597.

[67] Douglas E. Fox, "Ben Sira on OT Canon Again: The Date of Daniel," *WTJ* 49 (1987), 335–50.

Hasten the end and remember the appointed time...

God's judgment at this eschatological appointed time of the end is the theme in Sirach 36:1–11:[68]

> Have mercy upon us, O God of all,
> and put all the nations in fear of you.
> Lift up your hand against foreign nations
> and let them see your might.
> As you have used us to show your holiness to them,
> so use them to show your glory to us.
> Then they will know, as we have known
> that there is no God but you, O Lord.
> Give new signs, and work other wonders;
> make your hand and right arm glorious.
> Rouse your anger and pour out your wrath;
> destroy the adversary and wipe out the enemy.
> Hasten the end, and remember the appointed time,
> and let people recount your mighty deeds.
> Let survivors be consumed in the fiery wrath,
> and may those who harm your people meet destruction.

If we keep in mind Schechter's observation that "when the same phrase occurs in one of the canonical writers and in B.S., the balance of probability is strongly in favour of the supposition that B.S. was the imitator of the canonical writer and not *vice versa*"[69] we are led to the conclusion that Ben Sira was borrowing from Daniel at this point.

Ben Sira 36:22 (Daniel 9:17)

Ben Sira 36:22a says:

תשמע תפלת עבדיך...

Listen to the prayers of your servants...

---

[68] The translation is the NRSV except that in v. 10 I have substituted *end* for NRSV's *day*. NRSV is following the Greek text, which apparently misunderstood the Hebrew. The NRSV's decision to follow the Greek is probably an ideological one. It assumes that Ben Sira could not be borrowing from Daniel since critical opinion dates Daniel after Ben Sira.

[69] Schechter and Taylor, *Ben Sira*, 35.

The collocation of the Hebrew words שמע, תפלה, and עבד occurs only at Nehemiah 1:6 and Daniel 9:17. However, Nehemiah uses the infinitive construct לשמע, whereas Daniel uses the imperative שמע. Since תשמע in Ben Sira 36:22 is probably to be understood as an injunction, that is, a request,[70] (the Greek translates it with the imperative εἰσάκουσον) Daniel 9:17 has a much stronger claim as the source used by Ben Sira. Its syntax more easily aligns with the syntax in Ben Sira, whereas the syntax of Nehemiah 1:6 is much more distant.

These three verses in Ben Sira have clear parallels in Daniel. One could argue that the parallels are coincidence. However, since these parallels are of the same type as those to other OT books, one would have to deny practically every reference to other OT books. Since scholars generally view those other parallels as Ben Sira's use of the OT, this approach is precluded.

On the other hand, one could argue that Daniel borrowed from Ben Sira. Besides the fact that Ben Sira is known to be an adapter of other biblical material, this would also raise the question as to why Daniel borrowed at only these three places. The parallel in Ben Sira 36:10 to Daniel 8 and 11 could possibly be seen as Daniel adapting an eschatological passage for his own use since his book is eschatologically oriented, and the author might have been interested in using another well-respected book to boost his own. However, little reason could be found for the adopting of the other passages. Indeed, with the interest in wisdom in the first part of Daniel one would expect much more borrowing, especially in the contexts where wisdom is explicitly mentioned. However, we find only two other parallels and neither in the immediate proximity of references to wisdom. Indeed, Daniel 4 is a different kind of wisdom than found in Ben Sira—wisdom and insight that allows Daniel to interpret dreams, not the proverbial wisdom characteristic of Ben Sira. It would seem that Ben Sira is adopting Daniel for his purposes, as he does other biblical books.

Therefore, Ben Sira appears to have drawn upon Daniel chapters 4, 8 and 11 and most probably drew on chapter 9. This means that Ben Sira used even those chapters that scholars date as late compositions (8–12). Since he also used chapter 4, which some scholars date as earlier, Ben Sira appears to have been using the book of Daniel as we have it in the Hebrew OT or something very similar to it. Whether these parallels to Daniel are real or only apparent is an issue that has seldom been

---

[70] *IBHS*, 509, §31.5b

addressed. For the purposes of this study we can only state that there is no obvious reason, (other than the critical scholarly consensus on the date of Daniel) for maintaining that Ben Sira did not know and use Daniel.

### Summary of the Evidence from Ben Sira

From the use that Ben Sira makes of the OT the following conclusions may be drawn:

**Ben Sira as evidence for a canon.** Ben Sira knew and respected a group of Jewish literature as authoritative. Schechter states "...the impression produced by the perusal of B.S.'s original on the student who is at all familiar with the Hebrew Scriptures is that of reading the work of a post-canonical author, who already knew his Bible and was constantly quoting it."[71] This impression is especially strong in the Praise of Ancestors when Ben Sira completes his summary of OT figures with Nehemiah and closes with a reference again to Genesis before proceeding to praise a nonbiblical ancestor, the high priest Simeon. Even Skehan and Di Lella go as far as to say that Ben Sira considered the works of the OT he used to be "already viewed as sacred and virtually canonical."[72] (Their phrase "virtually canonical" is based on their opinion that the canon was officially defined in the last decade of the first century AD.)

**The content of Ben Sira's canon.** Ben Sira witnesses to a collection of books virtually identical to the Hebrew OT. The only book that is clearly not used by Ben Sira is the short book of Ruth. Esther most probably was a source for Ben Sira. Daniel appears to have been a source for Ben Sira, both the early chapters and the later chapters that are normally attributed to a Maccabean author by critical scholars (chapters 8 and 11, and probably 9). At most Ben Sira's canon is identical to the Hebrew OT we know, with the short book of Ruth being overlooked or perhaps grouped with the Judges, during whose time the narrative took place. At the very least Ben Sira's canon had all the books of the Hebrew OT except Ruth and possibly Esther and Daniel.

**The date of the closing of the canon.** By ending his praise of ancestors with Nehemiah and summarizing before praising his older contemporary Simeon, Ben Sira implies that the last books of the OT

---

[71] Schechter and Taylor, *Ben Sira*, 26.
[72] Skehan and Di Lella, *Ben Sira*, 45.

were books composed in the early Persian period (the late minor prophets, Ezra, Nehemiah, Chronicles, etc.).

**The organization of the canon.** Ben Sira supplies us with evidence that some groupings of books in the canon that are still recognized today were already formed in his day. Both the Torah (Pentateuch) and the Twelve Minor Prophets were collections in his day. He provides no evidence that the division of books outside the Law (Pentateuch) into Prophets and Writings had taken place in his day. He easily moves from Haggai (the Prophets) to Ezra to Nehemiah (both in the Writings) in the Praise of Ancestors. In addition, in this same section he incorporated references to Chronicles and Job (both in the Writings) while also using material from Kings and Ezekiel (both in the Prophets). This suggests that no division between these books was recognized in his day (cf. Ben Sira 49:11–13). Barton concludes:[73]

> There is little to suggest that Ben Sira himself knew a canon in which the Prophetic division ended where it does now. His list of the heroes of Israel includes Nehemiah, and almost certainly also Job, and he does not seem to make any distinction between Prophets and Writings as source material—nor, for that matter, between Prophets and Torah.

### The Greek Prologue to Sirach

As noted above, Ben Sira's grandson was responsible for translating his book into Greek sometime after 132 BC. Three times in his prologue he mentions books that his grandfather and other devout Jews studied. Some scholars have found evidence in this prologue that Ben Sira's grandson knew a tripartite canon similar or identical to the one in the present Hebrew OT.[74] Because this prologue is used by many to argue that by the end of the second century BC the OT was organized into three sections, we will need to look closely at this prologue.

Πολλῶν καὶ μεγάλων ἡμιν διὰ          Many great things have been

---

[73] John Barton, Oracles of God: Perceptions of Ancient Prophecy in Israel after the Exile. (New York: Oxford, 1986), 48.

[74] Beckwith, *Old Testament Canon,* 110–11; Ellis, *Old Testament,* 9–10; Leiman, *Canonization,* 29; McDonald, *Formation,* 35–37. McDonald raises doubts about the authenticity of the prologue, but views it as acknowledging a tripartite canon.

νόμου καὶ τῶν προφητῶν καὶ
ἄλλων τῶν κατ᾽ αὐτοὺς
ἠκολουθηκότον δεδομένων, ὑπὲρ ὧ
ν δέον ἐστιν ἐπαινεῖν τὸν Ἰσραηλ
παιδείας καὶ σοφίας, καὶ ὡς οὐ
μόνον αὐτοὺς τοὺς
ἀναγινώσκοντας δέον ἐστιν
ἐπιστήμονας γίνεσθαι, ἀλλὰ καὶ
τοῖς ἐκτὸς δύνασθαι τοὺς
φιλομαθοῦντας χρησίμους εἶναι
καὶ λέγοντας καὶ γράφοντας, ὁ
πάππος μου Ἰησοῦς ἐπι πλεῖον
ἑαυτὸν δοὺς εἴς τε τὴν τοῦ νόμου
καὶ τῶν προφητῶν καὶ τῶν ἄλλων
πατρίων βιβλίων ἀνάγνωσιν καὶ
ἐν τούτοις ἱκανὴν ἕξιν
περιποιησάμενος προήχθη καὶ
αὐτὸς συγγράψαι τι τῶν εἰς
παιδείαν καὶ σοφίαν ἀνηκόντων,
ὅπως οἱ φιλομαθεῖς καὶ τούτων
ἔνοχοι γενόμενοι πολλῷ μᾶλλον
ἐπιπροσθῶσιν διὰ τῆς ἐννόμου
βιώσεως.

Παρακέκλησθε οὖν μετ᾽
εὐνοίας καὶ προσοχῆς τὴν
ἀνάγνωσιν ποιεῖσθαι καὶ
συγγνώμην ἔχειν ἐφ᾽ οἷς ἄν
δοκῶμεν τῶν κατὰ τὴν ἑρμηνείαν
πεφιλοπονημένων τισὶν τῶν
λέξεων ἀδυναμεῖν· οὐ γὰρ
ἰσοδυναμεῖ αὐτὰ ἐν ἑαυτοις
Ἑβραϊστὶ λεγόμενα καὶ ὅταν
ματαχθῇ εἰς ἑτέραν γλῶσσαν· οὐ
μόνον δὲ ταῦτα, ἀλλὰ καὶ αὐτὸς ὁ
νόμος καὶ αἱ προφητεῖαι καὶ τὰ
λοιπὰ τῶν βιβλίων οὐ μικρὰν ἔχει
τὴν διαφορὰν ἐν ἑαυτοῖς λεγόμενα.

given to us through *the Law, and the Prophets, and the other books that followed them* for which we should praise Israel for instruction and wisdom. Moreover, since it is necessary that not only the readers themselves should acquire understanding but also as lovers of learning be able to help outsiders through the spoken and written word, my grandfather Jesus, who had dedicated himself to the reading of *both the Law and the Prophets and the other ancestral books* and had acquired sufficient proficiency in them, was led himself to compose something pertaining to instruction and wisdom so that those who love learning and become familiar with these things might make even greater progress in living by the law.

Therefore, you are invited to read it with good will and attention and to have tolerance where it seems something is lacking in the phrasing despite our diligent effort in translating. You see, what was originally expressed in Hebrew does not convey exactly the same sense when translated into another language. Not only this book but also *the Law itself and the Prophets and the rest of the books* contain no small differences when read in the original language....

Because on three occasions this prologue mentions the books that Ben Sira studied, and in all three cases they are divided into three categories, some scholars have assumed that this is early evidence for the tripartite Hebrew OT canon. Beckwith claims that it is evidence of a closed three-part canon in the time of Ben Sira and his grandson.[75] Leiman claims that the third category ("the other books that followed them," "the other ancestral books," "the rest of the books") was not closed in Ben Sira's time, but was closed shortly after the composition of Daniel in 164/163 BC.[76] McDonald assumes that the prologue does witness to three categories of sacred literature, though he believes that the third category is vague, and therefore indicates that the canon had not completely formed when the prologue was written.[77]

However, Barton has challenged this view. In his opinion, the third category does not refer to sacred books, but to other books in general.[78] Beckwith has challenged this interpretation of the Prologue, especially as it is outlined by Barton.[79] Beckwith insists that the Prologue indicates a three-part canon. He contends that the third group of books would not be mentioned three times if it were not a group in the canon like the Law and the Prophets. However, one could ask why Ben Sira's grandson was not careful to refer to this set of books with one description instead of three if it was sacred like the other two.

Secondly, he challenges Barton's view that the books in the third set were literature in general. Instead, he rightly observes that the Prologue implies they were religious books. Beckwith is certainly on firmer ground here. However, not all religious books are authoritative books of Scripture. Considering Ben's Sira's preoccupation with wisdom, he may not have made a sharp distinction between religious books and philosophical books, including Greek philosophy. In fact, such a distinction is a modern one. Ancient philosophy often was closely identified with religion. (Philo of Alexandria, whose writings we will treat later in this chapter, is a good example.)

Finally, Beckwith argues that the Prologue clearly distinguishes between the work of Ben Sira and all the other books in the three

---

[75] Beckwith, *Old Testament Canon*, 111.

[76] Leiman, *Canonization,* 29–30.

[77] McDonald, *Formation*, 35–37.

[78] Barton, *Oracles of God*, 47; see also John J. Collins, "Before the Canon," 230–31.

[79] Roger Beckwith, "A Modern Theory of the Old Testament Canon," *VT* 41 (1991), 385–95, esp. 388–89.

categories given in the Prologue. This proves little, however, because
these are in the category of books studied by Jews (including Ben Sira)
and upon which Ben Sira drew for his inspiration. The conclusion that
they were Scripture for Ben Sira or his grandson does not necessarily
follow. They could have studied Scripture *and* other books they found
useful for spiritual and devotional purposes as Christians and Jews do
today.

Barton's view is supported by a close reading of the Prologue itself
and his comments on its meaning are well taken:[80]

> ...the Prologue to Ecclesiasticus does not provide
> unequivocal evidence for the tripartite character of
> Scripture. It *could* [emphasis original] mean the Law and
> Prophets, in their present form, were already fixed, and
> the vague expressions 'the others that followed them',
> 'the other books of our fathers', and 'the rest of the
> books' might then imply that the third division has as yet
> no name and was not yet 'closed', as on the consensus
> view. *But the passage makes better sense, and coheres
> better with the evidence of the main body of the text itself,
> if we assume that 'the law and the prophets' refers to
> Scripture, the holy books of Ben Sira's people, and 'the
> rest of the books' means simply 'all other books'.*
> [emphasis mine] The author of the Prologue is arguing,
> after all, that books lose in translation: not just the
> Scriptures, but other books too—hence the reader should
> not expect the present work to be an exception; just as he
> is painting a picture of his grandfather as not simply
> learned in Scripture, in the sacred writings ('the law and
> the prophets'), but learned *tout court*, well versed not just
> in the holy books but in literature in general.

Thus, there are good arguments on both sides of the debate about
what Ben Sira's grandson meant by *other ancestral books* (ἄλλων
πατρίων βιβλίων).[81] Since it is impossible to know whether the
prologue is referring to a two-part or three-part canon, it is best not to be
too dogmatic on the issue. Therefore, we could draw the conclusion from
the translator's prologue to Sirach that he (and perhaps his grandfather

---

[80] Barton, *Oracles of God*, 47.

[81] Nothing should be read into the use of ἄλλων since ἄλλος cannot be clearly
distinguished in meaning from ἕτερος. (*TDNT* 1.264; *EDNT* 1.63–64).

also) knew of a canon of Scripture divided into two parts: the five books of the Law and all of the other books under the heading of the Prophets.

On the other hand, we could conclude that he knew of a three-part division of Law, Prophets, and other books. However, the third category should not be identified with the later Jewish section known as the Writings for several reasons. First, Ben Sira, the book to which the prologue is referring, treats several books presently in the Writings side-by-side with books from the Prophets without ever indicating a distinction, as was seen above. Second, as we will see later in this chapter and the next, Daniel, one of the current books in the Writings, is always treated as a prophet before the second century AD. Finally, if Ben Sira itself does indicate a third section of the canon, as he may at 39:1, it is composed only of wisdom books, not the disparate group of books currently making up the Writings.[82]

## *1 and 2 Maccabees*

Several passages in 1 and 2 Maccabees show some knowledge of the OT Scriptures as a collection. Both of these books relate events connected with the Hasmoneans and their rebellion against the Seleucid king Antiochus IV Epiphanes. 1 Maccabees appears to be written shortly after the death of the high priest John Hyrcanus I (134–104 BC) or perhaps even before his death.[83] 2 Maccabees is a condensation of a history by Jason of Cyrene (2 Macc 2:19–32). It is probably somewhat older than 1 Maccabees.[84] Since these books are roughly contemporaneous and deal with events of the late Hellenistic and early Hasmonean period, we will look at them together.

---

[82] However, 39:1 probably does not refer to a three-part canon, though it does mention devoting oneself to the study of the Law, wisdom and prophecies. Verses 2 and 3 extend this devotion to studying sayings of famous people, parables and proverbs. These six categories, if they are references to Scriptural books, would seem to refer to at least six types of literature, not a three-part canon.

[83] See the summary by Bruce Metzger, *The Oxford Annotated Apocrypha.* Expanded ed. (New York: Oxford, 1977), 211; the summary by Howard Clark Kee, *The Cambridge Annotated Study Apocrypha. New Revised Standard Version.* (Cambridge: Cambridge, 1994), xxiv; also R. K. Harrison, *Introduction to the Old Testament.* (Grand Rapids, MI: Eerdmans, 1969), 1260.

[84] Metzger, *Oxford Annotated Apocrypha,* 263; Kee, *Cambridge Annotated Apocrypha,* xxvii; Harrison, *Introduction,* 1267–74.

## The Loss of Books Due to the Destruction by Antiochus

In two passages we are told that Antiochus had Jewish holy books destroyed. In 1 Macc 1:56–57 we are told of the actions of Antiochus' agents.

> καὶ τὰ βιβλία τοῦ νόμου ἃ εὗρον ἐνεπύρισαν ἐν πυρὶ
> κατασχίσαντες καὶ ὅπου εὑρίσκετο παρά τινι βιβλίον
> διαθήκης καὶ εἴ τις συνευδόκει τῷ νόμῳ τὸ σύγκριμα
> τοῦ βασιλέως ἐθανάτου αὐτόν

> And the books of the law that they found they tore to shreds and burned. Anyone found having a book of the covenant or anyone who showed sympathy toward the law was condemned to death on the king's orders.

From this reference it would appear as if Antiochus' target was probably the Torah and not other books in the Hebrew OT. However, Leiman claims that the Syrians probably destroyed other sacred books of the Jews because they would have been unable to distinguish among them.[85] Leiman's suggestion would seem to be mere speculation if it were not for 2 Macc 2:14.[86] There we are told that just as Nehemiah assembled his memoirs [the book of Nehemiah?], the books about kings and prophets [Kings?], the writings of David [Psalms?] and letters of kings about votive offerings [Ezra? see Ezra 7:11–26; see further discussion on page 59]:

> ὡσαύτως δὲ καὶ Ιουδας τὰ διαπεπτωκότα διὰ τὸν
> γεγονότα πόλεμον ἡμῖν ἐπισυνήγαγεν πάντα καὶ ἔστιν
> παρ' ἡμῖν

> In the same way Judas [Maccabeus] collected for us the books that had perished in our recent war and they are in our possession.

Thus, it would appear that Antiochus' agents destroyed more than the books of the Law, as Leiman asserts. It would appear that Jews in the

---

[85] Leiman, *Canonization,* 151, n. 138.

[86] This section of 2 Maccabees is a letter from Judas Maccabeus to Aristobulus. Many have challenged the authenticity of this letter. However, Wacholder has made a strong case for its authenticity. See Ben Zion Wacholder, "The Letter from Judas Maccabee to Aristobulus: Is 2 Maccabees 1:10b–2:18 Authentic?" *HUCA* 49 (1978), 89–133.

late Hellenistic and early Maccabean periods regarded books such as Kings, Psalms, Nehemiah and Ezra as sacred, and the agents of the Seleucid king destroyed all they found. These references to sacred books appear to confirm what we have seen in Ben Sira and his grandson—that the entire OT canon or something very close to it was considered holy throughout the second century BC.

In addition, this passage in 2 Maccabees seems to imply that an official archive of these holy books was established (or reestablished) by Judas. It was from these official archives that copies of the books could be made for others who needed them.

## When Canonical Books Ceased to Be Written

Three passages in 1 Maccabees refer to the belief during the early Hasmonean period that prophecy had ceased sometime in the past and prophets were no longer being commissioned by God. Therefore, no more prophetic books could be produced for inclusion in the canon.

The first of these passages is 1 Maccabees 4:46. Here the reader is told that the priests removed from the temple all the stones that had been defiled by the Syrians and

> ...ἀπέθεντο τοὺς λίθους ἐν τῷ ὄρει τοῦ οἴκου ἐν τόπῳ ἐπιτηδείῳ μέχρι τοῦ παραγενηθῆναι προφήτην τοῦ ἀποκριθῆναι περὶ αὐτῶν

> ...they put them aside on the temple mount in a convenient place until a prophet who could tell them what to do with them would come.

In 9:27 we are told about the turmoil among the Jews after the death of Judas:

> καὶ ἐγένετο θλῖψις μεγάλη ἐν τῷ Ισραηλ ἥτις οὐκ ἐγένετο ἀφ᾽ ἧς ἡμέρας οὐκ ὤφθη προφήτης αὐτοῖς

> There was great distress in Israel. There had not been such distress since the days when prophets ceased to appear among them.

Finally, in 14:41 we are told that Simon was made priest.

καὶ ὅτι οἱ Ἰουδαῖοι καὶ οἱ ἱερεῖς εὐδόκησαν τοῦ εἶναι
αὐτῶν Σίμωνα ἡγούμενον καὶ ἀρχιερέα εἰς τὸν αἰῶνα
ἕως τοῦ ἀναστῆναι προφήτην πιστὸν

The Jews and the priests decided that Simon would be
their leader and high priest permanently until a trust-
worthy prophet would arise.

These three passages reinforce the notion that prophecy had ceased
and was no longer functioning. 1 Maccabees 9:27 implies that a consi-
derable period of time had lapsed since the last prophet. We cannot state
on the basis of these passages in 1 Maccabees when the period of
prophecy was believed to have ended. In the examination of Ben Sira,
however, we did note that he abruptly ended his treatment of praise for
ancestors with Nehemiah in the early Persian period (see page 49).
Whether 1 Maccabees is assuming that prophecy ceased in the Persian
period or later in the Hellenistic period, we cannot say. However, 1 Maccabees does clearly imply that prophecy had ceased for some time. The
logical conclusion from this is that the canon had been closed—if not
formally, at least in practice. The theoretical possibility of reopening it
could only be entertained if the gift of prophecy was given once again
and a new prophet arose.

## References to a Canon or Its Parts

Several passages in 1 and 2 Maccabees appear to refer to books seen
as authoritative and sacred. The first of these clearly indicates the status
of the Pentateuch as a section of the canon.

□καὶ ἐξεπέτασαν τὸ βιβλίον τοῦ νόμου περὶ ὧν
ἐξηρεύνων τὰ ἔθνη τὰ ὁμοιώματα τῶν εἰδώλων αὐτῶν

...and they studied the book of the Law for the type of
things about which the Gentiles consulted the images of
their gods. (1 Macc 3:48)

This passage demonstrates the canonical status of the Law. It was
consulted as an authoritative, inspired oracle and viewed in a way similar
to the oracles of the Gentile gods.

Two other passages indicate that certain books were considered holy.

ἡμεῖς οὖν ἀπροσδεεῖς τούτων ὄντες παράκλησιν ἔχοντες
τὰ βιβλία τὰ ἅγια τὰ ἐν ταῖς χερσὶν ἡμῶν

Although we have no need of these things, since we
receive consolation from the holy books that we possess.
(1 Macc 12:9)

ἔτι δὲ καὶ Ελεαζαρον παραναγνοὺς τὴν ἱερὰν βίβλον καὶ
δοὺς σύνθημα θεοῦ βοηθείας...

Besides, he appointed Eleazar to read the holy book aloud
and he gave them this motto: The Help of God... (2 Macc
8:23)

The first passage, from a letter the Jewish leaders sent to Sparta,
refers to holy books. Which books these were cannot be inferred from
context. The second passage tells of the preparation of Judas' troops by
Eleazar. The motto he gave them from the holy book is probably based
on Psalm 46:2, indicating that the book of Psalms was the holy book
from which Eleazar read.

Still another passage refers to the Law and the Prophets.

καὶ παραμυθούμενος αὐτοὺς ἐκ τοῦ νόμου καὶ τῶν
προφητῶν προσυπομνήσας δὲ αὐτοὺς καὶ τοὺς ἀγῶνας οὓς
ἦσαν ἐκτετελεκότες προθυμοτέρους αὐτοὺς κατέστησεν

And encouraging them from the Law and the Prophets
and reminding them of the struggles they had won, he
made them more eager. (2 Macc 15:9)

This verse is speaking about Judas' encouragement to his troops
before battle with Nicanor. It specifically mentions the Law and the
Prophets. However, we cannot be certain what the contents of the
Prophets were.

A final verse may indicate the status of Esther as an authoritative
book. In 2 Maccabees 15:36 we read:

ἐδογμάτισαν δὲ πάντες μετὰ κοινοῦ ψηφίσματος μηδαμῶς
ἐᾶσαι ἀπαρασήμαντον τήνδε τὴν ἡμέραν ἔχειν δὲ
ἐπίσημον τὴν τρισκαιδεκάτην τοῦ δωδεκάτου μηνὸς Αδαρ
λέγεται τῇ Συριακῇ φωνῇ πρὸ μιᾶς ἡμέρας τῆς
Μαρδοχαϊκῆς ἡμέρας

And they all decreed by public vote never to let this day
go unobserved, but to celebrate the thirteenth day of the
twelfth month (called Adar in the Aramaic language), the
day before Mordecai's day.

The reference to Purim as Mordecai's day is most probably based on
Esther 9:19–32 (though it is remotely possible that the label *Mordecai's
day* came from an independent tradition). Since Esther is poorly attested
in Ben Sira, this probable reference to it increases the likelihood that it
was known and considered among the holy books.

Therefore, on the basis of 1 and 2 Maccabees we can be reasonably
certain that a Scriptural canon did exist by the end of the first century. It
was divided into Law and Prophets, it was closed in practice, if not in
theory, and it contained Psalms and perhaps Esther.

## The Assembling of the Canon in an Archive

Beckwith has pointed out that the tradition of storing copies of holy
writings in a holy place is a tradition attested in the earliest history of
Israel.[87] We read of it in Exodus 25:16,21; 40:20, Deuteronomy 10:1–5;
31:24–26; Joshua 24:26 and 1 Samuel 10:25. The well-known incident of
the discovery of the book of the Law in the temple during Josiah's reign
(2 Kgs 22:8; 23:2, 24; 2 Chr 34:15, 30) assumes that the official archives
of the Scriptures were in the temple. Vasholz claims that "the placing of
writings in a nation's holy shrine is tantamount to and a consequence of
being deemed sacred and divine."[88] If he is correct, then the process of
canonization of books reaches back at least to the first storing of books in
the Temple. This tradition continued during the Second Temple period
and is attested in 2 Maccabees 2:13–15:

ἐξηγοῦντο δὲ καὶ ἐν ταῖς ἀναγραφαῖς καὶ ἐν τοῖς
ὑπομνηματισμοῖς τοῖς κατὰ τὸν Νεεμιαν τὰ αὐτὰ καὶ ὡς
καταβαλλόμενος βιβλιοθήκην ἐπισυνήγαγεν τὰ περὶ τῶν
βασιλέων βιβλία καὶ προφητῶν καὶ τὰ τοῦ Δαυιδ καὶ
ἐπιστολὰς βασιλέων περὶ ἀναθεμάτων ὡσαύτως δὲ καὶ
Ιουδας τὰ διαπεπτωκότα διὰ τὸν γεγονότα πόλεμον ἡμῖν
ἐπισυνήγαγεν πάντα καὶ ἔστιν παρ' ἡμῖν ὧν οὖν ἐὰν
χρείαν ἔχητε τοὺς ἀποκομιοῦντας ὑμῖν ἀποστέλλετε

---

[87] Roger Beckwith, "Formation," 41; also Beckwith, *Old Testament Canon,* 81–82.
[88] Robert I. Vasholz, *The Old Testament Canon in the Old Testament Church.* Ancient
Near Eastern Texts and Studies 7. (Lewiston, NY: Edwin Mellen, 1990), 19.

> The same things are narrated in the records and in the
> memoirs of Nehemiah, and also that he founded a library
> and collected the books about the kings and prophets, and
> the writings of David, and letters of kings about votive
> offerings. *In the same way* Judas [Maccabeus] collected
> for us the books that had perished in our recent war and
> they are in our possession. So if you have need of them,
> send people to get them for you.

This passage clearly states that Nehemiah placed certain writings in a
central archive. Nehemiah's memoirs should probably be identified with
the canonical book of Nehemiah. The books about kings and prophets are
probably Samuel and Kings. The writings of David most likely are the
Psalms, perhaps without any late psalms from the post-exilic period. The
letters of kings about votive offerings are contained in Ezra 7:11–26, and
the phrase here either refers to the book of Ezra or some of the source
material used to write it. As far the as the records mentioned at the
beginning of verse 13, their content is described in verses 1–12 and
include references to Jeremiah (vv. 1–8), Exodus (v. 8), Leviticus (v. 10),
and Chronicles (vv. 8–12, esp. v. 12). Thus, 2 Maccabees credits Nehemiah with reinstating the practice of archiving holy books in the temple.

It is on this passage that both Leiman and Beckwith build their
theory that the canon was closed by Judas Maccabeus about 160 BC.[89]
Strictly speaking, however, this passage only says that Judas restored
what had been lost in the war and made copies available to others who
needed them. (In this case the addressees are the Jews in Egypt led by the
priest Aristobulus.) This passage cannot be used to prove that the canon
was closed in Judas' day. Indeed, we have already seen that by Judas'
day it was acknowledged in 1 Maccabees that no prophet had arisen in
some time. Therefore, it is entirely possible that the canon was closed
earlier or that it was still in theory open.

On the other hand, this passage does imply that some books had been
destroyed and needed to be *replaced* in the official archives (from private
or synagogue collections?). This replacement is said to be analogous
(ὡσαύτως) to the work of Nehemiah assembling books in an archive.

---

[89] Leiman, *Canonization*, 9–30; Beckwith, *Old Testament Canon*, 152, 156–66. Beckwith
goes as far as to say that Judas closed the canon and organized it into the three sections
of Law, Prophets, and Writings. He even attempts to give Judas' logic for organizing
the canon and the order of its books based on a Talmudic barita that was recorded 250
years after Judas!

The analogy probably has its point of comparison in the overrunning of the temple by a foreign power. In Nehemiah's case it was the re-establishing of the temple archives after the Babylonian captivity when the Second Temple was built to replace the one destroyed by Nebuchadnezzar. In Judas' case it was the restoring of the Second Temple archives after their destruction by Antiochus. Thus, because of the analogy employed we cannot state that Judas closed the canon. For the analogy to hold Nehemiah would have had to do the same thing—close the canon! But, of course, the canon was not closed twice.

When the canon was closed cannot be stated on the basis of 2 Maccabees 2 alone. The passage itself leads us to believe that it could not have been closed before Nehemiah's day. The references in 1 Maccabees to the cessation of prophecy leads us to believe that it *may* have been closed before Judas' day. On the other hand, the canon could have been considered theoretically open at this time.

### Summary of the Evidence from 1 and 2 Maccabees

From the references to the OT in 1 and 2 Maccabees we can draw the following conclusions:

**The content of the canon.** These books confirm the evidence from Ben Sira and his grandson concerning the contents of the OT canon in the second century BC.

**The date of the closing of the canon.** 1 Maccabees implies that the canon had been closed in practice (but not necessarily in theory) for some time before Judas Maccabeus' day, but no earlier than the time of Nehemiah.

**The organization of the canon.** The canon appears to be divided into two sections—Law and Prophets, and it seems to have contained books such as Psalms under the rubric of Prophets. The existence of Esther in the canon that is weakly attested in Ben Sira is strengthened by a reference in 2 Maccabees.

**The canon as a collection of books.** The books of the canon were kept in an official repository. From this archive others (e.g., the Jews in Egypt) could make copies for use.

### Qumran

Beginning in 1947 ancient manuscripts were discovered at Khirbet Qumran near the Dead Sea. These Dead Sea Scrolls were hidden in caves

in ancient times, presumably by inhabitants of the nearby settlement of
Qumran. These manuscripts have been dated both by paleography and by
carbon dating to the period from the mid-second century BC to the mid-
first century AD.[90] Since all of the manuscripts are copies and not the
autographs, these manuscripts primarily give us a glimpse of Jewish
beliefs and practices in the second and first centuries BC.

These manuscripts have been instrumental in shaping many facets of
biblical studies. Their bearing on the question of canon, while important,
is limited. That the entire OT with the exception of Esther has been
found among the Qumran manuscripts is an often-repeated claim. In fact,
this claim is true only if one considers the manuscript 4QEzra to be a
scroll of a single book containing Ezra and Nehemiah as in later
manuscripts.[91] This manuscript contains only a few verses from Ezra 4–
5, and no other manuscript contains Nehemiah. The omission of Esther
and possibly Nehemiah could be happenstance. After all, Nehemiah and
Esther are relatively short books.

In the case of Nehemiah the omission appears to be an accident of
history or of the survival of manuscripts. Nehemiah is quoted or alluded
to several times in the Qumran documents (e.g., Neh 7:65, 9:14, 17, 29
and 10:1 are all used in the Damascus Document [4QD] according to
Campbell.[92])

On the other hand, the omission of Esther may be purposeful. It is
the only book of the Hebrew OT not to mention God. And its description
of events tied to the Jewish calendar does not fit into the calendar of 364
days (exactly 52 weeks) that was followed by the sectarians at Qumran.[93]
This calendar always placed the first day of the first month on a
Wednesday. In this way the yearly festivals such as Passover and Taber-
nacles would always be on a Wednesday, and never on a Sabbath.
However, the festival of Purim is on the fourteenth day of the twelfth

---

[90] For a short summary see Florentino García Martínez, *The Dead Sea Scrolls Translated:
The Qumran Texts in English.* Second ed. (Leiden: E. J. Brill, 1996), xlvii–xlviii.

[91] In addition, nothing of the short book of Obadiah has been found at Qumran. However,
since all of the twelve Minor Prophets were collected at an early time, and since several
scrolls from Qumran contain several of the minor prophets, it is safe to assume that
Obadiah was among the biblical books known at Qumran. Moreover, Obadiah has been
found among the manuscripts discovered at Wadi Murabba'at.

[92] Jonathan G. Campbell, *The Use of Scripture in the Damascus Document 1–8, 19–20.*
BZAW 228. (Berlin: Walter de Gruyter, 1995), esp. 182.

[93] This calendar is found in the books of Jubilees and Enoch (both of which were found at
Qumran) and in the Temple Scroll (11QTemple[a-b]).

month (Esth 9:21), a Sabbath in the Qumran calendar. Therefore, the lack of Esther from the Qumran scrolls may be an ideological rejection of this one book.

Recently, J. T. Milik has proposed that a precursor of Esther is among the Qumran manuscripts.[94] These fragments, which are given the sigla 4Qproto-Esther[a-f], contain several parallels to Esther. However, we cannot be certain whether these are one source used by the author of Esther, a parallel tradition or a story based on the book of Esther.[95] Moreover, Talmon has argued that Esther was known at Qumran because a number of biblical *hapax legomena* found only in the text of Esther also appear in several sectarian documents such as the Rule of the Community (1QS) and the War Scroll (1QM).[96]

### Biblical Interest at Qumran

Quite a few other works were found among the Qumran manuscripts. Three books of the wider OT canon (Tobit, Epistle of Jeremiah and Ben Sira) have been found. A host of sectarian writings has been uncovered. A number of works known from other sources (Jubilees, Enoch) have been discovered among the finds. This has led some scholars to assert that the sectarians at Qumran had a wider canon than other Jews.[97] However, the mere presence of books, even books that were obviously important to the community, does not in itself mean that those books were considered on a par with Scripture. Today many Christians highly value some books that can be found among their collections of religious books and even on the same bookshelf as their Bibles. However, that does not mean that these books are considered canonical. So too, the Qumran sect may have valued a number of books and stored them with canonical books without implying that these books were considered sacred. In order to determine their attitude toward these books, we need to assess the collection as a whole.

---

[94] J. T. Milik, "Les modéles araméens du livre d'Esther dan la grotte 4 de Qumrân" *RevQ* 15 (1991), 321–406.

[95] For a general discussion see Sidnie White Crawford, "Has Every Book of the Bible Been Found Among the Dead Sea Scrolls?" *BRev* 12 (1996), 28–33, 56.

[96] Shemaryahu Talmon, "Was the Book of Esther Known at Qumran?" [Hebrew] *Eretz Israel* 25 (1996), 377–82.

[97] McDonald, *Formation,* 72–74; Jacob Neusner, *The Talmud: A Close Encounter* (Minneapolis: Fortress, 1991), 174.

When we look at the collection of books from Qumran, it is probable that they accepted a canon similar to, if not identical to, the Hebrew OT. This can be inferred from the following:

1. The sectarians produced or preserved exegetical works on the OT, but not on other works. For instance, *pesharim* or commentaries on Genesis, Psalms, Isaiah, Hosea, Micah, Nahum, Habakkuk, Zephaniah, and Malachi are among the scrolls. The collection includes exegetical texts that contain explicit quotations from the Hebrew OT often strung together in catenae. These include 4QTanh (several quotations from Isaiah), 4QCatena[a] (quotations from Deuteronomy, Psalms, Isaiah, Ezekiel, Hosea, Micah, Nahum, Zechariah) and 4QFlorilegium (quotations from Exodus, 2 Samuel, Psalms, Isaiah, Ezekiel, Daniel, Amos). We might also include the targums on Leviticus (4QtgLev) and Job (4QtgJob and 11QtgJob). The collection contains no exegetical works on noncanonical books found at Qumran. Indeed, it is rare to find a quotation from noncanonical documents. Among the few quotations that are unambiguous are references in the Damascus Document to the Aramaic Testament of Levi (col. 4, lines 15–19[98]) and Jubilees (col. 16, lines 2–4, see discussion below beginning on page 67) and a quotation of the Psalms of Joshua (4QPsJoshua[b] lines 9–14) in 4QTestamonia (lines 23–29). This last quotation is significant because it is preceded by a quotation from the canonical book of Joshua (6:26). Apparently this was done to make it intelligible for readers since it follows a number of quotations from the Pentateuch. In order to place the quotation from the Psalms of Joshua in a context with the Pentateuch and make it intelligible evidently required an introduction from another holy book. Thus, it would seem that the Psalms of Joshua were understood to be of a lesser status than the Law or the book of Joshua.[99]

2. Many of the works are based upon OT books, persons, or incidents. A number of these have been classified as

---

[98] The line numbers are those in García Martínez, *The Dead Sea Scrolls.*

[99] This was first argued by I. H. Eybers, "Some Light on the Canon of the Qumran Sect" *Die Ou Testamentiese Werkgemeenskap in Suid-Afrika.* (Pretoria, 1962), 1–14.

paraphrases of biblical books or as para-biblical literature.[100]
These include the Reworked Pentateuch (4QRP), Biblical
Chronology (4Q559), Genesis Apocryphon (1QapGen ar),
Jubilees (1QJub$^{a-b}$; 2QJub$^{a-b}$; 3QJub; 4QJub$^{a-f}$; 11QJub); the
Book of Enoch (4QEn$^{a-g}$ ar), and various works attributed to
or written about Jacob, Judah, Joseph, Levi, Naphtali,
Kohath, Amram, Moses, Hur, Miriam, Joshua, Samuel,
Jeremiah and Daniel. These last works taken together seem
to indicate a pattern of attempting to bolster the authority of
a work by referring to a person from a holy book, thereby
giving indirect testimony to the authoritative status of many
of the books of the Hebrew OT.

3.  The sectarian documents refer to the familiar designation of
the canon as the Law and the Prophets:

כאשר אמר והגליתי את סכות מלככם ואת כיון צלמיכם
[כוכב אלהיכם אשר עשיתם לכם והגלתי אתכם מהלאה
ל]דמשק ספרי התורה הם סוכת המלך כאשר אמר
והקימותי את סוכת דוד הנופלת המלך הוא הקהל וכייי
בהצלמים [וכיון הצלמים] הם ספרי הנביאים אשר בזה
ישראל את דבריהם[101]

As he said, "I will deport Sikkuth your King and the
Kiyyun of your images [the star of your God that you
made for yourselves. I will deport you away from my tent
to] Damascus." (Amos 5:26–27) The *books of the law* are
the booth of the king, as he said, "I will lift up the fallen
booth of David," (Amos 9:11). The king is the assembly;
and the bases for the images [and the Kiyyun of the
images] are the *books of the prophets*, whose words Israel
despised. (Damascus Document A, col. 7, lines 14–18)[102]

היאה מדרש *התורה* [*אשר*] *צוה ביד* *מושה* לעשות ככול

[100] For a list see García Martínez, *The Dead Sea Scrolls*, x–xiii.
[101] For the Hebrew text and a discussion see S. Schechter, *Documents of Jewish Sectaries.* Vol. 1. (Cambridge: Cambridge, 1910; repr., New York: KTAV, 1970), 112. Also see Joseph Baumgarten, *Qumran Cave 4. XIII. The Damascus Document (4Q266– 273).* DJD 18. (Oxford: Clarendon, 1996) 44, 128.
[102] Also see García Martínez, *Dead Sea Scrolls*, 37–38.

הנגלה עת בעת וכאשר גלו הנביאים ברוח קדשו[103]

> This is the study of *the law which he commanded by the
> hand of Moses*, in order to act in keeping with all that has
> been revealed from age to age, and according to *what the
> prophets have revealed through his holy spirit*. (Rule of
> the Community, col. 8, lines 15–16; note that this follows
> col. 1, lines 2–3 which speak of things commanded by
> Moses and [God's] servants the prophets)[104]

Other references to Moses and the prophets include 4QDibHam[a]
3.12–13, and 4Q381 69.4–5. In addition, it should be noted that the
"words of [God's] servants, the prophets" are also mentioned in 1QpHab
2.9 and 7.5 and 4QpHos[a] 2.5.

While we cannot be certain what the books of the prophets are
assumed to be, we should note that in 4QFlorilegium, Daniel appears to
be grouped among the prophets. In column 2 line 3 we read:[105]

כתוב בספר דניאל הנביא...

> As is written in the book of the prophet Daniel...
> (Quotations from Dan 12:10 and 11:32 follow.)

This is identical to the earlier references to Isaiah and Ezekiel in
column 1 lines 15 and 16:

כתוב בספר ישעיה הנביא...

> As is written in the book of the prophet Isaiah... (A
> quotation from Isa 8:11 follows.)

כתוב עליהמה בספר יחזקאל הנביא...

> As is written about them in the book of the prophet
> Ezekiel... (A quotation from Ezek 44:10 follows.)

---

[103] The Hebrew text is from Millar Burrows, ed. *The Dead Sea Scrolls of St. Mark's
Monastery.* vol. 2. fasc. 2: *The Manual of Discipline.* (New Haven: American Schools
of Oriental Research, 1951), plate VIII.

[104] See also García Martínez, *Dead Sea Scrolls*, 3, 12.

[105] The Hebrew text is from John M. Allegro, *Qumrân Cave 4.* DJD V. (Oxford:
Clarendon, 1968), 53–54.

Therefore, it would appear that the Qumran documents display knowledge of a canon divided into Law and Prophets, with the designation *Prophets* including more books than in the present tripartite division known as the Prophets does.

Several of the nonbiblical works from Qumran have been suggested as having been viewed as authoritative books.[106] If this is the case, then perhaps the canon was still viewed as open (at least by the Qumran sectarians). The most often mentioned works in this category are Jubilees, several works that make up 1 Enoch, and the Temple Scroll. All of these are based on the Pentateuch. Jubilees, one of the most popular books at Qumran,[107] claims to be information revealed to Moses on Mt. Sinai, and is largely a reworking of Genesis and much of Exodus. The various books that make up 1 Enoch are based on the person by that name mentioned in Genesis. Jubilees and a few other texts from Qumran seem to make use of the Watcher story in 1 Enoch 1–36 (the Book of the Watchers). Like Jubilees, the Temple Scroll claims to be words revealed to Moses on Mt. Sinai.

Certainly Jubilees and Enoch were popular books at Qumran. Fifteen or sixteen copies of Jubilees were discovered at Qumran. As many as twenty copies of Enoch were found. Moreover, both of these books make claims as divine revelation with Jubilees explicitly stating this about itself. These books, then, were popular and claimed to be authoritative. Does that mean that they were canonical at Qumran?

The main problem with holding that the Qumran sectarians viewed any of these books as canonical is that they are based on the Law, a section of the canon that nearly everyone agrees was closed early—certainly before the writing of any of these works. Numerous references to the Law—the Mosaic portion of the canon—in the Qumran sectarian writings seem to attest to this fact (see especially the discussion of 4QMMT below, page 69). They could not have been included in the Prophets since at least two (Jubilees and the Temple Scroll) are Mosaic and the third (1 Enoch) is based on a figure from the Mosaic books. The Prophets are books that followed Moses.[108]

---

[106] See the general discussion in James C. VanderKam, *The Dead Sea Scrolls Today.* (Grand Rapids: Eerdmans, 1994), 153–57.

[107] There are more copies of Jubilees among the Qumran finds than all but four books of the OT.

[108] With the lone exception of Psalm 90, whose superscription attributes it to Moses, no work in the rest of the OT is attributed to Moses. Psalms is self-admittedly a composite

This seems to be confirmed by the only certain reference to any of these books, a reference to Jubilees (the Book of the Divisions of Times into their Jubilees and Weeks) in the Damascus Document (CD):[109]

על כן יקום האיש על נפשך לשוב אל תורת משה כי בה
הכל מדוקדק[.....]ופרוש   קציהם לעורון ישראל
מכל אלה הנה הוא מדוקדק על ספר מהלקות העתים
ליובלים ובשבועותיהם וביומאשר יקום האיש על נפשו
לשוב אל תורת משה...

> Therefore, that man will commit himself to returning to the Law of Moses because in it everything is defined. [.....] And the exact interpretation of the eras of Israel's blindness to all these things is defined in the Book of the Divisions of Times into their Jubilees and Weeks. And on the day when that man commits himself to return to the Law of Moses...

In this passage CD definitely makes a distinction between the Law of Moses and Jubilees. The Law (תורת משה) is what a person is to turn towards. Jubilees is an *interpretation* (פרוש) of times when Israel failed to live by the teachings in the Law. It would seem that somehow Jubilees is a prism through which canonical books are read, but it is not part of that canon. Perhaps it is part of a growing second canon of (official?) interpretation of the already accepted canon. Certainly the adoption of a second set of books that act as a prism through which an earlier accepted canon is read has later analogues: the Christian New Testament, the Jewish Talmud, even the Latter Day Saints' Book of Mormon. What seems to be clear, however, is that the Law is closed and these supposedly Mosaic books are not candidates for inclusion in it, nor are they (by their very nature) candidates for inclusion in the Prophets. Consequently, not even the most likely candidates among the Qumran scrolls provide us with evidence that the canon was in practice open at this time. (Though as we have seen earlier, we cannot rule out the possibility that it was open in theory.)

---

work, but is viewed even in ancient times as a Davidic, not a Mosaic book.

[109] The Damascus Document was first brought to light in modern times from the Cairo Genizah discovery. Additional copies have been found at Qumran. The text can be found in Chaim Rabin, *The Damascus Document: I. The Admonition II. The Law* (Clarendon: Oxford, 1954), 75 as well as in Baumgarten, DJD 18, 156–57 and 178–79.

We cannot state with absolute certainty that the Qumran sectarians did not attempt to include in their canon some books not found in the Hebrew OT. However, *the evidence strongly suggests that their canon was most likely the same as the Hebrew OT with the possible exception of the omission of Esther.* If they did assert authoritative, inspired status equal to the other books known to be among the Law and the Prophets for a few of their sectarian documents, the surprising lack of polemic against those who might have opposed the addition of such books is striking.

### 4QMMT and the Canon

While we have seen that the Scriptures were often classified into Law (the Pentateuch) and Prophets (the rest of the books), one document from Qumran, the Halakhic Letter (4QMMT), seems to indicate a different classification of the books. This letter is one of the oldest Qumran documents. It was written by a leader of the Qumran sect (perhaps the Teacher of Righteousness) to the leader of its opponents, perhaps Jonathan (160–143 BC) or Simon (143–135 BC).[110] Near the end in the epilogue we read:[111]

[כתב]נו אליכה שתבין בספר מושה [ו]בספר[י הנ]ביאים
ובדוי[ד    [ [במעשי] דור ודור...

...we have wr[itten] to you so that you may carefully study the book of M̲o̲ses [and] t̲h̲e̲ books of [the p]r̲ophets and Davi[d      events of] past generations.

This section from 4QMMT is fragmentary and difficult to recon-struct. However, because of some repetition in this section, a number of

---

[110] Elisha Qimron and John Strugnell, "An Unpublished Halakhic Letter from Qumran," *Biblical Archaeology Today: Proceedings of the International Congress on Biblical Archaeology, Jerusalem, 1984* (Israel Exploration Society, 1985), 400; Otto Betz, "The Qumran Halakhah Text Miqsat Ma'asê Ha-Torah (4QMMT) and Sadducean, Essene, and Early Pharisaic Tradition," in D. R. G. Beattie and M. J. McNamara, eds., *The Aramaic Bible: Targums in Their Historical Context* (JSOTSup 166; JSOT, 1994), 176–202. Betz identifies the writer of 4QMMT with the Teacher of Righteousness.

[111] The Hebrew text is from Elisha Qimron and John Strugnell, *Qumran Cave 4 V: Misqat Ma'ase HaTorah.* DJD 10. (Oxford: Oxford, 1994), 58.

the lacunae can be supplied with confidence. The only exception is the large gap at the end of line 10 and beginning of line 11.

We can see that the author of this Halakhic letter was probably working with a concept of a threefold division of the OT into Law and Prophets and David. This, however, is not identical to the later Jewish divisions of Law, Prophets and Writings. Only the book of Psalms in the section known as the Writings could reasonably be characterized as the words of David. Ruth, by its contents (without any reference to other factors that indicate authorship) could theoretically have been written by David, but no one, ancient or modern is known to have held that view. Proverbs, Song of Songs and Ecclesiastes could be assigned to Solomon, but not to David. It is impossible to see how Job, Lamentations, Esther, Daniel, Ezra, Nehemiah or Chronicles could be characterized as words of David. Therefore, it would appear that the author of 4QMMT is making a threefold distinction by singling out Psalms as unique.

The phrase that is reconstructed, [*events of pas*]*t generations*, may or may not refer to another book, depending on whether the reconstruction is accurate. Ellis would understand this phrase as referring to the book of Chronicles, preferring to translate "[and in the words of the days] from generation to generation." [112] Apparently, he is restoring the Hebrew text as [ובדברי הימים] דור ודור. Since הימים דברי is the Hebrew title of Chronicles, this would mean that two books of the Writings, Psalms and Chronicles, are mentioned together as a designation for the Writings as a whole. However, this restoration is completely speculative and without any hard evidence to support it. Since Ellis' suggestion is without foundation, we are on far firmer ground to believe that we are dealing with a slight modification of the twofold classification of Scriptures.

What conclusions can we draw from 4QMMT? We can probably come to three conclusions:

1. The author of 4QMMT is assuming that both he and his intended reader(s) accept a common set of authoritative books and that they can be divided ino three divisions. This assumption appears to point to a widespread (if not necessarily pan-Jewish) acceptance of a set of Scriptures.
2. The lone distinction made among non-Mosaic books was the singling out of Psalms. Perhaps this was recognition that some of the books in the second division were different in

---

[112] Ellis, *Old Testament*, 10. See the similar translation in García Martínez, *Dead Sea Scrolls*, 79.

genre. Psalms certainly is distinct in being a book of nothing but hymns. This distinction may have also been highlighted by the unique role Psalms played in liturgical usage.

3.  4QMMT may show us the beginning of the development of the threefold division of the OT books found in later rabbinic texts. ***In 4QMMT we do not have three distinct divisions identical to the divisions in the later Hebrew canon.***[113] The only conclusion one could draw from all the evidence to this point is that the canon may have been closed in two stages: first, the Law and later the Prophets and Psalms (including the books now classified among the Writings.)

## 11QPs[a] and the Canonical Psalter

Another find from Qumran that has been part of the discussion of the canon is 11QPs[a]. This manuscript contains psalms from books four and five of the Psalter, but not in the order of the MT. In addition, it contains a few noncanonical songs: a Plea for Deliverance, the Apostrophe to Zion, a Hymn to the Creator, Psalm 151 (known previously from the Septuagint) divided into two poems, and Psalms 154 and 155 (known previously in Syriac). Moreover, it also contains a notice about the number of songs written by David and two poems from other books: The Last Words of David (2 Samuel 23:1–7 [only v. 7 is extant in 11QPs[a]]) and Ben Sira 51:13–30. This manuscript dates from between AD 30 and 50.[114]

The problem this manuscript presents for the canon depends largely on how one understands its nature. Sanders argues that it demonstrates that the book of Psalms was not a closed collection in the early part of the first century, so the canon could not possibly be closed.[115] Wilson and

---

[113] Contra Beckwith, who is intent on imposing the later evidence for a tripartite canon onto the earlier evidence. R. T. Beckwith, "A Modern Theory," 388.

[114] J. A. Sanders, *The Dead Sea Psalms Scroll.* (Ithaca, NY: Cornell, 1967), 6. (=DJD 4)

[115] See James A. Sanders, "Cave 11 Surprises and the Questions of Canon," *McCormick Review* 21 (1969) 288 = *New Directions in Biblical Archaeology* ed. D. N. Freedman and J. C. Greenfield. (Garden City: Doubleday, 1969–71), 101–16; "Ps 151 in 11QPss," *ZAW* 75 (1963) 73–86; "The Qumran Psalms Scroll (11QPs[a]) Reviewed" in *On Language, Culture and Religion: In Honor of Eugene A Nida* (The Hague: Mouton, 1974), 79–99; "Two Non-canonical Psalms in 11QPs[a]," *ZAW* 76 (1964) 57–75; "Variorum in the Psalms Scroll (11QPs[a])," *HTR* 59 (1966) 86–87.

Flint appear to agree with him.[116] On the other hand, Talmon, Goshen-Gottstein, Skehan, and Beckwith argue that 11QPs[a] is not a manuscript of the book of Psalms but a liturgical arrangement of psalms and hymns.[117] In addition, Cross seems to be skeptical of the claim that this manuscript represents an alternate Psalter. He states, "If the so-called 11QPs[a] is indeed a Psalter, despite its bizarre order and noncanonical compositions, mostly of the Hellenistic era, then we must argue that one Psalms collection closed at the end of the Persian period (the canonical collection) and that another remained open well into the Greek period (11Q) but was rejected by the Rabbis."[118]

Sanders stresses the variability of the order of psalms in the various Qumran manuscripts. He lists these variations as (excluding 11QPs[a]):[119]

### Table 2
### Qumran Manuscripts Containing Noncanonical Psalms

| *Manuscript* | *Variation* |
|---|---|
| 4QPs[a]; 4QPs[q] | Psalm 32 missing between Psalms 31 and 33; Psalm 71 between Psalms 38 and 47 |
| 4QPs[b] | Psalms 104–111 missing |
| 4QPs[d] | Psalm 147 followed by Psalm 104; includes Plea for Deliverance |
| 4QPs[e] | Indications of Psalms 34 and 118 between Psalms 89 and 104 |
| 4QPs[f] | Psalm 109 followed by Apostrophe to Zion, Eschatological Hymn and Apostrophe to Judah |

---

[116] Gerald H. Wilson, "The Qumran Psalms Manuscripts and the Consecutive Arrangement of Psalms in the Hebrew Psalter," *CBQ* 45 (1983) 377–88; "The Qumran Psalms Scroll Reconsidered," *CBQ* 47 (1985) 624–42; Peter W. Flint, *The Dead Sea Psalms Scrolls and the Book of Psalms.* (STDJ 17. Leiden: Brill, 1997).

[117] Shemaryahu Talmon, "Pisqah Be'emsa' Pasuq and 11QPs[a]," *Textus* 5 (1965) 11–21; Moshe H. Goshen-Gottstein, "The Psalms Scroll (11QPs[a]): A Problem of Canon and Text," *Textus* 5 (1966) 22–33; Skehan, Patrick W. "A Liturgical Complex in 11QPs[a]," *CBQ* 35 (1973) 202–5; "Qumran and Old Testament Criticism," in M. Delcor, ed. *Qumran: sa piété, sa théologie et son milieu* BETL (Gembloux: Duculot, 1978), 163–82; Roger T. Beckwith, "The Courses of the Levites and the Eccentric Psalms Scrolls from Qumran" *RevQ* 11 (1984) 499–524.

[118] Frank Moore Cross, "The History of the Biblical Text in the Light of Discoveries in the Judaean Desert." *HTR* 57 (1964), 286.

[119] See Sanders, *Dead Sea Psalms Scroll*, 143–45; See also Beckwith, "The Courses of the Levites," 502.

| 11QPs[b] | Psalm 141 followed by Psalm 133, 144, Plea for Deliverance and verses from Psalm 118 |
|----------|-------------------------------------------------------------------------------------|
| 11QPsAp[a] | Psalm 91 followed by three apocryphal psalms |

From this Sanders concludes that the first three books of the Psalter were fixed earlier, but that the last two books were not fixed until the late first century AD. He cites 4QPs[a] and 4QPs[q] with their omission of Psalm 32 as the only place in the Qumran psalms scrolls where there is a departure in the Masoretic order in books 1–3.[120]

Flint has recently expanded Sander's argument. He argues that the *proportion* of the variations in order of the Psalms found in the Qumran manuscripts is much higher for books four and five than for books one through three. However, Flint's argument is undermined by the fact that he includes in his tally 11QPsAp[a], which he admits is possibly only a collection of psalms to be read over an ailing person.[121] Moreover, his statistics about the variation in the order of the psalms for books four and five contain data from 11QPs[a] and the allied manuscripts 4QPs[e] and 11QPs[b]. These manuscripts are at the heart of the dispute as to whether they are Psalters or liturgical collections of psalms, and yet they provide the vast majority of examples of differing order for psalms. To include them in the tally of variations in the order of the psalms involves a rather circular argument that states: Books four and five were not a fixed collection because of the variations in the order of the psalms in the Qumran manuscripts. 11QPs[a] is a collection of psalms with a different order and contents than the MT of books four and five and provides most of these variations. Therefore, books four and five of the psalms were not a fixed collection and 11QPs[a] is the prime example of this phenomenon.

Flint also expands Sanders' argument that 11QPs[a] was a Psalter and not a liturgical collection of psalms and poems. However, even he admits that most of the evidence he adduces can apply equally as well to arguing that 11QPs[a] is a liturgical compilation.[122] The additional evidence is also not convincing:

1.  Flint states that one of the apocryphal works included in 11QPs[a] is the basis for Jubilees 2:2–3. However, he admits that Jubilees may be older, nullifying his assertion that 11QPs[a] was used as

---

[120] Sanders, "Cave 11 Surprises," 109–13.

[121] Flint, *Dead Sea Psalms,* 139, 142, 145, 199.

[122] Flint, *Dead Sea Psalms,* 222.

scripture.[123] As Flint's table on page 220 of his book demonstrates, the only certain or reasonably certain quotations or allusions to the psalms in other Qumran manuscripts are to psalms from the canonical collection of 150 in the MT.[124]

2. Flint argues that the strong emphasis in the scroll on the Davidic authorship of psalms and his contention that their arrangement highlights this Davidic authorship means that 11QPs[a] was seen by its original audience as scripture.[125] However, the emphasis on David does not mean that the audience understood the entire collection to be Davidic and, therefore, inspired. How can one explain the inclusion of Psalm 137 with its obvious reference to the experience of the Jewish captives in Babylon as being Davidic? Or, more pointedly, how can one explain the inclusion of a poem from Sirach, which the audience surely knew to be non-Davidic? Even if the entire manuscript were only psalms attributed to David and it were forcefully stated that David wrote these psalms under inspiration, we could still not rule out that they were a compilation of such psalms for liturgical purposes.

3. Finally, Flint, following the lead of Wilson, notes that the psalms in 11QPs[a] have been organized into groupings of similar psalms on principles like those used in books four and five in the MT. From this he argues that 11QPs[a] was a parallel development with the ordering of books four and five in the MT. However, it could be that the compiler organized his collection of psalms and other poems by using already established books four and five as his guide.

Therefore, none of the arguments produced by Flint are convincing enough to conclude that 11QPs[a] demonstrates that the Psalms were not a closed and stabilized collection in the early first century AD.

On the other hand, Skehan concludes that 11QPs[a] is a liturgical collection of hymns and was not intended to be a standard psalms scroll. Though he makes a number of points, the main thrusts of his argument are that most of the Qumran psalms manuscripts contain only psalms found in the MT in the same order as the MT (when more than one psalm is preserved on a fragment); that only seven manuscripts depart from the

---

[123] Flint, *Dead Sea Psalms*, 223–24.

[124] Flint, *Dead Sea Psalms*, 220.

[125] Flint, *Dead Sea Psalms*, 224.

order found in the Masoretic Psalter; and that only four of those contain psalms not in the present canon.

In addition, Skehan notes that 11QPs[a] includes a prose catalogue of David's psalms following its inclusion of 2 Samuel 23:1–7. This catalogue reads:[126]

ויהי דויד בן ישי חכם ואור כאור השמש וסופר ונבון
ותמים בכול דרכיו לפני אל ואנשים ויתן לו יהוה רוח
נבונה ואורה ויכתוב תהלים שלושת אלפים ושש מאות
ושיר לשורר פלני המזבח על עולה התמיד לכול יום ויום
לכול ימי השנה ארבעה וששים ושלוש מאות ולקורבן
השבתות שנים וחמשים שיר ולקורבן ראשי החודשים ולכול
ימי המועדות ולי ם הכפורים שלושים שיר ויהי כול
השיר אשר דבר ששה וארבעים וארבע מאות ושיר לננן על
הפנועים ארבעה ויהי הכול ארבעת אלפים וחמשים כול
אלה דבר בנבואת אשר נתן לו מלפני העליון

> And David, the son of Jesse, was wise and a light like light of the sun and learned, discerning and perfect in all his ways before God and people. And God gave him a discerning and enlightened spirit. He wrote 3600 psalms and 364 songs to be sung in front of the perpetual offering every day for all the days of the year; 52 songs for the Sabbath offerings; 30 songs for the New Moon offerings and for all the Festivals and for the Day of Atonement. All the songs that he spoke were 446. There were four songs to be sung over the stricken. The total was 4050. All these he spoke prophetically as it was given to him from in front of the Most High.

Skehan notes that everything in this catalogue is liturgical with the possible exception of the four songs to be sung over the stricken, which are probably added to make the number of songs a round number: 450.[127] The 3600 psalms, the 450 songs and the total of 4050 are all divisible by 150, making it likely that the compiler of 11QPs[a] was working from the canonical Psalter of 150 psalms to compile a liturgical cycle of psalms. Beckwith points out that 3600 is 150 times 24, 24 being the number of Levitical courses appointed to sing the psalms in the temple according to

---

[126] Sanders, *The Dead Sea Psalms Scroll*, 86.
[127] Skehan, *Qumran and Old Testament Criticism*, 169.

1 Chronicles 25.[128] It should be noted that all of the scholars who deny that the standard collection of 150 psalms was a closed, stabilized collection (Sanders, Wilson and Flint) ignore the implication that 11QPs$^a$ itself is assuming that 150 is the basic number of psalms. These scholars never address this point and do not offer any defense for rejecting it as relevant.

Beckwith goes on to propose that each of the seven psalms manuscripts that depart from the standard order can probably be assigned to one of the four usages envisioned in this catalogue:[129]

### Table 3
### Beckwith's Proposal Concerning the Eccentric Psalms Scrolls from Qumran

| | |
|---|---|
| 11QPsAp$^a$ | Songs for the Stricken (it probably contained no more than 4 psalms) |
| 4QPs$^a$ and 4QPs$^b$ | Songs for the Sabbath (these contain no noncanonical psalms, keeping the Sabbath holy) |
| 4QPs$^d$ and 4QPs$^f$ | Songs for the Festivals |
| 11QPs$^a$ and 11QPs$^b$ | Daily Psalter |

Finally, Beckwith points out that although the Septuagint Psalter (attributed to the early second century BC) divides some psalms differently, it has the same order and number for the psalms as the Masoretic Text.[130] This would seem to be another indication that the number and order of the psalms was settled before the composition of the Qumran psalms manuscripts that display a different order or include additional psalms.

Therefore, it would seem unlikely that the Qumran psalms manuscripts such as 11QPs$^a$ represent anything more than liturgical adaptations of the psalms and other songs similar to those found in many church agendas to this day. If this is the case, 11QPs$^a$ is not an indication that either the Psalter or the canon was open or yet to be put in its final form in the second or first centuries BC or the first century AD.

---

[128] Beckwith, "The Courses of the Levites," 504.

[129] Beckwith, "The Courses of the Levites," 512–14

[130] Beckwith, "The Courses of the Levites," 503. Psalm 151 is included in the Septuagint but with the note that it is "outside the number" (ἔξωθεν τοῦ ἀριθμοῦ).

## Summary of the Evidence from Qumran

The evidence from the finds at Qumran corresponds to the other evidence examined in this chapter. The holy books recognized at Qumran appear to be identical to the Hebrew OT canon with the possible exception of Esther. Both the exegetical practice of the Qumran sectarians and their noncanonical literature appear to witness to the canon as we know it today. Moreover, the Qumran sectarians divided the canon, as others did, into the Law and the Prophets. The only significant new piece of information is that there appears to be the beginning of an awareness that some of the books contained in the section called *Prophets* are of a distinctly different type than most of the prophetic books. The singling out of the Psalms in one reference in 4QMMT shows this.

While the canon may have remained open in theory, there is a surprising lack of polemic at Qumran concerning which books are authoritative. The Qumran scrolls do not lack polemic against other Jews whose opinions and practice differ from theirs. However, they do not complain that other Jews do not accept certain holy books or that they do accept books that the sectarians reject. If they accepted some books as authoritative that other Jews did not, it is likely that they accepted the OT canon as the first canon and had adopted or were in the process of adopting a second set of books as a supplemental canon. If they rejected books other Jews accepted, the rejection was probably confined to Esther.

In fact, the common terminology *the Law and the Prophets* used by Ben Sira's grandson, 2 Maccabees and at Qumran suggests a widespread agreement on which books are being referred to by this phrase. We know which books comprised the Law—the five Mosaic books. The most natural reading of this phrase is that the Prophets also make up a well-defined collection (if not closed) group of books, even at Qumran.

### *The Samaritans*

It is well known that the Samaritan canon contains only the books of the Pentateuch. The Triple Canon Theory attributed this acceptance of the Pentateuch but rejection of the rest of the OT to a schism between the Samaritans and Jews in the days of Nehemiah (see Neh 2, 4, 6, 13).[131]

---

[131] Ryle, *Canon*, 91–93.

Thus, the Prophets were not recognized as canonical in the fifth century BC but were held to have been canonized in the third century BC (and the Writings in the first century AD). However, J. D. Purvis has demonstrated that the script, orthography, and textual tradition of the Samaritan Pentateuch are similar to that found in some manuscripts from Qumran.[132] Therefore, Purvis dated the Samaritan break with the Jews sometime in the Hasmonean era. Dexinger also dated the Samaritan schism to about 100 BC when John Hyrcanus destroyed Shechem and the Samaritan temple on Mt. Gerizim.[133] Judith Sanderson's analysis of 4QpaleoExod$^m$, a manuscript from Qumran with textual affinities to the Samaritan Pentateuch, confirms Purvis' view.[134]

The Samaritan canon, therefore, is not a reflection of the canon when the Samaritans broke from the Jews. Instead, it appears to be a conscious rejection of books that were considered sacred before the break in the late second or early first century BC. Moreover, the Samaritan canon sheds little light on other questions about the canon during this period. For instance, we cannot tell from the existence of the Samaritan Pentateuch alone whether they rejected other books in a canon that was open or in a canon that was closed.

### *Philo Judaeus*

Philo Judaeus was a leading member of the Jewish community in Alexandria. He was born about 25–20 BC and died about AD 45–50. His writings reveal him to be a philosopher and apologist for Judaism who was well versed in Greek thought, although he remained loyal to Jewish tradition. The main body of his work is concerned with the Pentateuch, but Beckwith demonstrates that he also considered Joshua, Judges, Samuel, Kings, Isaiah, Jeremiah, Hosea, Zechariah, Psalms, Job and Proverbs to be holy books.[135] Thus, there can be little doubt that Philo considered most, if not all, of the books of the OT as authoritative words of God.

---

[132] James D. Purvis, *The Samaritan Pentateuch and the Origin of the Samaritan Sect* (Cambridge: Harvard, 1968), 18–86.

[133] Ferdinand Dexinger, "Limits of Tolerance in Judaism: The Samaritan Example," in E. P. Sanders, ed. *Jewish and Christian Self-Definition.* Vol. 2 *Aspects of Judaism in the Graeco-Roman Period.* (Philadelphia: Fortress, 1981) 88–114, 327–38.

[134] Judith E. Sanderson, *An Exodus Scroll from Qumran: 4QPaleoExod$^m$ and the Samaritan Tradition.* HSS 30. (Cambridge: Harvard, 1986), 317–20.

[135] Beckwith, *Old Testament Canon,* 75–76.

In his work *The Contemplative Life* Philo tells of a Jewish sect called Therapeutae. From Philo's description of their practices this sect seems to be related to the Essenes, perhaps reflecting a stricter form of Essenism. One section of *The Contemplative Life* tells of the books revered by the Therapeutae:

> ἐν ἑκάστῃ δέ ἐστιν οἴκημα ἱερόν ὃ καεῖται
> σεμνεῖον καὶ μοναστήριον ἐν ᾧ μονούμενοι τὰ τοῦ
> σεμνοῦ βίου μυστήρια τελοῦνται μηδὲν
> εἰσκομίζοντες μὴ ποτόν μὴ σιτίον μηδέ τι ἄλλων
> ὅσα πρὸς τὰς τοῦ σώματος χρείας ἀναγκαῖα ἀλλὰ
> νόμος καὶ λόγια θεσπισθέντα διὰ προφητῶν καὶ
> ὕμνους καὶ τὰ ἄλλα οἷς ἐπιστήμη καὶ εὐσέβεια
> συναύξονται καὶ τελειοῦνται[136]

> In each [house] there is a consecrated room called a sanctuary or closet in which they are cloistered to be initiated into the mysteries of their sanctified life. They take nothing into it, neither drink nor food or anything else necessary for the needs of the body, except Law and words spoken by God through the prophets and Psalms and the other books that foster and perfect knowledge and piety.

This passage is often cited as proof of the existence of the tripartite canon in the early first century AD.[137] Philo's mention of *Psalms* is understood to be synecdoche for the third section of the canon, the Writings.

However, Barton has pointed out that Philo is a witness to *four* classes of books, not three: Law, Prophets, Psalms, other books.[138] Moreover, in light of the classification of the holy books found in 4QMMT (see discussion above beginning on page 69) where the third group can only consist of Psalms, it is much more likely that Philo's classification of the Therapeutae's Scriptures means that the third group is only the Psalms, and not his title for the Writings as we know them. In

---

[136] *The Contemplative Life*, 25.

[137] See Beckwith, *Old Testament Canon*, 117; Ellis, *Old Testament*, 8–9; Leiman, *Canonization*, 31.

[138] Barton, *Oracles of God*, 58.

addition, ὕμνοι is Philo's regular name for the Psalms, and he never uses it elsewhere to mean a group of books of which Psalms is a part.

Nor should we place too much weight on this one quotation from Philo because, as Barton points out, "Philo...has various ways of subdividing the books of Scripture, but it is clear that they come from only two sources: Moses, or the 'disciples of Moses'. This second expression is used to designate the Psalmist, Zechariah and Solomon."[139] Thus, Philo's separation of the Psalms from the Prophets does not indicate a radical departure from the generally held bipartite division of the canon into Law and Prophets.

But what of the fourth group of books, "the other books that foster and perfect knowledge and piety"? These are probably writings revered by the Therapeutae, but not considered part of their Scriptures, as Philo describes them slightly later in *The Contemplative Life*:[140]

> ἐντυγχάνοντες γὰρ τοῖς ἱεροις γράμμασι φιλοσοῦσι
> τὴν πάτριον φιλοσοφίαν ἀλληγοροῦντες...ἔστι δὲ
> αὐτοις καὶ συγγράμματα παλαιῶν ἀνδρῶν οἱ τῆς
> αἱρέσεως ἀρχηγέται γενόμενοι...ὥστε οὐ θεωροῦσι
> μόνον ἀλλὰ καὶ ποιοῦσιν ἄσματα καὶ ὕμνους εἰς
> τὸν θεόν...

> By reading the Holy Scriptures they seek wisdom from the ancestral philosophy, understanding the Scriptures as allegory...They also have writings of men of old, the founders of their sect...So they do not confine themselves to this [contemplation] alone, but also compose hymns and psalms to God...

This further information clarifies Philo's earlier statement. First of all, it makes clear that the Therapeutae did have a canon, which Philo refers to here as the Holy Scriptures (τοῖς ἱεροις γράμμασι).[141] This probably corresponds to the Law, Prophets and Psalms in the earlier section. In fact, Philo's usage may imply that he agrees with them on the limits of this canon since he does not call it "*their* Holy Scriptures" but simply "the Holy Scriptures." In addition, he also defines for us what he

---

[139] Barton, *Oracles of God*, 49. The references in Philo are *The Confusion of Language*, 39 and 62 and *The Embassy to Gaius*, 177.

[140] *The Contemplative Life*, 28–29.

[141] Note the parallel in 2 Tim 3:15.

meant by "the other books that foster and perfect knowledge and piety." These are probably "writings of men of old, the founders of their sect" which not only guide them in their quest for knowledge, but also move them to compose hymns and psalms (i.e., an act of piety).

While it might be argued that the earlier mention of Psalms refers to these psalms and not to the canonical book of Psalms, Philo states that the Psalms are taken into the cloister, but that the other hymns and psalms are produced while in contemplation in the cloister. This makes it unlikely that the compositions produced in the cloister are to be identified with the Psalms taken into the cloister. Instead, the first quotation is referring to the canonical book and the second to compositions that imitate the canonical book.

If the Therapeutae are linked somehow to the sectarians at Qumran (which many assume to be Essenes), their composition of hymns and psalms may shed further light on the manuscripts from Qumran that contain noncanonical psalms, and perhaps reinforce the opinion that those manuscripts were indeed liturgical compilations since the Therapeutae apparently used both canonical and noncanonical psalms in their meditation. Furthermore, if the Therapeutae are an offshoot of the Essenes and the Qumran sectarians were Essenes, the books that the Therapeutae took into their cloister may be essentially the nonbiblical books found at Qumran.

In summary, then, Philo's description of the Therapeutae leads to the following conclusions:

**The existence of a canon among the Therapeutae.** They had a canon, a collection of authoritative books that could simply be called *Holy Scripture.*

**The organization of the canon.** The canon could be subdivided into three groups: Law, Prophets and Psalms. The third group most likely consisted only of the book of Psalms, not the entire Writings as we know them.

**The canon as a closed collection.** The Therapeutae had a high regard for other books, but they were not considered canonical, and apparently they did not attempt to add them to the canon.

### *4 Maccabees*

4 Maccabees is a Jewish book, perhaps based on 2 Maccabees, that emphasized the martyrs in the early days of the Maccabean revolt. Originally written in Greek, it is dependent on Platonic and Stoic

philosophy for much of its thought and terminology. Dates from as early as 63 BC and as late as AD 70 are possible for its composition.[142] Since it mentions Syria and Cilicia as constituting a single Roman administrative region (4:2), the most likely date for its composition is AD 19–54, making it slightly younger than or contemporary with the earliest books of the NT.[143]

In chapter 18 the mother of seven martyred sons addresses them and reminds them of the things their father taught. Verses 10–19 read:

ὃς ἐδίδασκεν ὑμᾶς ἔτι ὢν σὺν ὑμῖν τὸν νόμον καὶ τοὺς προφήτας τὸν ἀναιρεθέντα Αβελ ὑπὸ Καιν ἀνεγίνωσκέν τε ὑμῖν καὶ τὸν ὁλοκαρπούμενον Ισαακ καὶ τὸν ἐν φυλακῇ Ιωσηφ ἔλεγεν δὲ ὑμῖν τὸν ζηλωτὴν Φινεες ἐδίδασκέν τε ὑμᾶς τοὺς ἐν πυρὶ Ανανιαν καὶ Αζαριαν καὶ Μισαηλ ἐδόξαζεν δὲ καὶ τὸν ἐν λάκκῳ λεόντων Δανιηλ ὃν ἐμακάριζεν ὑπεμίμνῃσκεν δὲ ὑμᾶς καὶ τὴν Ησαιου γραφὴν τὴν λέγουσαν κἂν διὰ πυρὸς διέλθῃς φλὸξ οὐ κατακαύσει σε τὸν ὑμνογράφον ἐμελῴδει ὑμῖν Δαυιδ λέγοντα πολλαὶ αἱ θλίψεις τῶν δικαίων τὸν Σαλωμῶντα ἐπαροιμίαζεν ὑμῖν λέγοντα ξύλον ζωῆς ἐστιν τοῖς ποιοῦσιν αὐτοῦ τὸ θέλημα τὸν Ιεζεκιηλ ἐπιστοποίει τὸν λέγοντα εἰ ζήσεται τὰ ὀστᾶ τὰ ξηρὰ ταῦτα ᾠδὴν μὲν γάρ ἦν ἐδίδαξεν Μωυσῆς οὐκ ἐπελάθετο διδάσκων τὴν λέγουσαν ἐγὼ ἀποκτενῶ καὶ ζῆν ποιήσω αὕτη ἡ ζωὴ ὑμῶν καὶ ἡ μακρότης τῶν ἡμερῶν

While he was still with you he taught you the Law and the Prophets. He read to you about the slaying of Abel by Cain, and the offering of Isaac as a burnt offering, and about Joseph in prison. He told you of the zeal of Phinehas, and he taught you about Hananiah, Azariah, and Mishael in the fire. He praised Daniel in the lions' den and blessed him. He reminded you of the scripture of Isaiah that says, "Although you go through fire, the flame shall not consume you." He sang to you songs of the psalmist David, who said, "Many are the afflictions of the righteous." He reminded you of Solomon's proverb, "There is a tree of life for those who do his will." He confirmed the question of Ezekiel, "Will these dry bones live?" For he did not forget to teach you the song that Moses taught that says, "I kill and I make alive" This is your life and the length of your days.

---

[142] H. Anderson, "4 Maccabees" OTP, v. 2, 533.
[143] H. Anderson, "4 Maccabees" OTP, v. 2, 534.

In this short passage the author of 4 Maccabees includes the following books under the rubric of the Law and the Prophets: Genesis (4:8; 22; 39:7–23), Numbers (25:7–13), Daniel (3 and 6), Isaiah (43:2), Psalms (34:19), Proverbs (3:18), Ezekiel (37:3) and Deuteronomy (32:39)—one-third (8 out of 24) of the books in the OT canon. Therefore, this book confirms what we have seen throughout this chapter: The canon was recognized as two parts with books later grouped in the Writings (Daniel, Psalms, Proverbs) considered among the Prophets. Nor can there be any doubt about which books he considered to be part of the Law, since in chapter 2, an excursus on the Law, he quotes or refers to all five books of the Pentateuch (*2:5* – Exod 20:17; *2:9* – Deut 15:9; 23:20; Exod 22:24; Lev 25:36–53; *2:14* – Deut 20:19; Exod 23:4; *2:17* – Num 16:23–30; *2:19* – Gen 34; *2:20* – Gen 49:7).

Therefore, slightly before or contemporaneous with the rise of Christianity, 4 Maccabees offers evidence of a canon similar, if not identical, to the Hebrew OT we know today except that it is divided into two sections, not three.

### *Summary*

In this chapter we have surveyed sources that shed light on the OT canon from the first two and a half centuries before Jesus. Figure 1 gives a chronological summary of our conclusions to this point.

## Figure 1
## Evidence for the BC Canon

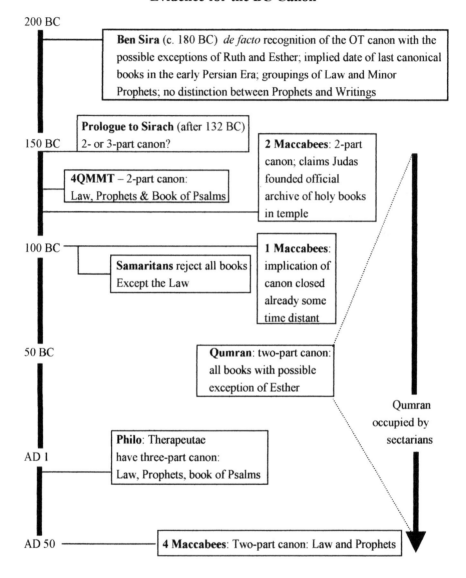

A number of general conclusions about the OT canon in this era can be drawn on the basis of the combined evidence:

**The assumption of a canon.** Most writers assume the existence of a set of authoritative Jewish holy books. This is implied in Ben Sira, assumed in the Greek Prologue, in 1 and 2 Maccabees, in the various manuscripts from Qumran, by Philo and in 4 Maccabees. These books appear to include all of the OT books in the Hebrew canon with the possible exception of Esther. Philo's designation of these books as *Holy Scripture* implies an accepted collection of books, a canon, and is similar to 1 & 2 Maccabees' mention of *holy books*.

**The subdivisions of the canon.** The books are in the process of being grouped into subdivisions of the canon. The two largest subdivisions generally are *Law* (the five books of Moses) and *Prophets* (all others including books later classified as *Writings*). This appears to be the oldest way of subdividing the canon. The Minor Prophets were probably already a collection within the prophets. Sometime around the middle of the second century BC the unique nature of the book of Psalms is recognized and it is sometimes placed in a subdivision by itself. This may be the beginning of the formation of the subdivision later called *Writings*. (No evidence exists to suggest that *Psalms* is a designation for all the books later known as *Writings*. In fact, the evidence of 4QMMT and Philo's own usage strongly argues that *Psalms* in Philo's account of the Theraputae means the book of Psalms alone.)

**The canon as an official collection in the Temple archives.** 2 Maccabees strongly suggests that the canon exists not as a list of authoritative holy books but as a collection of authoritative holy books archived in the Jerusalem temple.

**The closed canon.** For at least some Jews the canon was closed in practice, if not in theory, with books assumed to have been written no later than the early Persian period (fifth century BC). This is implied in Ben Sira and probably by 1 Maccabees.

**Agreement on the contents of the canon.** While the canon may have remained open in theory, there is a surprising lack of polemic at Qumran over which books are authoritative. The Qumran scrolls do not lack polemic against other Jews whose opinions and practices differ from theirs. However, they never complain that other Jews do not accept certain holy books or that they do accept books that the sectarians reject. During this period the only rejection of books otherwise considered holy by Jews is the Samaritan rejection of all books except the Law.

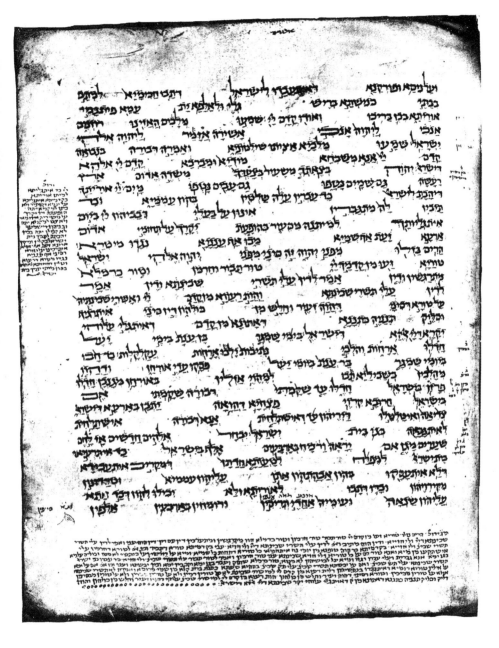

The Song of Deborah. Corpus Codicum Hebraicorum, Medii Aevi. *Codex Reuchlinianus,* No. 3 of the Badische Landsbibliothek in Karlsruhe. Copenhagen: Ejnar Munksgaard, 1956.

# 3

# The AD Canon: The First Century

The second half of the first century AD gave rise to many new witnesses to the OT canon. The beginnings of Christianity and the fall of Jerusalem to the Romans in AD 70 are two major events that shape the evidence for the canon that will be examined in this chapter. We will examine evidence from the NT here, assuming that, no matter what date is assigned to its various books by scholars, its attitude reflects the general attitude among Christians during the second half of the first century. We will also look at evidence from several Jewish sources: Flavius Josephus, whose life spanned the better part of the first century; the attitude of the Pharisees, Saduceees, and Essenes toward holy books (these sects arose in the mid-second century BC, but were still active in the first century); 2 Esdras, a Jewish work from the end of the first century; and Talmudic recollections of the first century.

## *The New Testament*

### The Divisions of the Canon

The NT's most common way of referring to the canon is γραφή, Scripture. But when the NT does refer to the canon by parts, its most common designation is "the Law and the Prophets" (ὁ νόμος καὶ οἱ προφῆται) or its equivalent "Moses and the Prophets" (Μωϋσέως καὶ τῶν προφητῶν).[144] Clearly, the NT evidence demonstrates a continuation of the tradition established in the previous centuries. Moreover, both Daniel and Psalms are included in this category as is

---

[144] The Law (of Moses) and the Prophets: Matt 5:17; 7:12; 11:13; 22:24; Luke 16:16; John 1:45; Acts 13:15; 24:14; 28:23; Rom 3:21; Moses and the Prophets: Luke 16:29,31; 24:27; Acts 26:22.

evident from the reference to their writers as prophets in Matthew 24:15 (referring to Dan 9:27 and 11:31) and Acts 2:30 (referring to Pss 15:8–11 and 109:1, cf. vv. 25–28 and 34–35). However, one passage in the NT does refer to Scripture in a slightly different way. Luke 24:44 reads:

> Εἶπεν δὲ πρὸς αὐτούς, Οὗτοι οἱ λόγοι μου οὓς ἐλάλησα πρὸς ὑμᾶς ἔτι ὢν σὺν ὑμῖν, ὅτι δεῖ πληρωθῆναι πάντα τὰ γεγραμμένα ἐν τῷ νόμῳ Μωϋσέως καὶ τοῖς προφήταις καὶ ψαλμοῖς περὶ ἐμοῦ.

> He said to them, "These are my words that I spoke to you when I was still with you, that it was necessary to fulfill everything that is written in the law of Moses and the Prophets and Psalms concerning me."

This passage has been used by some to argue that the canon was already divided into three sections, with Psalms designating the third division of the Hebrew OT later known as the Writings by means of synecdoche.[145] (For the similar treatment of the evidence from Philo see page 79.) However, the facts militate against this view:

1. As was seen in the previous chapter, especially in the discussion of 4QMMT (see page 69), this expression means the book of Psalms only. Since this was established practice, it is unlikely that Luke is innovating here. He most likely is using a well-established expression.
2. Ψαλμοί is never used in any other first century documents to mean a third section of the canon. It can mean the book of Psalms or describe other songs, but not a section of the canon.

The reading of ψαλμοί as synedoche for the later section known as Writings is a retrojection back into history from later evidence from the Talmud and even later sources. Such a procedure risks an anachronistic reading of the evidence. A more reliable method is reading history forward, not backward.[146] While it is true that already in the first century

---

[145] Beckwith, *Old Testament Canon*, 111; Ellis, *Old Testament*, 9; Leiman, *Canonization*, 40.

[146] McDonald, "Integrity," 104 rightly points out the error of imposing later terminology about the canon on earlier evidence. "This is the basic problem with Roger Beckwith's otherwise excellent work on *The Old Testament Canon of the New Testament Church* (Grand Rapids: Eerdmans, 1985). He regularly attributes to the first century CE features of Judaism that were represented for the first time, so far as current evidence allows, only in rabbinic Judaism in the second and third century and even later.

*Law* can be synechdoche for the entire canon (e.g., John 10:34; 12:34; 15:25), there is no evidence from the first century that *Psalms* is used as synechdoche for the Writings. However, there is evidence from both 4QMMT and Philo (see the discussion in chapter 2). They contain expressions parallel to Luke 24:44, suggesting that its third division contains only the book of Psalms.

In summary, Luke 24:44 at best demonstrates a threefold division of the canon identical to that found in Philo's *The Contemplative Life* (see discussion beginning on page 79) where the third section of the canon consists only of the book of Psalms. However, the most common designation for the canon is still *the Law and the Prophets* at this time. The section designated *Prophets* includes books later placed in the Writings. This also is in general agreement with Philo, who commonly views the canon as bipartite.

## The Books in the Canon

Like the works examined in the previous chapter, the NT has no list of books considered authoritative and inspired. However, the NT does quote many works as "Scripture" or as "The Law" or as spoken by a prophet, or even with the simple formula "[as] it is written" (καθὼς γέγραπται; ὡς γέγραπται; ὥσπερ γέγραπται; simply γέγραπται,

---

Beckwith, for example, in an attempt to equate Jesus' reference to the 'psalms' in Luke 24:44 with the whole of the later established Hagiographa, shows how in the Talmudic literature the 'fifths' sometimes referred to the Psalms and to the whole of the Hagiographa.... If 'Fifths' is used as a reference to the Psalms and if the term "psalms," because it stood in the first place in the Hagiographa, is also used for the third part of the Hebrew Bible, as Beckwith claims, then the reference to Psalms in Luke 24:44 may stand for the whole collection of Writings, but the evidence simply is not there to make the jump backward to the first century and argue that this is what Jesus had in mind in this text."

etc.). This formula for sighting Scripture is significant. It apparently is the Greek equivalent of כבתוב, a formula found already at Qumran for citing Scripture.[147] In the NT this formula is used only to cite passages from the OT and never from other works, Jewish or Greek.

The evidence for which books are Scripture by the way they are quoted in the NT is summarized in Tables 4–7.

### Table 4
### Quotations of Scripture (γράφη/γράμματα) in the NT

| | | | |
|---|---|---|---|
| Matt 2:42 | Ps 118:22–23 | Acts 1:16 | Ps 41:10 |
| Matt 22:29 (32) | Exod 3:6 | Acts 8:32,35 | Is 53:7–8 |
| Mark 12:10 | Ps 118:22–23 | Rom 4:3 | Gen 15:6 |
| Mark 12:24 | Exod 3:6 | Rom 9:17 | Exod 9:16 |
| Luke 4:21 (18–19) | Isa 61:1–2 | Rom 10:11 | Isa 28:16 |
| John 7:38 | Isa 58:1(?) | Rom 11:2 (3–4) | 1 Kgs 19:10,14 |
| | Song 4:15(?) | Gal 3:8 | Gen 12:3 |
| John 7:42 | Mic 5:1 | Gal 4:30 | Gen 21:10 |
| John 10:35 (34) | Ps 82:6 | 1 Tim 5:18 | Deut 25:4 |
| John 13:18 | Ps 41:10 | | Luke 10:7(?) |
| John 19:24 | Ps 22:19 | Jas 2:8 | Lev 19:18 |
| John 19:28 | Ps 22:15 (?) | Jas 2:23 | Gen 15:6 |
| John 19:36 | Exod 12:10,46 | Jas 4:5 | Prov 3:34 |
| John 19:37 | Zech 12:10 | 1 Pet 2:6 | Isa 28:16 |

### Table 5
### Quotations of the Law (ὁ νομός) in the NT

| | | | |
|---|---|---|---|
| Matt 22:36 (37,39) | Deut 6:5 | John 7:51 | Deut 1:16–17 |
| | Lev 19:18 | John 8:17 | Deut 17:6 |
| Luke 2:22 | Lev 12:2–4 | John 10:34 | Ps 82:6 |
| Luke 2:23 | Exod 12:2,12,15 | John 12:34 | Ps 89:37 (?) |
| Luke 2:24 | Lev 5:11 | | Ezek 37:25 (?) |
| Luke 10:26 (27) | Deut 6:5 | John 15:25 | Ps 35:19 |
| | Lev 18:5 | | Ps 69:5 |
| | Josh 22:5 (?) | John 19:7 | Lev 24:16 |
| John 7:23 | Gen 17:10–12 | Rom 10:5 | Lev 18:5 |
| | Lev 12:3 | 1 Cor 9:9 | Deut 25:4 |

---

[147] See the discussion in Beckwith, *Old Testament Canon*, 69–70.

| | | | |
|---|---|---|---|
| 1 Cor 14:21 | Isa 28:11–12 | Heb 9:19 (20) | Exod 24:8 |
| 1 Cor 14:34 | Gen 3:15 | Jas 2:6 | Lev 19:18 |
| Gal 5:14 | Lev 19:18 | Jas 2:10 (11) | Exod 20:13–14 |
| Heb 7:5 | Num 18:21 | | Deut 5:17–18 |

Note: *The Law* is often used in its proper sense to mean only the five books of Moses. However, as this list demonstrates, by use of synecdoche it can be a generic term for the whole of the canon (note the quotations of Psalms, and possibly Joshua and Ezekiel).

## Table 6
### Quotations of the Prophets (προφήτης) in the NT

| | | | |
|---|---|---|---|
| Matt 1:22 | Isa 7:14 | Luke 3:4 (5–6) | Isa 40:3–5 |
| Matt 2:5 (6) | Mic 5:1,3 | Luke 4:17 (18–19) | Isa 61:1–2; 58:6 |
| Matt 2:15 | Hos 11:1 | John 1:23 | Isa 40:3 |
| Matt 2:17 (18) | Jer 31:15 | John 6:45 | Isa 54:13 |
| Matt 3:3 | Isa 40:3 | John 12:38 | Isa 53:1 |
| Matt 4:14 (15–16) | Isa 8:23–9:1 | Acts 2:16 (17–21) | Joel 3:1–5 |
| Matt 8:17 | Isa 53:4 | Acts 2:30 (25–28, 34–35) | |
| Matt 12:17 (18–21) | Isa 42:1–4,9 | | Ps 16:8–11 |
| Matt 12:39 | Jonah | | Ps 110:1 |
| Matt 13:35 | Ps 78:2 | Acts 7:42 (43) | Amos 5:25–27 |
| Matt 21:4 (5) | Isa 62:11 | Acts 7:48 (49) | Isa 66:1–2 |
| | Zech 9:9 | Acts 8:28,30,34 (32–33) | |
| Matt 24:15 | Dan 9:27; 11:31 | | Isa 53:7–8 |
| Matt 27:9 (10) | Jer 18:2–3 (?) | Acts 13:40 (41) | Hab 1:5 |
| | Zech 9:9 | Acts 15:15 (16–18) | Amos 9:11–12 |
| Mark 1:2 (3) | Exod 23:20 | | Isa 45:21 |
| | Mal 3:1 | Acts 28:25 (26–27) | Isa 6:9 |
| | Isa 40:3 | | |

Note: Matt 2:23 quotes "prophets" (plural as opposed to the singular elsewhere in Matthew). The source of the quotation is not known. Matthew's unique plural may indicate that he is not quoting Scripture but some other source (oral?). Since the NT also contains references to contemporary prophecy, also note that every book that appears in this table except Daniel also appears in Tables 4, 5 or 7 (counting the Twelve Prophets as one book). Finally note that the Prophets always refers to books outside the Pentateuch in this list (Mark 1:2 does refer to Exodus, but only in conjunction with Malachi and Isaiah). However, it does refer to two books, Psalms and Daniel that are classified as Writings in the Jewish canon. Apparently, both David and Daniel were considered prophets.

## Table 7
### Quotations of the OT as "It Is Written" (γέγραπται)

| | | | |
|---|---|---|---|
| Matt 4:4 | Deut 8:3 | Rom 9:33 | Isa 28:16; 8:14 |
| Matt 4:6 | Ps 91:11 | Rom 10:15 | Isa 52:7 |
| Matt 4:7 | Deut 6:16 | | Nah 2:1 |
| Matt 11:10 | Exod 23:20 | Rom 11:8 | Deut 29:3 |
| | Mal 3:1 | | Isa 29:10 |
| Matt 21:13 | Isa 56:7 | Rom 11:26 (27) | Isa 49:20–21; 27:9 |
| | Jer 7:11 | Rom 12:19 (20) | Prov 25:21–22 |
| Matt 26:31 | Zech 13:7 | Rom 14:11 | Isa 49:18 |
| Mark 7:6 | Isa 29:13 | | Jer 22:24 |
| Mark 11:17 | Isa 56:7 | | Ezek 5:11 |
| | Jer 7:11 | | Isa 45:23 |
| Mark 14:27 | Zech 13:7 | Rom 15:3 | Ps 68:10 |
| Luke 4:4 | Deut 8:3 | Rom 15:9 (10–12) | Ps 17:20 |
| Luke 4:8 | Deut 6:13; 10:20 | | 2 Sam 22:50 |
| Luke 4:10 | Ps 91:11 | | Deut 32:43 |
| Luke 7:27 | Exod 23:20 | | Ps 117:1 |
| | Mal 3:1 | | Isa 11:10 |
| Luke 19:46 | Isa 56:7 | Rom 15:21 | Isa 52:15 |
| | Jer 7:11 | 1 Cor 1:19 | Isa 29:4 |
| Acts 15:15 | Amos 9:11–12 | 1 Cor 1:31 | Jer 9:22–23 |
| Acts 23:5 | Exod 22:27 | 1 Cor 2:9 | Isa 63:3 |
| Rom 1:17 | Hab 2:4 | 1 Cor 3:19 (20) | Job 5:12–13 |
| Rom 2:24 | Isa 52:5 | 1 Cor 10:7 | Exod 32:6 |
| Rom 3:4 | Ps 50:6 | 1 Cor 15:45 | Gen 2:7 |
| Rom 3:10 (11–18) | Eccl 7:20 | 2 Cor 8:15 | Exod 16:18 |
| | Ps 14:1–3; 5:10 | 2 Cor 9:9 | Ps 111:9 |
| | Ps 139:4; 10:7 | Gal 3:10 | Deut 27:26 |
| | Ps 59:7–8 | Gal 3:13 | Deut 27:26; 21:23 |
| | Prov 1:16 | Gal 4:27 | Isa 54:1 |
| | Ps 35:2 | 1 Pet 1:16 | Lev 11:44–45; |
| Rom 4:17 | Gen 17:5 | | Lev 19:2 |
| Rom 8:36 | Ps 43:23 | | |
| Rom 9:13 | Mal 1:2–3 | | |

The combined weight of this evidence is twofold. First, every book of the Hebrew OT canon is quoted except Judges, Ruth, Chronicles, Ezra, Nehemiah, Esther, Obadiah and Zephaniah and possibly Joshua and Song of Songs.[148] Since the Twelve Prophets are known as a group long before the writing of the NT, the omission of Obadiah and Zephaniah is not significant.[149] Judges, Ruth, Chronicles, Ezra and Nehemiah are definitely known by the NT writers (Matt 1:5, 12; Luke 1:5) and were considered Scripture as early as Ben Sira. The NT writers apparently had no need to quote them. The only book left uncertain is Esther, which, as we have seen, is weakly attested up to this time.

On the other hand, no books outside the Hebrew OT canon are ever cited as Scripture by any of these formulae. This is true even though the twenty-seventh edition of Nestle-Aland lists many parallels and allusions to other Jewish works including 110 to Sirach, 65 to 1 Enoch and 109 to the Wisdom of Solomon. The 65 allusions to 1 Enoch are more than quotations and allusions to Amos, Jonah, Nahum, Haggai and Malachi combined, yet each of these books is clearly indicated to be Scripture by the NT writers, and 1 Enoch is not. In fact, Greek authors are quoted more often in the NT (though not as Scripture) than any book of the Apocrypha or Pseudepigrapha (three or four quotations, see the discussion on page 103).[150] While this cannot be said to be conclusive proof, as others have pointed out, *the weight of the evidence strongly indicates that the NT writers recognized a canon identical to the Hebrew OT canon (with the possible exception of Esther).*[151]

---

[148] Although Haggai does not appear in the tables, it is quoted in Hebrews as "God said." The quotation in John 7:38 (Table 4) is similar to Isaiah 58:1 and Song of Songs 4:15. It is impossible to determine which is being quoted. The quotations in Luke 10:26–27 (Table 5) contain language that appear to be Deut 6:5 and Lev 18:5 (since these are in the context of a discussion of the Law), but they are similar to Josh 22:5.

[149] The book of Acts probably refers to the Minor Prophets as a collection when it quotes Amos 5:25–27 as occurring "in the book of the Prophets" (ἐν βίβλῳ τῶν προφητῶν; Acts 7:42).

[150] Aratus is quoted in Acts 17:28, Epimenides in Tit 1:12; Euripides (by Jesus himself!) in Acts 26:14; Heraclitus in 2 Pet 2:22 and Menander in 1 Cor 15:33.

[151] McDonald, *Formation*, 95 correctly states that "the NT does not help us know *precisely* what the canon of Jesus or the early church was." However, his assertion that we cannot rule out other books because they are not quoted as Scripture is incorrect in light of the evidence. It would be true if we had no or few quotations from the OT canonical books identifying them as Scripture. However, the complete

## The Canon of Scripture: Did the NT Writers Recognize One?

Several passages in the NT imply that the Scripture was closed in practice, if not in theory. The most important of these is John 5:39:

ἐραυνᾶτε τὰς γραφάς, ὅτι ὑμεῖς δοκεῖτε ἐν αὐταῖς ζωὴν
αἰώνιον ἔχειν· καὶ ἐκεῖναί εἰσιν αἱ μαρτυροῦσαι περὶ
ἐμοῦ·

You study the Scriptures because you think that in them
you have eternal life. They testify about me.

This verse is set in the context of Jesus disputing with some Jews about the Sabbath and about his claims concerning himself (John 5:18). Within this context he discusses witnesses to his identity. This verse states that these Jews studied the Scriptures because they give eternal life. That statement by itself implies a circumscribed set of books that distinguish themselves as ones which are presumed to offer eternal life and which the Jews studied.

Moreover, Jesus is quoted as claiming that these books *testify* about him. That is, they are a legal witness to who he is. Surely it is a misreading of this passage to think that Jesus is implying that any and all books that the Jews could have studied testify about him. In fact, the citing of these books as witnesses rules out anything but a clearly defined set of books *that both he and the Jews agree on* (i.e., there is general agreement on what the canon contains). Otherwise, the force of Jesus' statement is useless to his argument because he cannot identify the witnesses that make his case, and his opponents would not agree that they are reliable witnesses.

While this statement in John does not tell us *which* books were canonical, it loses its force if it is not referring to a defined set of books that make up Scripture (i.e., a canon). Read in conjunction with passages such as Luke 24:44 (see page 90), John 1:45 and Acts 28:23 where Jesus or others claim that the Law and Prophets contain information about him, this passage can only mean that the canon was a discrete collection and not an open, fluid, ill-defined set of books.

---

lack of quotation as Scripture for other books, even the most popular ones such as Sirach or 1 Enoch, in the face of the overwhelming number of quotations of the canonical books is forceful evidence.

That the Law and Prophets act as a witness (and therefore must be well-defined) is affirmed by Paul in Romans 3:21:

> Νυνὶ δὲ χωρὶς νόμου δικαιοσύνη θεοῦ πεφανέρωται μαρτυρουμένη ὑπὸ τοῦ νόμου καὶ τῶν προφητῶν,

> But now, apart from law, the righteousness of God has been disclosed, and is witnessed to by the Law and the Prophets.

Another passage from the NT' that assumes that the Scriptures are a discrete set of books is 2 Timothy 3:15–17:

> ...καὶ ὅτι ἀπὸ βρέφους [τὰ] ἱερὰ γράμματα οἶδας, τὰ δυνάμενά σε σοφίσαι εἰς σωτηρίαν διὰ πίστεως τῆς ἐν Χριστῷ Ἰησοῦ. πᾶσα γραφὴ θεόπνευστος καὶ ὠφέλιμος πρὸς διδασκαλίαν, πρὸς ἐλεγμόν, πρὸς ἐπανόρθωσιν, πρὸς παιδείαν τὴν ἐν δικαιοσύνῃ, ἵνα ἄρτιος ᾖ ὁ τοῦ θεοῦ ἄνθρωπος, πρὸς πᾶν ἔργον ἀγαθὸν ἐξηρτισμένος.

> ...and how from infancy you have known the Holy Writings that are able to give you wisdom for salvation through faith in Christ Jesus. All Scripture is inspired by God and is useful for teaching, for reproof, for correction, and for training in righteousness, so that the person who belongs to God may be proficient, equipped for every good work.

This passage assumes that Timothy has known a specific set of holy books his entire life and it affirms that they are inspired by God. To state that all Scripture is inspired, but not to have a definite set of books in mind is to deny that inspiration, making it a useless assertion, since one could not truly distinguish between inspired and uninspired books and know which are useful for the purposes listed here. This statement in 2 Timothy only makes sense if the author and his readers can assume there is a defined canon.

Other passages in the NT operate under the same assumption about a canon. Among them are Matthew 5:17, Acts 18:28, Acts 28:23 and 1 Corinthians 15:3–5. These passages do not tell us *which* books are in the canon, but they do witness to the existence of a commonly accepted canon.

## The Order of the Canonical Books

One saying of Jesus in the Gospels has been adduced by some as supplying evidence for the order of the canonical books because it seems to refer to the first and last books of the canon in the traditional Jewish order (Genesis and Chronicles).[152] This is Matthew 23:34–36 and its parallel in Luke 11:49–51:

διὰ τοῦτο ἰδοὺ ἐγὼ ἀποστέλλω πρὸς ὑμᾶς προφήτας καὶ σοφοὺς καὶ γραμματεῖς· ἐξ αὐτῶν ἀποκτενεῖτε καὶ σταυρώσετε καὶ ἐξ αὐτῶν μαστιγώσετε ἐν ταῖς συναγωγαῖς ὑμῶν καὶ διώξετε ἀπὸ πόλεως εἰς πόλιν· ὅπως ἔλθῃ ἐφ᾽ ὑμᾶς πᾶν αἷμα δίκαιον ἐκχυννόμενον ἐπὶ τῆς γῆς ἀπὸ τοῦ αἵματος ῞Αβελ τοῦ δικαίου ἕως τοῦ αἵματος Ζαχαρίου υἱοῦ Βαραχίου, ὃν ἐφονεύσατε μεταξὺ τοῦ ναοῦ καὶ τοῦ θυσιαστηρίου. ἀμὴν λέγω ὑμῖν, ἥξει ταῦτα πάντα ἐπὶ τὴν γενεὰν ταύτην.

Therefore I send you prophets, wise men and scribes, some of whom you will kill and crucify, and some you will flog in your synagogues and pursue from town to town, so that on you may come all the righteous blood shed on earth, from the blood of righteous Abel to the blood of Zechariah son of Berechiah, whom you murdered between the sanctuary and the altar. Truly I tell you, all this will come upon this generation. (Matthew 23:34–36)

διὰ τοῦτο καὶ ἡ σοφία τοῦ θεοῦ εἶπεν, ᾿Αποστελῶ εἰς αὐτοὺς προφήτας καὶ ἀποστόλους, καὶ ἐξ αὐτῶν ἀποκτενοῦσιν καὶ διώξουσιν, ἵνα ἐκζητηθῇ τὸ αἷμα πάντων τῶν προφητῶν τὸ ἐκκεχυμένον ἀπὸ καταβολῆς κόσμου ἀπὸ τῆς γενεᾶς ταύτης, ἀπὸ αἵματος ῞Αβελ ἕως αἵματος Ζαχαρίου τοῦ ἀπολομένου μεταξὺ τοῦ θυσιαστηρίου καὶ τοῦ οἴκου· ναί λέγω ὑμῖν, ἐκζητηθήσεται ἀπὸ τῆς γενεᾶς ταύτης.

Therefore also the Wisdom of God said, "I will send them prophets and apostles, some of whom they will kill and persecute," so that this generation may be charged with the blood of all the prophets shed since the world was founded, from the blood of Abel to the blood of

---

[152] E.g., Beckwith, *Old Testament Canon*, 212–22; VanderKam, *Dead Sea Scrolls*, p 146 (though VanderKam himself does not endorse this use of Matt 23:35).

> Zechariah, who perished between the altar and the
> sanctuary. Yes, I tell you, it will be charged against this
> generation. (Luke 11:49–51)

This statement traces the prophets from Abel in Genesis 4 to a certain Zechariah who was slain in the Temple courtyard between the altar for burnt offerings and the Temple itself. As far as we know only two men by this name come close to fitting this description: Zechariah, son of Jehoiada whose murder is recorded in 2 Chronicles 24:19–22 and Zechariah, son of Baruch (perhaps a shortened form of the name Berekiah given in Matthew), whose murder is described by Josephus in *The Jewish War*, 4.334–44. The second Zechariah, whose death took place in AD 67 or 68, would have died more than thirty years after the ministry of Jesus. Even if it is assumed that Luke was written after AD 70, it is difficult to understand how this Zechariah could have been thought to have been murdered prior to or during Jesus' ministry.

On the other hand, the first Zechariah (mentioned in 2 Chr 24) does prophecy under the power of the Holy Spirit (2 Chr 24:19). However, he is nowhere known to have a father named Berechiah, as Matthew indicates.[153] Since Jehoiada was 130 years old when he died (2 Chr 24:15), some have proposed that Jehoiada was actually the grandfather of Zechariah (since Hebrew אב can apply to any male ancestor) and that his father was actually Berechiah.[154] Unfortunately, there is no evidence to support this theory.

Beckwith seeks to identify this Zechariah with the Zechariah of 2 Chronicles 24 by way of a rabbinic midrashic technique. According to Beckwith he is to be identified as the Zechariah of 2 Chronicles but associated with the canonical prophet Zechariah whose father was named Berekiah (Zech 1:1).[155] While Beckwith produces a number of rabbinic illustrations of this technique, he does not provide one example from the NT, making it highly suspect.

Thus, we do not know who this Zechariah that Jesus is referring to in these two passages was. He may be a recent Zechariah whose death was not recorded in any written account. But why is this passage

---

[153] There is no indication that the words υἱοῦ Βαραχίου were a later (mistaken) addition to Matthew's text. They are missing only in the original hand in Codex Sinaiticus, but occur in all other witnesses.

[154] See the discussion in Beckwith, *Old Testament Canon*, 216, where this suggestion is rejected.

[155] Beckwith, *Old Testament Canon*, 217–20.

important at all? The answer lies in the fact that if this Zechariah is the Zechariah in 2 Chronicles, then Jesus may be saying "all the prophets in the canon from Genesis to Chronicles." Since Chronicles is the last book in the canon according to the arrangement of the books given in the Talmud (*Baba Bathra* 14–15), Beckwith takes this passage to be an indication that the Scriptures were arranged in the order later found in the Talmud. He notes that Jesus' statement cannot mean from the first to the last martyred prophet in the OT chronologically, since the last martyred prophet chronologically was Uriah, son of Shemaiah (Jer 26:20–23).

The order of the OT canon given in the Talmud is not the only order for the books of the OT in Hebrew. As McDonald notes,[156]

> [David Noel] Freedman has contended convincingly that the Chronicles is not the last book in the Hebrew biblical canon, but stands first in the Writings. This position is supported by the major medieval manuscripts including the standard MT Aleppo Codex and the Leningrad Codex. A further substantiation for Freedman's position is the fact that the last paragraph of 2 Chronicles is the first paragraph in Ezra. This clearly suggests that 1 and 2 Chronicles were first in the sequence and indicates that the books were separated spatially, since if the books had been connected there would have been no need for the repetition. The primary historical books that are connected, that is, the Samuels and the Kings, have no repetitive texts connecting the books.

Therefore, even the later evidence for the order of the canonical books is mixed. Since we cannot even be certain that Jesus' statement refers to Chronicles, this passage proves nothing about the order of the canon in Jesus' day (if there was a standard order).

However, even if we were to concede that the Zechariah mentioned by Jesus is the Zechariah of 2 Chronicles 24, Beckwith's case still is not proven. Jesus could mean "from the first martyred prophet in one of the first canonical books to be written to the last martyred prophet in one of the last books to be written." The NT generally assumes the books of the Pentateuch were the first books, written by Moses himself (e.g., Matt 8:4; Mark 1:44; Luke 20:28; 2 Cor 3:15). Certainly

---

[156] McDonald, *Formation*, 46–47.

Chronicles is one of the last OT books to be written. Scholars could date a few books later or contemporary with it (e.g., Ezra-Nehemiah; Daniel is assumed in the NT to be earlier [Matt 24:15]). In these last books to be written, Zechariah is the last martyr mentioned.

Of course, one could argue that Chronicles is the *first* book in the Writings (as in the Aleppo and Leningrad codices) and Jesus means to say "every martyr from the first section of Scripture to the last" and cites the first martyr in the first book in the first section and the last martyr in the first book in the last section. But this would argue that the order of the books in these medieval codices is more ancient than that given in the Talmud, a doubtful proposition. In fact, the argument that Chronicles was in a third section of the canon in the first century is not supported by any source. This is especially true of the NT, which never depicts Jesus as elsewhere referring to the three-part canon of the Talmud or of the codices. Instead, in the one instance where he mentions a three-part canon, the third part contains only the book of Psalms (see the discussion at the beginning of this chapter).

In short, Matthew 23:34–36 and Luke 11:49–51 do not offer us any reliable information about the accepted order of the books OT canon in Jesus' day—they only give us the opportunity for speculative conclusions. The Zechariah mentioned in this passage cannot be identified with any degree of confidence. Even if we could identify him as the Zechariah of 2 Chronicles we cannot state the significance of this. It *could* mean that Jesus is referring to the order of the arrangement of the books of the canon in his day. But it is equally possible that he is referring to the order in which the books of the canon were presumed to be written. (Perhaps he could be referring to both.) If the latter view is the correct one, then Jesus is confirming that the canon was closed in the Persian period. Since we have already seen this implication in Ben Sira and 1 Maccabees (see pages 49 and 56), this is more likely than reading the talmudic order of the canon back into the NT. However, even this rests on the assumption that Jesus is referring to 2 Chronicles 24, an assumption that lacks confirming evidence.

## Prophecy As an Ongoing Phenomenon

While the author of 1 Maccabees appears to have believed that prophecy ceased sometime before the beginning of the first century BC, the NT views prophecy as an ongoing phenomenon. The synoptic gospels report that many of the Jewish people believed John the Baptist to be a prophet (Matt 21:26, Mark 11:32, Luke 20:6). Similar reports circulated about Jesus (Matt 21:11). The prophets Anna (Luke 2:36), Agabus (Acts 21:10), Barnabas, Simeon, Lucius, and Manaen (Acts 13:1), Judas and Silas (Acts 15:32), and some anonymous prophets from Jerusalem (Acts 11:27) are all mentioned in the NT. Paul mentions ongoing prophecy in his letters to the Corinthian, Ephesian, and Thessalonian congregations (1 Cor 14; Eph 3:5; 4:11; 1 Thess 5:20–22). Does this mean that the NT sees the OT canon as open and Christians expected to add to it?

Despite the fact that prophecy is found in the NT, we have no evidence that the early Christians sought to add words of any of the prophets (even Jesus!) to the OT canon. In fact, when Christians do adopt new books, they are seen as distinct. The apostolic revelation is not mixed with the old prophetic revelation, but is placed in its own canon. This distinction can be seen already in 2 Peter 3:1–2:

> Ταύτην ἤδη, ἀγαπητοί, δευτέραν ὑμῖν γράφω ἐπιστολήν, ἐν αἷς διεγείρω ὑμῶν ἐν ὑπομνήσει τὴν εἰλικρινῆ διάνοιαν μνησθῆναι τῶν προειρημένων ῥημάτων ὑπὸ τῶν ἁγίων προφητῶν καὶ τῆς τῶν ἀποστόλων ὑμῶν ἐντολῆς τοῦ κυρίου καὶ σωτῆρος,

> Beloved, this is now the second letter I am writing to you. In them I am trying to stir up your sincere intention by reminding you that you should remember the words spoken in the past by the holy prophets, and the commandment of the Lord and Savior spoken through your apostles.

2 Peter does recognize Christian writings as Scripture, at least the letters of Paul (2 Pet 3:15–16). But this passage makes a distinction between these later Christian Scriptures and the OT.

The writer to the Hebrews makes a similar distinction at the beginning of his letter:

> Πολυμερῶς καὶ πολυτρόπως πάλαι ὁ θεὸς λαλήσας τοῖς πατράσιν ἐν τοῖς προφήταις ἐπ' ἐσχάτου τῶν ἡμερῶν τούτων ἐλάλησεν ἡμῖν ἐν υἱῷ, ὃν ἔθηκεν κληρονόμον πάντων, δι' οὗ καὶ ἐποίησεν τοὺς αἰῶνας·

> Long ago God spoke to our ancestors in many and
> various ways through the prophets. In these last days he
> has spoken to us by a Son, whom he made heir of
> everything, through whom he also created the worlds.

Clearly, already by the time of the writing of the NT Christians saw
the older prophetic books as complete. The writer to the Hebrews
clearly states that the prophets spoke "long ago" (πάλαι), implying that
enduring authoritative prophetic revelation had ceased for some
extended period of time, later Christian prophecy notwithstanding. The
later Christian double canon of OT and NT preserves the NT attitude
toward the OT as a closed canon to which nothing can be added. The
recognition of prophecy during the first century does not alter this
view. In fact, Paul always subordinates Christian prophecy to the
apostolic revelation (1 Cor 12:28–29; Eph 3:5; 4:11). Thus, for the NT
not all prophecy is to be viewed as eligible for inclusion in the canon.
This is not necessarily an innovation with Christians, since the OT
itself refers to prophesy that was not included in the canon (Num
11:25–26; 1 Sam 10:10–13; 2 Chr 9:29) and to prophets who
contributed no known books to the canon (Judg 6:8; 1 Sam 22:5; 2 Sam
7:2; 12:25; 1 Kgs 11:29; 13:11; 16:7; 18:36; 19:16; 20:13; 2 Kgs 9:4;
14:25; 2 Chr 13:22; 34:22).

## The Apocrypha and Pseudepigrapha in the New Testament

The NT contains many thoughts and phrases drawn from or parallel
to thoughts and phrases in the Apocrypha and Pseudepigrapha.[157] In
addition, it may contain two quotations from Sirach and does contain
one quotation from 1 Enoch. McDonald, who believes this demonstrates that the NT writers did not recognize a closed canon,
summarizes this evidence:[158]

> Stuhlmacher, however, has found a number of the
> parallels and allusions to extracanonical literature in the
> NT writings. We will list some of them here. Mark
> 10:19 appears to make use of Sir 4:1 along with Exod
> 20:12–16 and Deut 5:16–20. Second Timothy appears to
> cite Sir 17:26 along with Num 16:5. It is likely that

---

[157] See the list in the twenty-seventh edition of *Novum Testamentum Graece*, pages
769–75.

[158] McDonald, *Formation*, 101.

> Paul, in Rom 1:24–32, makes use of Wis 14:22–31 and
> in Rom 5:12–21 he apparently makes use of the ideas
> present in Wis 2:23–24. Wisdom of Solomon's
> canonicity does not appear to concern Paul, but only the
> theological arguments in it. In 1 Cor 2:9, Paul cites as
> "scripture" either the Ascension of Isaiah 11:34 or a lost
> Elijah Apocalypse derived from Isa 64:3. Jude 14
> expressly cites the pseudepigraphal 1 Enoch 1:9. The
> author of 2 Pet also shows knowledge or awareness of 1
> Enoch in 2:4 and 3:6. The author of Heb 1:3 makes
> clear reference to Wis 7:25–26 and Jas 4:5 appears to
> cite an unknown scripture.

What, however, is the nature of this evidence that McDonald considers to be proof? Certainly we cannot argue that whenever adopting phraseology or ideas from a source that a NT author considered that source authoritative revelation. He may have considered it correct and useful in the same way Paul quotes Menander in 1 Corinthians 15:33 and Epimenides in Titus 1:12. Luke tells us that Paul also quoted Aratus to the Athenians as part of his theological argument (Acts 17:28). No one holds that Paul or the early Christians argued that these Greek authors should be considered on a par with the OT prophets. Thus, we can eliminate all the passages that are used as source material to inform or bolster an argument, since these prove nothing. We are then left with two passages that appear to quote some book, though we cannot identify it with certainty: 1 Corinthians 2:9 and James 4:5, and three passages whose quotations appear to be identifiable: Mark 10:19 (Sirach 4:1), 2 Timothy 2:19 (Sirach 17:26) and Jude 14 (1 Enoch 1:9). In addition, we should examine the quotation in Jude 9 which some Church Fathers claimed was based on a lost work, The Assumption of Moses.

## The Two Undetermined Quotations

Both of these quotations cannot be used as proof because they are inconclusive. 1 Corinthians 2:9 has long been a controversial passage because the form of the quotation does not match any known text (hence McDonald proposes Ascension of Isaiah 11:34 or a lost Elijah Apocalypse [as held by Origen]). However, even McDonald admits that this quotation has a striking similarity to Isaiah 64:3.

ἀλλὰ καθὼς γέγραπται, "Α ὀφθαλμὸς οὐκ εἶδεν καὶ οὖς οὐκ ἤκουσεν καὶ ἐπὶ καρδίαν ἀνθρώπου οὐκ ἀνέβη, ἃ ἡτοίμασεν ὁ θεὸς τοῖς ἀγαπῶσιν αὐτόν.

But, as it is written, "What an eye has not seen, nor an ear heard, nor the human heart conceived, what God has prepared for those who love him." (1 Corinthians 2:9)

וּמֵעוֹלָם לֹא־שָׁמְעוּ לֹא הֶאֱזִינוּ עַיִן לֹא־רָאָתָה אֱלֹהִים
זוּלָתְךָ יַעֲשֶׂה לִמְחַכֵּה־לוֹ:

From ages past no one has listened, no ear has heard, no eye has seen any God besides you, who works for those who wait for him. (Isaiah 64:3)

ἀπὸ τοῦ αἰῶνος οὐκ ἠκούσαμεν οὐδὲ οἱ ὀφθαλμοὶ ἡμῶν εἶδον θεὸν πλὴν σοῦ καὶ τὰ ἔργα σου ἃ ποιήσεις τοῖς ὑπομένουσιν ἔλεον

From ages past no one has listened, no eye has seen any God besides you and your works that you will do for those who wait for mercy. (Isaiah 64:3, Septuagint)

Since both Jesus and Paul occasionally quoted the OT periphrastically (e.g., John 7:38 [several OT passages]; 1 Cor 15:45 [Gen 2:7]), this may simply be another example.

As for James 4:5, we simply do not know the source of the quote, so we can draw no reliable conclusions from it. In fact, it may not be a direct quotation at all but a periphrastic summary of concepts found in the OT (the quotation is introduced by "the Scripture says" [γραφὴ λέγει]). No matter what the nature of this citation of Scripture is, we should refrain from drawing conclusions about the extent of the OT from it.

## Mark 10:19 (Sirach 4:1)

τὰς ἐντολὰς οἶδας· Μὴ φονεύσῃς, Μὴ μοιχεύσῃς, Μὴ κλέψῃς, Μὴ ψευδομαρτυρήσῃς, Μὴ ἀποστερήσῃς, Τίμα τὸν πατέρα σου καὶ τὴν μητέρα.

You know the commandments: 'Do not murder. Do not commit adultery. Do not steal. Do not bear false witness. Do not defraud. Honor your father and mother.'

All the commandments quoted here are from Exodus 20 and Deuteronomy 5 except "Do not defraud." This appears to be taken from Sirach 4:1

τέκνον τὴν ζωὴν τοῦ πτωχοῦ μὴ ἀποστερήσῃς καὶ μὴ παρελκύσῃς ὀφθαλμοὺς ἐπιδεεῖς

My child, do not defraud the poor of their living, and do not keep needy eyes waiting.

However, Sirach 4:1 is itself based on Deuteronomy 24:14:

לֹא־תַעֲשֹׁק שָׂכִיר עָנִי וְאֶבְיוֹן מֵאַחֶיךָ אוֹ מִגֵּרְךָ אֲשֶׁר
בְּאַרְצְךָ בִּשְׁעָרֶיךָ:

You shall not withhold the wages of poor and needy workers, whether among your relatives or aliens who reside in your land in one of your towns.

Therefore, Sirach 4:1 derives its authority from the Law of Moses and is a paraphrase of it. Since this is the case, the use of Sirach in this case does not prove that Jesus or the Gospel writer attributes authority to Sirach apart from its derived authority from Deuteronomy. In fact, the wording here may simply be a summary of Deuteronomy 24:14 and is only coincidentally the same as a two-word phrase from Sirach.

## 2 Timothy 2:19 (Sirach 17:26)

ὁ μέντοι στερεὸς θεμέλιος τοῦ θεοῦ ἕστηκεν, ἔχων τὴν σφραγῖδα ταύτην· Ἔγνω κύριος τοὺς ὄντας αὐτοῦ, καί, Ἀποστήτω ἀπὸ ἀδικίας πᾶς ὁ ὀνομάζων τὸ ὄνομα κυρίου.

Indeed, God's firm foundation stands, bearing this inscription: "The Lord knows those who are his," and, "Turn away from wickedness, everyone who calls on the name of the Lord."

This first quotation is from Numbers 16:5. The second quotation is not found in this form in any known work. The first part of this quotation appears to be from Sirach 17:26 (although note that Sirach uses a present imperative whereas 2 Timothy uses an aorist imperative).

ἐπάναγε ἐπὶ ὕψιστον καὶ ἀπόστρεφε ἀπὸ ἀδικίας καὶ
σφόδρα μίσησον βδέλυγμα

Return to the Most High, turn away from wickedness,
and hate intensely the things he finds detestable.

But the first part of the second quotation could also be based on Job
36:10 (although the Greek appears to be closer to Sirach 17:26):

וַיִּגֶל אָזְנָם לַמּוּסָר וַיֹּאמֶר כִּי יְשֻׁבוּן מֵאָוֶן:

He opens their ears to instruction, and orders that they
return from wickedness.

ἀλλὰ τοῦ δικαίου εἰσακούσεται καὶ εἶπεν ὅτι
ἐπιστραφήσονται ἐξ ἀδικίας

But he will listen to the righteous, and he has said that
they should turn from their wickedness (Septuagint).

The second part of the second quotation in 2 Timothy 2:19 is based
on Septuagint Isaiah 26:13:

κύριε ὁ θεὸς ἡμῶν κτῆσαι ἡμᾶς κύριε ἐκτὸς σοῦ ἄλλον
οὐκ οἴδαμεν τὸ ὄνομά σου ὀνομάζομεν

O Lord our God, take possession of us. We know no
other [god] besides you. We acknowledge your name
alone.

Note that the second part of the second quotation in 2 Timothy is a
paraphrase of Isaiah 26:13. Therefore, it is entirely possible that the
first part is a paraphrase of Job 36:10 even though Sirach 17:26 appears
to be closer to the form of the quotation in 2 Timothy. Thus, we have
no firm proof that 2 Timothy quotes Sirach.

## Jude 14 (1 Enoch 1:9)

> Προεφήτευσεν δὲ καὶ τούτοις ἕβδομος ἀπὸ ᾿Αδὰμ ᾿Ενὼχ
> λέγων, ᾿Ιδοὺ ἦλθεν κύριος ἐν ἁγίαις μυριάσιν αὐτου
> ποιῆσαι κρίσιν κατὰ πάντων καὶ ἐλέγξαι πᾶσαν ψυχὴν
> περὶ πάντων τῶν ἔργων ἀσεβείας αὐτῶν ὧν ἠσέβησαν
> καὶ περὶ πάντων τῶν σκληρῶν ὧν ἐλάλησαν κατ᾿
> αὐτοῦ ἁμαρτωλοὶ ἀσεβεῖς.

> It was also about these that Enoch, in the seventh
> generation after Adam, prophesied, saying, "See, the
> Lord is coming with tens of thousands of his holy ones
> to execute judgment on all and to convict everyone of
> all their deeds of ungodliness that they have committed
> in such an ungodly way and of all the harsh things that
> ungodly sinners have spoken against him."

This passage definitely quotes 1 Enoch 1:9 as words prophesied by
Enoch. However, as we saw earlier, prophecy in the NT is not limited
to canonical works. In fact, of the twenty-seven times the verb
προφετεύω occurs elsewhere in the NT, only in Mark 7:6 and 1 Peter
1:10 does it refer to prophecies in the OT canon. Thus, this quotation of
1 Enoch does not guarantee that it is considered canonical, only that
Jude considered it a true prophecy on the same level as that spoken by
Zechariah in Luke 1:68–79 and other prophecies recorded in the NT. In
addition, Jude's extensive use of the Pentateuch for source material
would argue against his including 1 Enoch as canonical. The
recognition of the Pentateuch as the foundational canonical collection
from Moses, the foundational prophet, would appear to rule out any
book thought to be from a person earlier than Moses. Thus, Jude 14
quotes 1 Enoch as *factual*, but it is doubtful that he quotes it as
*canonical*.

## Jude 9 (The Assumption of Moses)

> ὁ δὲ Μιχαὴλ ὁ ἀρχάγγελος, ὅτε τῷ διαβόλῳ
> διακρινόμενος διελέγετο περὶ τοῦ Μωϋσέως σώματος,
> οὐκ ἐτόλμησεν κρίσιν ἐπενεγκεῖν βλασφημίας ἀλλὰ
> εἶπεν, ᾿Επιτιμήσαι σοι κύριος.

> But when the archangel Michael contended with the
> devil and disputed about the body of Moses, he did not
> dare judge him guilty of blasphemy against him, but
> said, "The Lord rebuke you!"

The first thing to notice about Jude 9 is that, unlike Jude 14, it does not claim to be prophecy. Like Jude 14 it does appear to be presented as factual. Whether it is a quote from the lost Assumption of Moses we cannot judge. However, the words "The Lord rebuke you" (ἐπιτιμήσαι σοι κύριος) do occur in Zechariah 3:2 (LXX: ἐπιτιμήσαι κύριος ἐν σοί) as a rebuke to the devil. Thus, Jude could have included these words as reflecting canonical thought.

To summarize, there is no indication that any book outside the Hebrew OT canon was treated as canonical by the NT writers. Their adopting thoughts, phrases or even quotations in and of itself is not an indication of canonicity or authority. Rather, only when they explicitly cite a book or quotation as scriptural can we draw a conclusion about their view of the OT canon.

## Summary of the NT Evidence for the OT Canon

From the NT we can draw the following conclusions about the OT canon in the last half of the first century:

**The organization of the canon.** The NT continues the practice of dividing the OT canon into two sections: Law and Prophets. The only exception is Luke 24:44 which places the book of Psalms in its own section in a threefold division identical to that found in Philo's *The Contemplative Life.*

**The assumption of the existence of the canon.** The NT assumes that there is a well-defined, discrete collection of authoritative books, i.e., a canon. Furthermore, it assumes that there is general agreement on what this canon is.

**The order of the canonical books and the date of the closing of the canon.** Matthew 23:34–36 and its parallel, Luke 11:49–51, do not witness to the order of the books of the canon later attested in the Talmud with Genesis as the first book and Chronicles as the last book. If these passages imply anything it is that the last canonical books were assumed to be from the early Persian period. However, even this conclusion is tentative because we cannot positively identify the Zechariah mentioned in Matthew 23.

**Prophecy as a continuing phenomenon.** While the early Christians did recognize prophecy as an ongoing phenomenon, they did not believe that this would allow further prophetic writings to be added to the OT canon. In fact, the evidence from the NT indicates that the prophetic books already received as authoritative and inspired could not be supplemented with further works. The NT maintains a careful distinction between the older prophetic revelation preserved in the OT canon and the newer apostolic revelation preserved in Christian writings.

**The canon as a closed collection of books.** While the NT does borrow thoughts and phraseology from the Apocrypha and Pseudepigrapha, even occasionally quoting from them, it never gives any indication that it considers any book outside the Hebrew OT canon as authoritative, inspired canonical books.

### *Flavius Josephus*

Flavius Josephus was born into a Jewish priestly family in AD 37 or 38 and died around 100 in Rome. Although he studied under Pharisees, Sadducees and Essenes, at the age of nineteen he joined the Pharisees and followed their practices for the rest of his life. At first he opposed the Jewish rebellion against Rome, but he eventually joined the Jewish forces as general in Galilee and was captured by Vespasian in 67. He prophesied that Vespasian would become emperor, which probably led to Vespasian sparing his life. When Vespasian was made emperor in 69 he had Josephus set free and Josephus took Vespasian's family name, Flavius. Josephus was taken to Jerusalem by Vespasian's son Titus and was there to witness the fall of the city in 70. When Titus returned to Rome, Josephus accompanied him and became an author and favorite of the imperial court. During this time Josephus produced four works: *The Jewish War* (completed 75–79) which contains his account of the Jewish rebellion in 66–70; *The Jewish Antiquities* (completed 93–94), a history of the Jews based on the OT and later historical sources; *The Life*, his autobiography appended to the *Antiquities*; and *Against Apion* (completed 93–96), a defense of the Jewish people against anti-Jewish polemic. Since Josephus left Palestine in AD 70, his view of the canon probably reflected the Jewish practice in Palestine up to that time and not in the nineties when his last books were written.

## The Temple Archives

In a number of passages in his writings Josephus confirms what we have seen earlier—the holy books were officially archived in the Temple in Jerusalem. In *Antiquities* 3.38 he notes that either Exodus or Numbers was part of this archive:

> δηλοῖ δὲ ἐν τῷ ἱερῷ ἀνακειμένη γραφὴ τὸν θεὸν προειπεῖν Μωυσεῖ οὕτως ἐκ τῆς πέτρας ἀναδοθήσεσθαι ὕδωρ.

> In a writing archived in the Temple it is revealed that God predicted to Moses that water would gush from the rock. (cf. Exod 17:6; Num 20:8)

In *Antiquities* 4.303–304, after summarizing the works of Moses, he mentions that the works of Moses were stored in the Temple:

> ἔπειτα ποίησιν ἑξάμετρον αὐτοῖς ἀνέγνω, ἣν καὶ καταλέλοιπεν ἐν βίβλιῳ ἐν τῷ ἱερῷ

> Then he [Moses] recited to them a poem in hexameter which is also archived in a book in the Temple...(cf. Deut 33)

The book of Joshua is likewise mentioned as a book in the Temple archives in *Antiquities* 5.61:

> ὅτι δὲ τὸ μῆκος τῆς ἡμέρας ἐπέδωκε τότε καὶ τοῦ συνήθους ἐπλεόνασέ δηλοῦνται διὰ τῶν ἀνακειμένων ἐν τῷ ἱερῷ γραμμάτων.

> That the length of the day was increased then and was greater than what is customary is revealed in the Scriptures that are archived in the Temple. (cf. Josh 10:12–13).

These Temple archives were captured by the Romans, and Josephus mentions them as some of the spoils of war taken from the Temple (*War* 7.148–150).

λάφυρα δὲ τὰ μὲν ἄλλα χύδην ἐφέρετο, διέπρεπε δὲ
πάντων τὰ ἐγκαταληφθέντα τῷ ἐν Ἱεποσολύμοις ἱερωῦὅ
τε νόμος ὁ τῶν Ἰουδαίων ἐπὶ τούτος ἐφέρετο τῶν
λαφύρων τελευταῖος.

The spoils were borne in large heaps, but conspicuous
of all of them were those captured in the Jerusalem
Temple... And after these the Jewish Law was carried as
the last of the spoils.

Thus, Josephus confirms on several occasions that the sacred
Jewish books were in an archive in the Temple. This archive ceased to
exist when Jerusalem was captured and looted by the Romans.
Therefore, the normative character of this archive in the Temple was
lost, and the canon could not be defined as the holy books that were
recognized as such by their special place in the Temple archives.

However, Josephus does note that the Temple not only stored
Scriptures but also official priestly records. In *Against Apion* 1.34–36
he speaks of the practice of carefully recording priestly genealogical
information and archiving it:

πόλεμος δ' εἰ κατάσχοι, καθάπερ ἤδη γέγονε πολλάκις,
Ἀντιόχου τε τοῦ Ἐπιφανοῦς εἰς τὴν χώραν ἐμβαλ-
όντος καὶ Πομπηίου Μάγνου καὶ Κυντιλίου Οὐάρου
μάλιστα δὲ καὶ ἐν τοῖς καθ' ἡμᾶς χρόνοις, οἱ περι-
λειπόμενοι τὸν ἱερέων καινὰ πάλιν ἐκ τῶν ἀρχείων
γράμματα συνίστανταιΠτεκμήριον δὲ μέγιστον τῆς
ἀκριβείας· οἱ γὰρ ἀρχιερεῖς οἱ παρ' ἡμῖν ἀπὸ
δισχιλίων ἐτῶν ὀνομαστοὶ παῖδες ἐκ πατρός εἰσιν ἐν
ταῖς ἀναγραφαῖς.

In the frequent event of war, for instance when our
country was invaded by Antiochus Epiphanes, by
Pompey the Great, by Quintilius Varus, and above all,
in our own times, the surviving priests compile a new
set of records from the archives... But the most
impressive proof of our accuracy is that the records
contain the names of our high priests from father to son
for [the last] two thousand years.

Therefore, the Temple was the place to store the Scriptures and the
records that allowed the priests to prove their legitimacy so that they
could participate in the sacrifices and other duties. He notes that the
Temple archives included records from Jews in other parts of the world

so that their priestly lines could be verified against the master list in the Jerusalem archives (*Against Apion* 1.33). Even if we allow that Josephus is exaggerating when he contends that the names of the high priests for the last two thousand years were recorded in the Temple records, his point is not invalidated. The Temple library was a place for archiving the most holy of books and records. These included the Scriptures, the holy books for Jews. While Josephus gives us details about the various archives in the Temple, his treatment of this subject is not the first. We saw it already in 2 Maccabees, and archiving holy books in the Temple is attested in the OT itself.

Just as the Temple records of priestly lineage served as a definitive official collection of records, the books archived in the Temple as Scripture must have served as a definitive collection of those sacred books. *The clear implication of the evidence is that before the fall of Jerusalem in AD 70 canonicity was determined by a book's admission to the archives of Scripture in the Temple, not by being a part of a list of accepted books as in later times.*

## The Number and Classification of the Canonical Books

The section in *Against Apion* we have just examined continues with Josephus' account of other archival books, in this case the Scriptures themselves. In paragraphs 37–43 he states:

Ἐικότος οὖν, μᾶλλον δὲ ἀναγκαίως, ἅτε μήτε τοῦ γράφειν αὐτεξουσίου πᾶσιν ὄντος μήτε τινὸς ἐν τοῖς γραφομένοις ἐνούσης διαφωνίας, ἀλλὰ μόνον τῶν προφητῶν τὰ μὲν ἀνωτάτω καὶ παλαιότατα κατὰ τὴν ἐπίπνοιαν τὴν ἀπὸ τοῦ θεοῦ μαθόντων, τὰ δὲ καθ' αὑτοὺς ὡς ἐγένετο σαφῶς συγγραφόντων, οὐ μυριάδες βιβλίων εἰσὶ παρ' ἡμῖν ἀσυμφώνων καὶ μαχομένων, δύο δὲ μόνα πρὸς τοῖς εἴκοσι βιβλία τοῦ παντὸς ἔχοντα χρόνου τὴν ἀναγραφήν, τὰ δικαίως πεπιστευμένα. καὶ τούτων πέντε μέν ἐστι τὰ Μωυσέως, ἃ τούς τε νόμους περιέχει καὶ τήν ἀπ'ἀνθρωπογονίας

It naturally, or rather necessarily, follows (in as much as it is not everyone's prerogative to write the records and that there is no discrepancy in what is written; rather only the prophets who knew the highest and most ancient history according to the inspiration from God, and committing to writing clear account of what happened in their own times) that we do not have myriads of inconsistent and conflicting books. Our books, the ones justly trusted, are but twenty-two, containing the record of all time. Of these five are from Moses. They contain the law

παράδοσιν μέχρι τῆς αὐτοῦ τελευτῆς· οὗτος ὁ χρόνος ἀπολείπει τρισχιλίων ὀλίγον ἐτῶν ἀπὸ δὲ τῆς Μωυσέως τελευτῆς μέχρις ᾿αρταξέρξου τοῦ μετὰ Ξέρξην Περσῶν βασιλέως οἱ μετὰ Μωυσῆν προφῆται τὰ κατ᾿ αὐτοὺς πραχ- θέντα συνέγραψαν ἐν τρισὶ καὶ δέκα βιβλίοις. αἱ δὲ λοιπαὶ τέσσαρες ὕμνους εἰς τὸν θεὸν καὶ τοῖς ἀνθρώποις ὑποθήκας τοῦ βίου περιέχουσιν. ἀπὸ δὲ ᾿Αρταξέρξου μέχρι τοῦ καθ᾿ ἡμᾶς χρόνου γέγραπται μὲν ἕκαστα, πίστεως δ᾿ οὐχ ὁμοίας ἠξίωται τοῖς πρὸ αὐτῶν διὰ τὸ μὴ γενέσθαι τὴν τῶν προφητῶν ἀκριβῆ διαδοχήν.

Δῆλον δ᾿ ἐστὶν ἔργῳ πῶς ἡμεῖς πρόσιμεν τοῖς ἰδίοις γράμμασι· τοσούτου γὰρ αἰῶνος ἤδη παρῳχηκότος οὔτε προσθεῖναί τις οὐδὲν οὔτε ἀφελεῖν αὐτῶν οὔτε μεταθεῖναι τετόλμηκεν, πᾶσι δὲ σύμφυτόν ἐστιν εὐθὺς ἐκ τῆς πρώτης γενέσεως ᾿Ιουδαίοις τὸ νομίζειν αὐτὰ θεοῦ δόγματα καὶ τούτοις ἐμμένειν καὶ ὑπερ αὐτῶν, εἰ δέοι, θνήσκειν ἡδέως. ἤδη οὖν πολλοὶ πολλάκις ἑώρανται τῶν αἰχμαλώντων στρέβλας καὶ παντοίων θανάτων τρόπους ἐν θεάτροις ὑπομένοντες ἐπὶ τῷ μηδὲν ῥῆμα προέσθαι παρὰ τοὺς νόμους καὶ τὰς μετὰ τούτων ἀναγραφάς.

and the history handed down from the beginning of humans until the death of Moses. This period is slightly less than three thousand years. From the death of Moses until Artaxerxes, who succeeded Xerxes as Persian king, the prophets after Moses recorded the events of their own times in thirteen books. The remaining four books are hymns to God and counsel for the conduct of life. From Artaxerxes until our time the complete history has been written, but is not considered worthy of equal stature with the earlier works because of the failure of the exact succession of the prophets.

Our work has made clear how we approach our own Scriptures. Although long ages have already passed, no one has dared to add or delete anything or alter them. It is instinctual with every Jew immediately from the day of birth to consider them God's decrees, to keep them and, if necessary, to die for them. Therefore, already many times people have seen prisoners tortured and endure every kind of death in the theaters rather than speak a single word against the laws and the documents that belong with them.

Since this statement of Josephus immediately follows his description of the priestly records, we can infer from context that the Scriptural books he describes here were considered an official collection, not merely his private opinion.

However, others have argued that Josephus is expressing only a private opinion. D. J. Silver claims that this passage contains Josephus' wish about the extent of the canon, rather than the actual state of affairs in his day.[159] McDonald also doubts whether Josephus' statement is more than his own view.[160] The doubts arise because of Josephus' obvious hyperbole—that the Scriptures have never been altered (as if Josephus was completely unaware of differing textual witnesses), that it is instinctual with every Jew to accept, defend and even die for them, etc. However, Josephus' hyperbole does not mean that *nothing* he writes is to be trusted. Josephus is defending his people against Apion and his anti-Jewish rhetoric. That he would adorn the facts with hyperbole is understandable. That he would seek to mount a defense on the basis of completely fabricated facts is very improbable. Moreover, we know from other sources that some facts Josephus assumes in this passage are true—there was a Temple archive, the Greeks did have many sacred texts, other sources assume that the canonical books were from the Persian period or earlier, and some Jews did defend their faith (and their Scriptures) at the cost of their lives.

Therefore, the best approach to Josephus' testimony is to assume that the core of his testimony about the extent and number of the books is true, though he may have defended the canon with some hyperbolic claims about Jewish sensibilities toward it. This would match much of what we know about Josephus' writing. He reports the facts as he knows them, but often also overstates the evidence to cast the Jewish people in a better light.

What does this passage tell us about the canon that existed in Josephus' day (i.e., in the decades preceding and following the fall of Jerusalem)? We can draw a number of conclusions about it:

1. The canon Josephus knew was probably identical to the Hebrew OT.
    A. Like all other ancient Jewish sources, he acknowledges the five books of Moses.
    B. His thirteen prophetic books are probably Joshua, Judges-Ruth, Samuel, Kings, Chronicles, Ezra-Nehemiah, Esther, Job, Isaiah, Jeremiah-Lamentations, Ezekiel, Daniel, the Twelve Prophets. Of these, Josephus names Joshua (*Antiquities* 5.612), Kings (*Antiquities* 9.28, 46; *War* 6.103–105), Isaiah (*Antiquities*

---

[159] D. J. Silver, *The Story of Scripture: From Oral Tradition to the Written Word* (New York: Basic Books, 1990) 134.

[160] McDonald, *Formation*, 55–58 and *Integrity*, 108–11.

11.4–6, 10.35, 13.64, 68, *War* 7.432), Jeremiah-Lamentations (*Antiquities* 10.78–79, 11.1–2; *War* 5.391), Ezekiel (*Antiquities* 10:79), Daniel (*Antiquities* 10.210, 266–81; 11.337; 12.322) and the Minor Prophets (*Antiquities* 10.35). Josephus drew on Judges and Samuel for his *Antiquities* books 5–7. He treats Ruth immediately after Judges (*Antiquities* 5.318–337), making it likely that he is counting Judges and Ruth as one book. His mention of Artaxerxes here ties in with his identification of Artaxerxes as Esther's husband in his treatment of Esther (*Antiquities* 11.184–274). Artaxerxes is also the son of Xerxes, during whose reign Josephus places his account of Ezra and Nehemiah in *Antiquities* book 11. This leaves only Job and Chronicles as not mentioned by Josephus. Since these books are attested as early as Ben Sira, we have no reason to doubt that Josephus' list includes these books also.

C. The four hymns to God and counsel for the conduct of life are Psalms and Proverbs and most likely Songs of Songs and Ecclesiastes, books also attested as early as Ben Sira. Ben Sira, though fitting the description of a book giving counsel for the conduct of life, is ruled out since it mentions the high priest Simeon whom Josephus dates much later than Artaxerxes (*Antiquities* 12.43).

2. Josephus definitely acknowledges other religious books after the time of Artaxerxes, but does not consider them authoritative or inspired. The reason for this is that the exact succession prophets ceased in the early Persian period. In this statement Josephus is more nuanced than 1 Maccabees. Josephus does not state that prophets did not arise after the reign of Artaxerxes, just that the succession from one prophet to the next was broken, bringing to the end the writing of authoritative and inspired books. Indeed, Josephus, like the NT, acknowledges the existence of

prophets after the exact succession of the old prophetic line was broken (e.g., *War* 6.286; *Antiquities* 13:311–312).[161]

3. Josephus considers these books as revered by all Jews. Josephus knows of different Jewish sects and reports the differences in their beliefs (*Antiquities* 18.11–27). However, nowhere does he report any differences in opinion among Jews as to the contents of their holy books. Indeed, in this passage from *Against Apion* he considers the canon the acknowledged common heritage of every Jew.

4. Josephus' list divides the canon into two historical periods: the period up to the death of Moses (the Pentateuch) and the period from the death of Moses to the reign of Artaxerxes. The books of the later period are subdivided into two groups: thirteen historical books and four hymnic and wisdom books. While Josephus could be seen as having a tripartite canon, he is probably enumerating a two-part canon with the second part divided into two sections. Indeed Barton notes,[162]

> This may indeed mean that the prophets wrote thirteen books, and someone else the other four books accepted by the Jews as authoritative; but it could equally well mean that thirteen of the books written by prophets are histories, and four hymnographic and sapiential. Even apart from this, it seems that Josephus' understanding of Scripture allows only a basic twofold division. There is the Law, and there are the books of prophets, and no other books are authoritative in the same way. Books of prophets are books written by the properly authorized successors of Moses—not the Torah, but the next best thing.

Certainly at the end of the section quoted above from *Against Apion* Josephus reverts to a twofold division of Scripture: "the laws and the documents that belong with them." Therefore, Josephus' list may be seen as a further development along the way to the three-part canon, but it is not a three-part canon.

---

[161] David E. Aune, "The Use of ΠΡΟΦΗΤΗΣ in Josephus," *JBL* 101 (1982), 420; Joseph Blenkinsopp, "Prophecy and Priesthood in Josephus," *JJS* 25 (1974), 239–62.

[162] Barton, "The Law and the Prophets," 5–6; see also Barton, *Oracles of God*, 48–49.

Thus, Josephus tells of a Jewish canon whose contents appear to be identical to the Hebrew OT. He also is the first source known to us that enumerates the books in the canon. The number of books, twenty-two, corresponds to the number of letters in the Hebrew alphabet. Whether this is deliberate, as we will see that it is in a later list by Origen, we cannot say. That Josephus is the first to enumerate the books may well have to do with the time of his writing—about two decades after the destruction of the Temple and the looting of its contents. The fact that one can no longer consult the archives because they no longer exist leads to the importance of a more precise accounting of what books were considered authoritative, inspired books. Josephus, therefore, probably stands at the beginning of a process whereby the canon makes a transition from a collection of scrolls in the Temple archives to a list of books.

In addition, Josephus is also the first source we have to date the closing of the canon. While we have seen implications of this in earlier sources, Josephus is the first to explicitly state that the canon was closed with the cessation of the line of the prophets in the early Persian period. Once again, this may have been deliberately stated because the Temple no longer existed. While the Temple existed it would have been theoretically possible for the line of the prophets to be re-established and new authoritative books to be added (1 Maccabees 4:46 and 14:41 imply that this would be possible, see page 56). However, once the Temple archives ceased to exist, there would be no way of receiving another book into them. Josephus' notice gives us an explicit statement about the closing of the canon in practical terms and implies that even the theoretical possibility of adding to the canon is no longer available.

### Pharisees, Sadducees, and Essenes

Now that we have examined both the NT and Josephus, we should also determine whether any evidence points to differences of opinion about the canon among Jewish groups of the late second Temple period. Josephus' statement about the canon states that all Jews accepted the same canon. Moreover in *Antiquities* 18.11–25 he describes the Jewish sects in his day. While he mentions many differences among them, he never claims that they differed on the contents of the Scriptures.

Certainly Josephus, as a Pharisee, is at least presenting their view of the canon as do the later rabbinic teachings that affirm the Hebrew OT as we know it today. Moreover, if we can identify the Therapeutae and the Qumran sectarians as Essenes, then, as we have already seen, it is likely that they accepted the same canon as the Pharisees. Furthermore, if we can identify the Herodians mentioned in the Gospels as Essenes (see *Antiquities* 15.373–378; Matt 22:16; Mark 12:13) then the alliance between the Pharisees and the Herodians to kill Jesus reported in Mark 3:6 shows that there were no strong impediments preventing close cooperation between the Pharisees and the Essenes.

While the Gospels report that the Pharisees and Sadducees could work together to attempt to trap Jesus in his words (Matt 16:1), the NT reports more animosity and competition between these groups than cooperation (Matt 22:34; Acts 23:6–8). Perhaps they also were divided on their view of the canon. Beckwith has examined the canonical views of the Sadducees, and his treatment provides us with ample evidence that the Sadducees also accepted the same canon as the Pharisees.[163] He makes the following points:

1. The Sadducees rejected belief in the resurrection (Matt 22:23; Mark 12:18; Luke 20:27; Acts 4:1; Acts 23:8; *Antiquities* 18:16) which is clearly taught in the Prophets (Isa 26:19; Ezek 37:1–4; Dan 12:2). This does not mean that they rejected all books outside the Pentateuch, however. Since they also rejected belief in angels (Acts 23:8) they would have had to reject even the Pentateuch (since angels are mentioned in Genesis, Exodus and Numbers) if they had no way to explain their beliefs. However, Hyppolytus tells us that the Sadducees explained the resurrection in a non-literal manner (*Refutation* 9:29). Moreover, a late midrash, the *Printed Tanhuma*, reports that the Sadducees used Job 7:9 to defend their view of the resurrection.[164]

2. Josephus makes the following statement about the Sadducees:

Σαδδουκαίοις δὲ τὰς ψυχὰς ὁ λόγος συναφανίζει τοῖς σώμασι, φυλακῇ δὲ οὐδαμῶς τινων μεταποίησις αὐτοῖς ἢ τῶν νόμων....

---

[163] Beckwith, *Formation*, 73–76; *Old Testament Canon*, 86–91.

[164] Jean Le Moyne, *Les Sadducéens*. Etudes bibliques. (Paris: Gabalda, 1972), 173.

> "The Sadducees hold that the soul perishes with the body. They accept no practices apart from the laws...."
> (Antiquities 18.16)

Besides telling us of the reason for the Sadducees' rejection of the resurrection, this passage also tells us of their aversion to religious practices imposed apart from the explicit statements in the Law. However, this passage does not mean that the Sadducees did not accept any books outside the Pentateuch. Instead, it means they rejected the oral law followed by the Pharisees (*Antiquities* 18.12).

3. Most of the high priests and the more prominent priests after John Hyrcanus were Sadducees. Matthew 2:1–6 speaks of the chief priests as expecting the "Christ" or the "Son of David" and quoting Micah 5:2 in reference to him. These titles occur in 2 Samuel 7:8–16, Isaiah 61:1, Psalm 2:2, 89:3–4; Psalms 28–37, Daniel 9:25 and 1 Chronicles 17:7–14, but never in the Pentateuch. Therefore, the Sadducees must have accepted more than the Law.

4. The Sadducees were in control of the Temple where the Scriptures were archived. They inherited this archive when they gained control of the Temple in the late second century BC. This archive was probably the common heritage of all Jewish sects.

5. Many of the church Fathers beginning with Hippolytus and Origen in the third century AD clearly state that the Sadducees' canon consisted only of the Pentateuch. However, Hippolytus explicitly identified the Sadducees with the Samaritans. In addition, Pseudo-Tertullian describes the Sadducees as an offshoot of the Dositheans, a Samaritan sect. This is repeated in other Fathers, including Epiphanius. Later in the fourteenth century Abu 'l-Fath in his *Chronicle* states that the subdivisions of the Dositheans included some who claimed to be Sadducees. All this seems to point to the Sadducees joining with the Samaritans sometime in the second or third century AD, about the time rabbinic literature indicates that they were dying out among the Jews. Therefore, the Sadducees' belief about the canon reported by the Fathers is not a reflection of their beliefs in the first

century or earlier, but an indication of their beliefs under the influence of the Samaritans in the late second century or later.

Thus, during the first century AD and earlier the three Jewish sects we know of from ancient writings appear to have been in agreement on the extent of the canon. It was not a point of contention among them and no ancient writer of this period indicates otherwise.

### 2 Esdras

In the book of 2 Esdras (4 Ezra) one passage appears to refer to the OT canon. This book was written in the late first century, probably about AD 100. Though it was most likely written in a Semitic language, it survives only in Latin, Syriac, Coptic, Ethiopic, Arabic, Armenian, and Georgian. In chapter 14, Ezra is instructed to set aside forty days during which he will receive inspiration to write books based on words that Moses received, some of which were to be published and others of which were to be hidden (2 Esdras 14:4–6). In verses 44–47 we read:

> scripti sunt autem in quadraginta diebus libri nongenti quattuor. et factum est cum conpleti essent quadraginta dies, et locutus est Altissimus dicens: priora quae scripsisti in palam pone, et legant digni et indigni. novissimos autem septuaginta conservabis, ut tradas eos sapientibus de populo tuo. in his enim est vena intellectus et sapientiae fons et scientiae flumen. et feci sic.

> So during the forty days, ninety-four books were written. When the forty days were completed, the Most High said to me, "Publish the twenty-four books that you wrote first, and let the worthy and the unworthy read them. But keep the seventy that were written last to give them to the wise among your people. In them is the spring of understanding, the fountain of wisdom, and the river of knowledge."

This passage is the first to enumerate the OT canon as twenty-four books. The additional seventy are probably apocryphal or pseudepigraphal books. The writer of 2 Esdras is clearly attempting to use the status of the twenty-four books to boost the status of the other seventy.

He acknowledges the public nature of the canon, but uses this to argue that the seventy other books are not public because they are reserved for only those who are worthy to learn their wisdom. This in itself is an acknowledgment of the status of the twenty-four books as well-known and well-accepted canon. Moreover, the connection of the writing of the canonical books with Ezra and the attempt to boost the authority of the other seventy by their connection with him and the twenty-four book canon are implicit evidence for the closing of the canon in the early Persian period, confirming what we have seen in other sources.

While we cannot unequivocally state that these twenty-four books are the same as the twenty-four book canon accepted in Judaism and as witnessed later in the Talmud, the evidence certainly points in this direction. That is, this is most likely the same canon enumerated by Josephus as twenty-two books with Ruth and Lamentations counted as separate books.[165] In addition, this work connects the completion of the canon with Ezra, confirming the line of evidence stretching back to Ben Sira that the canon was closed (at least in practical terms) in the early Persian period.

### Talmudic Recollections of the First Century

Several passages in the Talmud and allied documents contain recollections of questions concerning the canon from the first century. Each one of these passages concerns ritual purity laws and whether a book "defiles the hands." This phrase refers to a rabbinic ruling intended to guard certain items from being destroyed. Leiman has argued convincingly that this decree could have been promulgated no later than the middle of the first century and was probably much older.[166] Broyde summarizes the concept of sacred books defiling the hands:[167]

---

[165] McDonald, *Formation*, 60 agrees that this twenty-four book canon probably corresponds to the later twenty-four book canon. However, because the books are not listed, he states that there is no way to know whether this twenty-four book canon or Josephus' twenty-two book canon contains Ruth, Lamentations, Ezekiel, Daniel, Ecclesiastes or Song of Songs. However, as we have seen in our discussion of Josephus, the only books that Josephus does not mention or treat are Ecclesiastes and Song of Songs, and these books have strong evidence behind them to indicate that they were accepted as Scripture before Josephus' time (see page 115).

[166] Leiman, *Canonization*, 118–19.

[167] Michael J. Broyde, "Defilement of the Hands, Canonization of the Bible, and the Special Status of Esther, Ecclesiastes, and Song of Songs," *Judaism* 44 (1995), 66.

Defiling the hands is a status of ritual purity (or impurity) that is completely rabbinic in nature and was enacted by the Talmudic Sages not to promote ritual purity, but to protect holy works from destruction or desecration. Essentially, the Sages of the Talmud observed people would store terumah (a "sacred" food) in the ark with holy scrolls saying, "both are holy." In order to prevent this conduct, which apparently led to rats, mice, and weasels eating the scrolls as well as the sacred food, the Sages enacted a series of rabbinic decrees designed to deter this conduct. The initial decree was that the torah scrolls defiled one's hands; thus, a person could not directly touch sacred scrolls and then sacred food. Secondly, they decreed that if one touched a sacred scroll and then touched sacred food, that food became ritually unclean (and could not be eaten). Finally, they decreed that when one touched sacred food it defiled one's hands, thus preventing one from first touching food and then touching sacred scrolls. The effect of these decrees was to prevent one from storing food and scrolls together or to go immediately from one to another without first washing the hands. From the Talmud, however, it is clear that this decree was limited to certain types of sacred texts: not all sacred texts defiled the hands. Thus Tosephta (Yadayim 2:12) recounts that written-out blessings and certain verses do not defile the hands. While the Talmud does not explain this particular insight directly, the discussion in Talmud Shabbat 116–118 concerning those sacred texts which can be saved from a fire on the Sabbath does explicitly link salvation from the fire with the presence of God's name.

Thus, the issue of the defiling of hands is not a direct indication of canonical status, since other holy texts also can defile the hands. However, many scholars have understood Talmudic discussions of whether certain biblical books defile the hands as discussions of their canonical status.

The relevant passages that concern the first century are:[168]

---

[168] All the relevant passages in the Talmud and Midrash are collected in Leiman, *Canonization*, 102–20.

משנה כלים כו:ו
כל הספרים מטמאין את הידים חוץ מספר העזרה

Mishnah Kelim 15:6
All books [of Scripture] defile the hands except the
Book of [the Law copied by] Ezra. [169]

תוספתא כלים בבא מציעא ה:ח
ספר עזרא שיצא לחוץ מטמא את הידים ולא ספר
עזרא בלבד אלא אפילו נביאים וחומשים וספר אחר
נכנס לשם מטמא את הידים

Tosefta Kelim, Baba Metzia 5:8
The Book of [the Law copied by] Ezra when taken
outside [the Temple Courtyard] defiles the hands. Not
only the Book of Ezra, but also the Prophetic books and
scrolls containing one of the five [books of Moses]. A
book [of Scripture] brought into the Temple Courtyard
defiles the hands.

These two passages are both concerned with scrolls of Scripture
that were in the Temple. These scrolls were said not to defile the hands
only while in the Temple courtyard. While we cannot know exactly
why these scrolls did not defile the hands, it may have been practical
considerations that lead to this exception. The priests who would read
from these scrolls in the Temple would also be involved in receiving
sacred food. To make them wash their hands before each reading from
these scrolls would have involved them in almost endless delays.
Therefore, these scrolls were exempt. However, if they were taken
outside the Temple they were to be treated like other biblical scrolls,
since there would then be no need for the exception. Likewise, other
books of Scripture whether the Prophets[170] or the Law would defile the
hands even if brought into the Temple court, because they were not
official copies for Temple use and did not need to be in the Temple.

---

[169] This is not a reference to the biblical book of Ezra, but to a scroll of the Law in the
Temple whose production was attributed to Ezra.

[170] I believe that the term *Prophets* here probably refers to all the rest of the Scripture,
not the later section of the OT that was distinct from the Law.

משנה עדויות ה:ג

רבי שמעון אומר שלשה דברים מקלי בית שמאי
ומחמרי בית הלל קהלת אינה מטמא את הידים
כדברי בית שמאי ובית הלל אומרים מטמא את
הידים

Mishnah Eduyoth 5:3

Rabbi Simeon[171] says, "In three cases the School of
Shammai is more lenient and the School of Hillel[172] is
more strict. The book of Ecclesiastes does not defile the
hands according to the School of Shammai. The School
of Hillel says that it does defile the hands."

משנה ידים ג:ה

כל כתבי הקדש מטמאין את הידים שיר השירים
וקהלת מטמאות את הידים רבי יהודה אומר שיר
השירים מטמא את הידים וקהלת מהלקת רבי יוסי
אומר קהלת אינה מטמא את הידים ושיר השירים
מחלקת רבי שמעון אומר קהלת מקלי בית שמאי
ומחמרי בית הלל אמר רב שמעון בן עזאי מקבל
אני מפי שבעים ושנים זקן ביום שהושיבו את רבי
אלעזר בן עזריה בישיבה ששיר השירים
וקהלת מטמאות את הידים אמר רבי עקיבא חס
ושלום לא נחלק אדם מישראל על שיר השירים
שלא חטמא את הידים שאין כל העולם כלו כדאי
כיום שנתנה בו שיר השירים לישראל שכל
הכתובים קדש ושיר השורים קדש קדשים ואם
נחלקו לא נחלקו אלא על קהלת אמר רבי יוחנן
בן יהושע בן חמיו שלרבי עקיבא כדברי בן עזאי
כן נחלקו וכן גמרו

*Mishnah Yadayim* 3:5

All the Holy Scriptures defile the hands. The Song of
Songs and Ecclesiastes defile the hands. Rabbi Judah
says, "The Songs of Songs defiles the hands, but there is
a dispute about Ecclesiastes." Rabbi Jose says, "Ec-

---

[171] Active AD 135–170.

[172] Shammai and Hillel were active at the beginning of the first century. This passage
gives the opinion of their successors.

clesiastes does not defile the hands, but there is a dispute about Song of Songs." Rabbi Simeon says, "Ecclesiastes is among the lenient decisions of the School of Shammai and among the stringent decisions of the School of Hillel. Rabbi Simeon, son of Azzai said, "I have heard a tradition from the seventy-two elders on the day that Rabbi Eleazar, son of Azariah was appointed head of the academy, that the Song of Songs and Ecclesiastes defile the hands." Rabbi Akiba said, "God forbid. No one in Israel ever disputed the status of the Song of Songs by saying that it does not defile the hands, for the entire world is not worth the day when the Song of Songs was given to Israel. All the Holy Scripture is holy. But the Song of Songs is the most holy. If there was a dispute it was about Ecclesiastes." Rabbi Jonathan, son of Joshua, the son of Rabbi Akiba's father-in-law, said, "Ben Azzai's version of the dispute is the correct one."

Both of these passages report disagreements over whether Ecclesiastes defiles the hands. The second passage includes the Song of Songs and was the basis for the Council of Jamnia Hypothesis about the closing of the canon. While they both record sayings of rabbis active in the second century, the rabbis are in some cases reporting what they understood to be the case in the first century. In the passage from Mishnah Yadayim a report is given of the day when Rabbi Eleazar was appointed head of the academy at Jamnia. Most scholars date this to about AD 90.

According to many scholars the debate about Ecclesiastes and Songs of Songs was a debate about their canonicty. If this were the case, then one of two conclusions would have to be drawn. One conclusion would be that the canon was not closed until much later because the Talmud records disputes into the third century about whether Ecclesiastes, Song of Songs and Esther defile the hands. However, since the earliest references to the tripartite division of the canon come from the early second century, it is unlikely that the canon remained open for Jews as late as the third century. (Leiman solves the problem by declaring that these books were canonical, but not inspired. He contends that the discussion was a disagreement over whether these

books were inspired. [173] Leiman's solution, though creative, is doubtful.
See page 16.) The other conclusion would be that the canon was closed
early, but some later questioned whether certain books belonged in the
canon (much like Luther's questions about certain NT books). This line
of reasoning is perhaps a little more sound since we know of no
disputes over whether other books outside the present canon defile the
hands. [174]

However, the problem may be with the premise that discussion of
books defiling the hands may not be an indication of disputes about
canonicity. Broyde argues that this is precisely the case. [175] Broyde
notes one characteristic shared by Song of Songs, Ecclesiastes and
Esther and by no other books of the canon: the Tetragrammaton is
absent from all three. He notes that the concept of defiling the hands is
at least partially connected to the presence of God's name in the text.
For instance, *Tosefta Yadayim* 2:12–13:

הברכות אף על פי שיש בהן מאותות השם ומעניינות
הרבה שבתורה אינן מטמאות את הידים הגליונים
וספרי המינין אינן מטמאות את הידים ספרי בן סירא
וכל ספרים שנכתבו מכאן ואילך אינןמטמאין את
הידים

> Blessings, although they contain abbreviations of God's
> name and many citations from the Torah, do not defile
> the hands. The Gospels and [other] heretical books do
> not defile the hands. The book of Ben Sira and all books
> written from then on do not defile the hands.

Note the Talmudic discussion of the Gospels and Ben Sira not
defiling the hands. Ben Sira contains the divine name and the Gospels
quote books that contain the divine name and defile the hands, but
neither Ben Sira or the Gospels defile the hands. Therefore, Broyde
concludes: [176]

---

[173] Note that Leiman makes a distinction between inspired canonical books and
uninspired canonical books. He believes the books were already accepted as
canonical before the first century. See Leiman, *Canonization*, 120.

[174] The Talmud does record statements denying that other books such as Ben Sira and
the Gospels defile the hands. See Leiman, *Canonization*, 92–102, 109.

[175] Broyde, *Defilement*.

[176] Broyde, *Defilement*, 73–74.

It is through a clear understanding of the rules and rationale for why texts defile the hands that one can understand why one might doubt if Esther, Song of Songs, and Ecclesiastes defile the hands but are still members of the Biblical canon. Indeed, part of this understanding of the difference between the names of God generally, and the Tetragrammaton (שם המפורש) in particular, can be understood in the context of saving scrolls from destruction....

This article surveyed three issues: the rabbinic understanding of the dispute as to whether Esther, Song of Songs and Ecclesiastes defile the hands; how that issue is resolved in Jewish law; and a possible rationale for the unique status of these three books. While at first glance it might appear that these three issues are unrelated, in fact they all revolve around a discussion of the special status of Esther, Ecclesiastes, and Song of Songs. Each of these works have their status discussed in the Talmud and each has various rabbinic authorities who question whether its status is similar to that of other books of the Writings since each of these lacks the presence of the Tetragrammaton (שם המפורש).

Broyde's conclusion seems to be correct, especially in light of Mishnah Yadayim 3:5 (see page 125).[177] There it is stated that all the Scriptures defile the hands. Then it is stated specifically that Songs of Songs and Ecclesiastes defile the hands. Then contrary opinions are given. The logic seems to be:

1.  All Scriptures defile the hands.
2.  This includes some books that some rabbis would have excluded from the decree about defiling the hands.
3.  These are the comments of the rabbis who would have excluded these books from the decree concerning defiling the hands.

The references to the differences between the Schools of Shammai and Hillel mentioned in *Mishnah Eduyoth* 5:3 and *Mishnah Yadayim* 3:5 appear to be differences based on the same premise. The School of Shammai applied the decree to all books of the canon. The School of Hillel applied the rule only to those books that contained the divine

---

[177] Barr, *Holy Scripture*, 50–51 and Barton, *Oracles of God*, 69 come to the same conclusion.

name. That Esther is not mentioned in this early discussion may reinforce what we have seen from the very beginning: If there was one book whose canonical status might have been doubted by some, it was Esther.

Therefore, the Talmud not only gives no evidence that the canon was closed at Jamnia as the old Council of Jamnia Hypothesis held, but also its discussion of books that defile the hands does not argue for an open canon late in the first century. If Broyde is correct about the concept of defiling the hands (and I believe he is), then the Talmudic references to the discussions of books that defile the hands are only peripherally relevant to the question of canonicity. If scholars who equate questions of defilement of the hands with canonicity are right (which I believe is unlikely), then some rabbis during the first three centuries AD challenged the presence of some books in the canon. However, there is no evidence that they considered the canon open and capable of having books added to it.

### *Summary*

This chapter has surveyed sources on the OT canon from the time of Jesus to the end of the first century. Figure 2 gives a chronological summary of the evidence from the first century in this chapter and chapter 2.

The first century provides us with indications of change in the view of the canon that sets the stage for developments that will be seen in the history of the canon in later centuries. Among these are the organization of canon into sections and numbering of the canonical books. The most influential factor effecting the canon during this century was the destruction of the Temple in Jerusalem in AD 70. With the fall of the Temple the norm for the canon could no longer be the Temple archives. No longer would the mode for canonical definition be the archiving of a book in the Temple as a book recognized by consensus to be a prophetic book written under inspiration. In fact, though a number of sources examined in this chapter and in chapter 2 have pointed toward the early Persian period as the point where the canon was closed, the destruction of the Temple closes the canon in its older sense permanently. The canon will have to take on a new standard for its definition. This begins with the enumeration of books in the canon. Josephus and 2 Esdras, written within three decades of Jerusalem's fall are the first indications in this direction.

## Figure 2
## Evidence for the Canon in the First Century

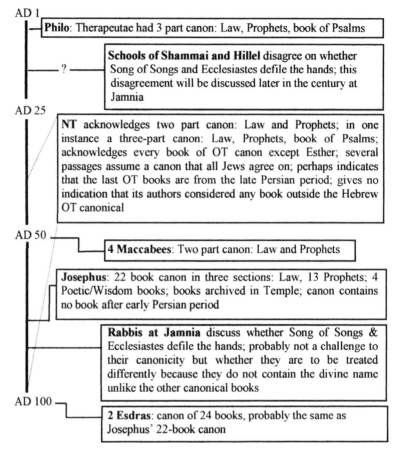

AD 1

**Philo**: Therapeutae had 3 part canon: Law, Prophets, book of Psalms

? — **Schools of Shammai and Hillel** disagree on whether Song of Songs and Ecclesiastes defile the hands; this disagreement will be discussed later in the century at Jamnia

AD 25

**NT** acknowledges two part canon: Law and Prophets; in one instance a three-part canon: Law, Prophets, book of Psalms; acknowledges every book of OT canon except Esther; several passages assume a canon that all Jews agree on; perhaps indicates that the last OT books are from the late Persian period; gives no indication that its authors considered any book outside the Hebrew OT canonical

AD 50

**4 Maccabees**: Two part canon: Law and Prophets

**Josephus**: 22 book canon in three sections: Law, 13 Prophets; 4 Poetic/Wisdom books; books archived in Temple; canon contains no book after early Persian period

**Rabbis at Jamnia** discuss whether Song of Songs & Ecclesiastes defile the hands; probably not a challenge to their canonicity but whether they are to be treated differently because they do not contain the divine name unlike the other canonical books

AD 100

**2 Esdras**: canon of 24 books, probably the same as Josephus' 22-book canon

Thus, the first century is pivotal in the discussion of the OT canon. During this century one can observe a number of strands of evidence about the canon:

**The sections of the canon.** The canon divided into two parts—Law and Prophets—persists throughout this century. However, movement toward the three-part canon first witnessed in the first century BC continues. Philo and the NT both witness to the separation of the Psalms from the Prophets. Josephus' three-part canon develops this further grouping three other books (probably Proverbs, Song of Songs and Ecclesiastes) with Psalms. In all cases the order of the sections is Law, Prophets, other book(s). This is the developing Jewish order of the divisions of the canon and is distinct from the Christian order that places the Poetic/Wisdom books in the middle of the canon. Apparently the Christian order is a development from the two-part canon and this allowed the Poetic/Wisdom books to be placed among the prophetic books. In addition, it should be noted that all books outside the Pentateuch could be classified as Prophets, since they were part of the Prophets sections of the two-part canon.

**Agreement on the limits of the canon.** Several passages in the NT assume there is general agreement on the extent of the canon. Josephus claims that Jews are agreed on the contents of the canon, and 2 Esdras' evidence also points in this direction. Thus, both Christians and Jews have a common heritage from the first century for the OT canon.

**The closing of the canon.** Matthew 23:34–36 and Luke 11:49–51 may be an indication that the Gospel writers believed the OT canon was closed in the late Persian period. Josephus clearly states this, and 2 Esdras supports this view. Unlike 1 Maccabees, the NT and Josephus recognize prophecy as a continuing phenomenon. However, neither consider prophecy in their age capable of adding new books to the canon. The fall of the Temple eliminated the theoretical possibility of adding a book by an inspired prophet to the canonical archives.

**The change in the mode of definition of the canon.** Before the fall of Jerusalem the canon was a set of books recognized by all Jews as authoritative, inspired books. These books were distinguished from noncanonical books because copies of them were preserved as holy books in the Temple archives. After the fall of Jerusalem a new way of distinguishing canonical books from noncanonical books was needed. The beginning steps toward this new definition of canon is taken with the enumeration of the books as twenty-two or twenty-four.

**Rabbinic discussions of books that defile the hands.** This was not a discussion of whether certain books belonged in the canon, but rather a discussion about whether certain canonical books that did not contain the divine name needed to be kept from possible desecration. Some rabbis did not include canonical books without the divine name among the books that defile the hands (Songs of Songs, Ecclesiastes and in later centuries Esther), but eventually the rabbis decided that all the Scriptures defile the hands. In later centuries the rabbis explicitly stated that books or other writings that contained the divine name (Ben Sira, blessings) or that contained portions of canonical books that contained the divine name (the Gospels) were deemed not to defile the hands.

Deuteronomy. Michael L. Klein, *Genizah Manuscript of the Palestinian Targum to the Pentateuch*. Cincinnati: Hebrew Union College Press, 1986.

**4**

# The AD Canon: After the First Century

In the second century and beyond the church and the synagogue diverge in their treatment of the canon. The canon is known in Jewish circles as a collection of Hebrew books that continue to be written on scrolls. The canon in Christian circles has a different history owing to the increasingly non-Jewish character of the church. For the church the OT canon is known as ancient Jewish books in their Greek translation. In many places Christians translate these books into the vernacular. Christian books take on the form of the codex in which several books or even an entire canon can be bound. These are only a few of the differences in the canon between church and synagogue. In this chapter we will examine the OT canon's history in two separate ways. First, we will look at the evidence for the history of the canon in Jewish circles during the second and third centuries. Then we will examine the evidence for the history of the canon in the church during those same centuries and even glance beyond them into the fourth century.

### The OT Canon in Rabbinic Judaism: The Talmud and Midrash

The Talmud provides evidence for the canon in the second and third centuries in a number of different ways. However, when working with the evidence from the Talmud we must always keep in mind that it was not reduced to writing until sometime in the fourth century. Therefore, the evidence is somewhat provisional and we can never discount the possibility that it records older teachings but modifies them through the lens of later practice. Nevertheless, the Talmud and other rabbinic writings do provide us with evidence for two areas of interest for the OT

canon: the way in which the canon was divided and the contents of the
canon itself.

## The Subdivisions of the Canon

The Jerusalem and Babylonian Talmuds and Midrash give us the
first evidence of the threefold division of the canon into Law, Prophets,
and Writings.[178] The oldest of these date to the early second century or
late first century.

ירושלמי חגינה 77b

א"ר אליעזר לר' יהושע עד דאינון נעוסקין בדידון
נעסוק אנן בדידן וישבו ונתעסקו בדברי תורה מן
התורה לנביאים ומן הנביאים לכתובים וירדה אש מן
השמים והקיפה אותם

*Jerusalem Hagigah 77b*
[Elisha son of Abuyah related that] Rabbi Eliezer said to
Rabbi Joshua, "While they are occupying themselves with
their matters, let's occupy ourselves with ours." So they
sat and studied the words of the Torah. From the Torah
they went on to the Prophets, and from the Prophets they
went on to the Writings. Fire came down from heaven and
surrounded them.

Elisha was active from about AD 110–135. Rabbis Eliezer and
Joshua were active from about AD 80–110. If this passage is not an
imposition of Elisha's view of the canon on Eliezer and Joshua or a later
view of the canon on Elisha then it provides evidence for the tripartite
division of the canon around AD 100. Otherwise, it may provide
evidence for the tripartite division for Elisha's time during the first third
of the second century. However, because it does not quote Eliezer and
Joshua directly, it may be a later view of the canon imposed on the report
of Elisha.

סנהדרין צ:
שאלו מינין את רבן גמליאל מניין שהקדוש ברוך הוא
מחיה מתים אמר להם מן התורה ומן הנביאים ומן

---

[178] For a complete compilation of passages see Leiman, *Canonization*, 56–72.

הכתובים ולא קיבלו ממנו

*Sanhedrin* 90b
Some heretics asked Rabban Gamaliel, "From what do we
know that the Holy One, Blessed be He, will resurrect the
dead?" He answered them from the Torah, the Prophets,
and the Writings, but they were not convinced.

Gamaliel was active at the end of the first century. At best, this
passage places the tripartite canon into the late first century. However,
this passage does not directly quote him as recognizing a tripartite canon.
Therefore, we cannot be certain that it is not imposing a later organization of the canon upon an earlier incident.

ויקרא רבה טו:ד

בן עזאי היה יושב ודורש ואש מלהטת סביבותיו אמרו
ליה שמא בסדרי מרכבה אתה עוסק אמר להן לאו
אלא מחריז דברי תורה לנביאים ונביאים לכרובים
ודברי תורה שמחין כיום נתינתן בסיני

*Vayyikra Rabbah* 16:4
Ben Azzai was sitting and interpreting Scripture, and a
flame was burning around him. They asked him, "Are you
studying the Merkabah passages?" He replied, "No. I am
joining words of the Torah with the Prophets and the
Prophets with the Writings. The words of the Torah are
glowing as on the day they were given at Sinai."

Ben Azzai was active in the first third of the second century. This
passages attributes to him a saying that acknowledges a tripartite canon.
We have seen, then, that the canon could not have been subdivided
into its present-day three-part structure before the late first century or
early second century, if these passages are correctly attributed to the
rabbis and not an imposition of later canonical terminology on them.
Leiman provides evidence that later canonical terminology was imposed
on the recollections of the rabbis in the first and second centuries, though
he is not willing to draw this conclusion towards which his evidence
points. This evidence comes from parallel passages in which one passage
divides the canon into two parts and the other into three parts. Two
parallels are given below, with the older passage first in each case.

תוספתא מגילה ד:כ

נותנים תורה על גבי תורה וחומשין על גבי חומשין
תורה וחומשין על בני נביאיםאבל לא נביאים גבי
תורה וחומשין

*Tosefta Megillah* 4:20
A Torah scroll may be placed on another Torah and
*homashin* on other *homashin*. A Torah and *homashin* may
be placed on Prophets, but Prophets may not be placed on
a Torah and *homashin*.

ירושלמי מגילה 73d

נותנים תורה על גבי תורה וחומשין על בני הומשין
תורה וחומשין על גבי נביאים וכתובים אבל נביאים
וכתובים על תורה וחומשין

*Jerusalem Megillah* 73d
A Torah scroll may be placed on another Torah and
*homashin* on other *homashin*. A Torah and *homashin* may
be placed on Prophets and Writings, but Prophets and
Writings may not be placed on Torah and *homashin*.

תוספתא מגילה ד:כ

מכרכין תורה במטפחות תורה וחמשין במטפחות
חומשין תורה וחומשין במטפחות נביאים אבל לא
נביאים במטפחות תורה וחומשין

*Tosefta Megillah* 4:20
A Torah scroll may be wrapped in Torah wrappings and
*homashin* in *homashin* wrappings. Torah and *homashin*
may be wrapped in Prophets wrappings, but Prophets may
not be wrapped in Torah or *homashin* wrappings.

ירושלמי מגילה 73d

כורכין תורה במטפחות תורה חומשין במטפחות חומשין
נביאים במטפחות נביאיםתורה וחומשין במטפחות
נביאים וכתובים אבל לא נביאים וכתובים במטפחות
תורה וחומשין

*Jerusalem Megillah* 73d
A Torah scroll may be wrapped in Torah wrappings,
*homashin* in *homashin* wrappings, and Prophets in

Prophets wrappings. Torah and *homashin* may be wrapped in Prophets and Writings wrappings, but Prophets and Writings may not be wrapped in Torah and *homashin* wrappings.

Leiman also notes several other passages in the rabbinic sayings that indicate a two-part canon of Law and Prophets (*Mishnah Rosh Hashana* 4:6 compared with *Tosefta Rosh Hashana* 4:6; *Jerusalem Megillah* 73d–74a and *Baba. Bathra* 13b compared with *Sopherim.* 3:1). Barton comments that Leiman's own evidence points toward the distinction between Prophets and Writings being a late one since the Mishnah knows only of a two-part canon:[179]

> Leiman is uneasy about drawing the conclusion he points towards, noting that in another example, Baba Bathra 13b (cf. j. Megillah 73d–74a), the parallel which lacks the explicit reference to the Writings is in Soferim 3:1, which is hardly likely to be earlier. He also holds that the shorter versions may be abbreviated from the longer, or that there may be other reasons for the difference which are now not recoverable. Naturally, in the absence of any sure way of dating talmudic passages, one can only agree that these examples do not *prove* the tripartite division to be late. Nevertheless the difference is suggestive, especially in view of the fact that the original mishnah thinks in terms of only two divisions; the way Leiman discounts this evidence which he himself so scrupulously assembled looks a little lame to me. At all events he correctly concludes that 'the talmudic view…contrasts sharply with the medieval view that the three sections of the biblical canon represent three different degrees of inspired writing' and the 'the halakhic codes reflect the early, talmudic view'. He should, I believe, have gone on to draw a more far-reaching conclusion from this accurate observation: that the distinction between Prophets and Writings is itself a late arrival, and that much material even in the Talmud reflects the same inability to find a function for the distinction that eventually led to the artificial "concentric circles" theory[180] of medieval commentators.

---

[179] Barton, *Oracles of God*, 53–54.

[180] I.e., differing degrees of inspiration for the three sections.

Thus, the earliest Talmudic passages most likely point to the received tradition of a two-part canon from the first century. Barton's assertions are not new. Already in 1924 Wolfenson, in a study of the position of Ruth in manuscripts and editions of the OT, noted that Melito in the second century, Origen in the third century and Jerome in the fourth century all consulted Jewish authorities and reported that Ruth was placed after Judges, not in a third section of the canon.[181] Based on this and other evidence, Wolfenson argued "All this proves, I believe, that Jews did not have any fixed classification of Prophets and 'Writings', originally. These divisions are the arbitrary arrangement of the Rabbis of the Mishnaic period in the 2d century."[182] Barton and Wolfenson are probably correct, given the evidence. The tripartite canon is most likely a result of a reclassification of the non-Mosaic books during the middle of the second century.

What, then, is the reason for the division of the non-Mosaic books into Prophets and Writings? It has long been noted that the Prophets comprise those books along with the Torah that are part of the Sabbath liturgical readings in synagogues. Even Leiman, who, as we have seen, attempts to place the tripartite division of the canon in the earliest history of the canon, advocates this view, as does Barton.[183] However, we should note that some books in the Writings are read on festivals in synagogues today. These are the five *Megillot*: Ruth, Song of Songs, Lamentations, Ecclesiastes and Esther. Yet, Wolfenson points out there is no evidence that they were read as part of the liturgy before the eleventh century, although Esther was read at Purim from very early times.[184]

It would seem, then, that the tripartite canon was a development of rabbinic Judaism after AD 70. While we have seen that some movement toward a tripartite canon was evident earlier, we have no evidence for the tripartite OT canon as we know it today before the late first century at the earliest. Josephus, whose knowledge of developments in Palestinian Judaism probably ended in AD 70 when he was taken to Rome, perhaps gives evidence that this development was underway before AD 70. However, his classification of books into Prophets and Hymns/Wisdom

---

[181] Wolfenson, "Implications of the Place of the Book of Ruth in Editions, Manuscripts, and Canon of the Old Testament" *HUCA* 1 (1924), 172.

[182] L. B. Wolfenson, "Implications," 175.

[183] Leiman, *Canonization*, 168; note also that Barton, *Oracles of God*, 75–82 argues that the development of the tripartite canon is due to liturgical practice.

[184] Wolfenson, "Implications," 164–65.

is based on content, not liturgical use. The post-second Temple synagogue developed a liturgical use for the canonical books in the absence of worship in the Temple. It was the vacuum created by the destruction of the Temple that led to the division of the canon into three parts, a process that was completed by the middle of the second century. Those books that became part of the Prophetic liturgical readings (the *haftaroth*) remained in a section called *Prophets* (נביאים). Those books that were relegated to private reading or that were used in worship apart from the assigned readings became part of a section entitled *Writings* (כתובים; perhaps the general term *Scriptures* would be a better translation).[185]

## The Number of Canonical Books

The later sections of the Talmud regularly assume that the canon consists of twenty-four books. Leiman lists ten examples that derive mostly from late Midrashim. One example is:

קוהלת רבה יב:יא

ר' חייא נותן אחד עשר מכאן ושלשה עשר מכאן כנגד
עשרים וארבעה ספריםמה הספרים כ"ד אף המשמרות
כ"ד ומה המשמרות כ"ד אף מסמרים כ"ד

---

[185] That some books were excluded from public reading by some rabbis does not prove that the canon was open, as McDonald, *Formation*, 82 suggests. He notes that according to the Talmud some rabbis would have excluded one or more of the following from public reading in the synagogue: Songs of Songs, Ecclesiastes, Ruth, Esther and Ezekiel. Therefore, he concludes that the canon remained open until the fourth century. However, all that the passages he cites from the Talmud prove is that some rabbis found public readings from certain books to be inappropriate. (Esther did, however, continue to be read publicly at Purim.) That Ezekiel, whose credentials as a recognized inspired and authoritative prophetic book unquestionably predate the Talmud, was a candidate for such treatment should in itself call McDonald's assertion into question. However, even modern liturgical practice casts doubt on McDonald's thesis. For instance, one modern Christian lectionary contains no readings from Ezra, Esther, Song of Songs, Obadiah, Nahum and Haggai in the OT and none from 2 or 3 John in the NT (see "Index to the Three-Year Lectionary," *Lutheran Worship: Agenda* (St. Louis: Concordia, 1982), 571–77). Each of these books is considered canonical in all Christian churches. Yet the contents of these books apparently did not lend them to liturgical reading in the opinion of those who compiled this lectionary.

*Koheleth Rabbah* 12:11
Rabbi Hiyya inserted eleven in one and thirteen in the
other corresponding to the twenty-four books [of the
canon]. As there are twenty-four books, so there were
twenty-four watches [of Levites]. And as there were
twenty-four watches, so the number of nails should be
twenty-four.

Leiman comments:[186]

Thus, at the earliest, these passages reflect the consensus
of the amoraic period.[187] A biblical canon of precisely
twenty-four books is nowhere mentioned in early
talmudic or midrashic materials such as Mekhilta, Sifré,
Tosefta and Mishnah. Though it is certain that all twenty-
four books were known (they are all cited and commented
upon as Scripture) in the early tannaitic period,[188] it is
possible that another system of counting the biblical
books was in use (such as the twenty-two book count of
Josephus, *Against Apion*, Book I, paragraph 38). It seems
likely, however, that the twenty-four book count was
already known and in use during the tannaitic period. Its
oldest attestation appears in the Fourth Book of Ezra,
whose final redaction dates to ca. 100 C.E.

That Josephus, whose firsthand knowledge of Jewish practice in
Palestine predates AD 70, counted the books as twenty-two whereas the
Talmud and 2 Esdras (4 Ezra) counted them as twenty-four could be
significant. The process that would lead to the tripartite canon would
have to split Ruth from Judges and Lamentations from Jeremiah in order
to include Ruth and Lamentations in the Writings. This made a twenty-
two book count into a twenty-four book count. Therefore, the first
Talmudic reference to the twenty-four book canon around AD 200
confirms that the tripartite canon was a late development that took place
in the second century. Moreover, since most of the rabbinical writings
have a Babylonian, not a Palestinian provenance, the development of the
twenty-four book tripartite canon may be a Babylonian one, and not
Palestinian. However, the mention of a twenty-four book canon in 2

---

[186] Leiman, *Canonization*, 56.

[187] Ca. AD 200–500.

[188] Beginning in the first century BC. About AD 200 Rabbi Judah, the last of the tannaitic
scholars, codified the Tannaim's traditions.

Esdras indicates that the process was underway at the very beginning of that century.

## The Contents of the Canon

The contents of the OT canon in its tripartite form is given in *Baba Bathra* 14b:

תנו רבנן סדרן של נביאים יהושע ושופטים שמואל
ומלכים ירמיה ויחזקאל ישעיה ושנים עשר
...[תנו רבנן] סידרן של כתובים רות וספר תהלים
קהלת שיר השירים ואיוב ומשלי וקינות דניאל ומגילת
אסתר עזרא ודברי הימים

Our Rabbis taught, "The order of the prophets is: Joshua and Judges, Samuel and Kings, Jeremiah and Ezekiel, Isaiah and the Twelve Prophets... [Our Rabbis taught], "The order of the Writings is Ruth and the Book of Psalms and Job and Proverbs, Ecclesiastes, Song of Songs and Lamentations, Daniel and the Scroll of Esther, Ezra and Chronicles."

This list assumes the five-book Torah. The Prophets comprise eight books and the Writings eleven books. (The Twelve Prophets count as one. Ezra includes Nehemiah).

The only question about this passage concerns what is implied by *order*. Sarna has argued that the order is that in which the scrolls were shelved in ancient Jewish libraries.[189] Barton and Brunswick disagree and argue that the order is probably a rabbinic opinion of the order in which the books in each section were written.[190] Beckwith holds that the order was determined by a number of factors when the canon was closed.[191] While these and other theories have their strengths and weaknesses, we

---

[189] Nahum M. Sarna *Ancient Libraries and the Ordering of the Biblical Books.* Center for the Book Viewpoint 25. (Washington: Library of Congress, 1989); "The Order of the Books," in Charles Berlin, ed., *Studies in Jewish Bibliography, History and Literature in Honor of I. Edward Kiev.* (New York, 1971), 407–13.

[190] Barton, *Oracles of God*, 88–91; Sheldon R. Brunswick "The Order of the Books" in Mishael M. Caspi, ed., *Jewish Tradition in the Diaspora: Studies in Memory of Professor Walter J. Fischel.* (Berkeley: Judah L. Magnes Memorial Museum 1981), 91.

[191] Beckwith, *Old Testament Canon,* 156–66. Note that Beckwith believes that the canon was closed (and arranged in tripartite form) around 160 BC by Judas Maccabeus.

simply cannot state with any degree of certainty what the significance of
the order in *Baba Bathra* 14b is. No matter what it was intended to
signify, it is interesting to note that this order was not considered
normative when the Hebrew Bible was put in codex form, since the
codices show several variations in the order of the books.[192]

The Storing Away of Books

In a number of passages in talmudic literature the rabbis propose
storing away of books and other objects. This would have, in effect,
removed them from public circulation. The books of Ezekiel, Ecclesiastes and Proverbs were candidates to be stored away. Ezekiel was
considered for storing away because it appeared to contradict the Torah
(*Shabbath* 13b). Ecclesiastes and Proverbs were considered for such
treatment because their words appeared to be self-contradictory
(*Shabbath* 30b). In the past these passages were understood as discussions of whether these books were canonical (and were used to
bolster the Council of Jamnia Hypothesis of the closing of the canon).
However, Leiman has assembled all the passages dealing with storing
away objects. He has argued convincingly that this procedure was not a
discussion of whether a book belonged in the canon. Leiman concludes
his analysis by stating:[193]

> According to the talmudic and midrashic evidence, then
> גנז means "to store away" or "to put away for
> safekeeping." When used with books which clearly were
> never biblical, גנז implies reverence. That the withdrawal
> of non-biblical books implies a reverent attitude toward
> them, is also attested by Origen (ca. 185–255), who was
> informed by Jewish friends that the apocryphal books of
> Tobit and Judith were not even among the "Hebrew
> hidden books." Apparently, Origen's informants knew of
> a collection of Hebrew books, all of which were with-
> drawn from circulation. It probably consisted of such
> books as Ben Sira and the book of Genealogies. It may
> even have been a fixed collection, for the informants were
> certain that Tobit and Judith were not among the "Hebrew
> hidden books"; a fixed collection of hidden books,
> however, is nowhere attested in talmudic or midrashic
> literature. The import of Origen's remarks was that Tobit

---

[192] Beckwith, *Old Testament Canon*, 450–64; Wolfenson, "Implications," 160–61.
[193] Leiman, *Canonization*, 85–86.

> and Judith were not accorded any esteem whatever by the Jews. The two apocryphal works did not even merit special legislation requiring their withdrawal from circulation. Only biblical books, or books revered on other grounds, qualified for גניזה.
>
> When used with biblical books, גנז does not refer to initial canonical activity, i.e. whether or not a book should enter the biblical canon....With the possible exception of [*Aboth of Rabbi Nathan* 1:4] and [*Sanhedrin* 100b] (whose ambiguous nature has been noted), there is no evidence that any biblical book was, in fact, withdrawn from circulation or delcared uncanonical.

Therefore, the discussion of withdrawing biblical books from public circulation in the Talmud is not an indication of canonical activity.

## The Cessation of Prophecy

Like earlier sources, in the Talmud and Midrash we find references to the cessation of prophecy. The most important passage is *Tosefta Sotah* 13:2:[194]

תוספתא סותה יג:ב

משנת חגי זכריה ומלאכי נביאים האחרורים פסקה רוח
הקודש מישראל ואף על פי כן היו משמיעין להן בבת
קול

> After the last prophets—Haggai, Zechariah and Malachi—died, the Holy Spirit ceased in Israel. Nevertheless, they were informed by means of the *Bat Qol*.

This passage continues the tradition we have seen from other sources: inspiration ceased in the Persian period. However, like Josephus, it would appear that some type of prophetic activity continued in the *Bat Qol*. Therefore, Jewish sources in the second and third centuries also imply that the canon was complete (at least in practical terms) sometime in the Persian period.

---

[194] See also *m. Sota* 9.12; *b. Sanh.* 11a and *S. 'Olam Rab.* 30.

Summary: The Jewish Scriptures in the Second and Third Centuries

The evidence from Talmud and Midrash suggest three conclusions about the canon among Jews in the second and third centuries:

**The origin of the tripartite canon.** The canon was divided into the familiar three sections sometime after AD 70 and most probably not until the second century. We have no evidence for the tripartite canon before the late first century at the earliest. The process that led to the separation of the Writings from the Prophets was probably begun at that time and completed by the middle of the second century. The separation of the books in the Writings from the Prophets was probably done to correspond to liturgical usage. The Prophets consisted of those books that were part of the regular Sabbath liturgical readings. The Writings were those books that had no portions designated for such readings. The evidence from earlier periods points to most, if not all of these books as being included in the Prophets: Prior to the late first century Daniel was always referred to as a prophet. Josephus treats Ruth, Esther, Chronicles and Ezra-Nehemiah in ways similar to Joshua, Judges, Samuel and Kings in his *History*, and they most likely are not included in his third section of the canon, but his second (Prophets). Only Proverbs, Ecclesiastes and Song of Songs are candidates for inclusion in a third section of the canon in any source before the late first century, and then only in the latest source—Josephus.

**The origin of the canon as twenty-four books.** Corresponding to the organizing of the canon into three parts was the adoption of a twenty-four book numbering of the canon. This reckoning of the canonical books became permanent with the reclassification of books outside the Torah into the Prophets and Writings and the accompanying separation of Ruth from Judges and Lamentations from Jeremiah. Thus, the earliest Talmudic reference to the twenty-four book canon is from about AD 200. Since neither the twenty-four book reckoning nor the tripartite canon was known to Palestinian sources in the second and third centuries, the development of the Jewish arrangement of the canon was probably accomplished in a Babylonian setting.

**The discussion of storing away some books of the canon.** The discussion of whether certain books were to be stored away was not a discussion of their canonicity. Instead, this concept implies a certain reverence for these books.

**The final books of the canon.** Jewish sources of the second and third centuries imply what was seen in earlier sources: the canon was completed in the Persian period.

## Christians in the Second and Third Centuries

By the second century the Christian church was largely Gentile in nature. The language of the church was Greek, and the OT was familiar to most Christians in this language or in translations based on the Greek OT. Since Christians definitely received a tradition of Scripture as witnessed by the NT, we need to determine how Christians viewed this scriptural tradition. We will concentrate on the second and third centuries in order to parallel most of the Talmudic evidence we have already examined.

### Melito, Bishop of Sardis

The earliest account of the OT canon by a Christian is from Melito, bishop of Sardis, who died about AD 190. His list of canonical books is preserved for us by Eusebius of Caesarea (ca. 260–ca. 339) in his *Church History*. Melito writes:[195]

Μελίτων Ὀνησίμῳ τῷ ἀδελφῷ χαίρειν. Ἐπειδὴ πολλάκις ἠξίωσας σπουδῇ τῇ πρὸς τὸν λόγον χρώμενος, γενέσθαι σοι ἐκλογάς ἔκ τε τοῦ νόμου καὶ τῶν προφητῶν περὶ τοῦ Σωτῆρος καὶ πάσης τῆς πίστεως ἡμων, ἔτι δὲ καὶ μαθεῖν τὴν τῶν παλαιῶν βιβλίων ἐβουλήθης ἀκρίβειαν, πόσα τόν ἀριθμὸν καὶ ὁποῖα τὴν τάξιν εἶ εν, ἐσπούδασα τὸ τοιοῦτο πρᾶξαι, ἐπιστάμενός σου τὸ σπουδαῖον περὶ τὴν πίστιν, καὶ φιλομαθὲς περὶ τὸν λόγον, ὅτι τε μάλιστα πάντων πόθῳ τῷ πρὸς Θεὸν ταῦτα προκρίνεις, περὶ τῆς αἰωνίου σωτηρίας

Melito to his brother Onesimus; Greetings. You have often in your zeal for the word expressed a desire to have extracts concerning the Savior from the Law and the Prophets and concerning our entire faith, and you also wished to learn the details about the ancient books, especially their number and order. I have been eager to do this for you, since I know your zeal for the faith and your desire to learn the word and especially above all else how you value these things in your yearning for God as you struggle to gain eternal sal-

---

[195] Eusebius, *Church History* 4.26, *PG* 10:396–97.

ἀγωιζόμενος. Ἀνελθὼν ουν εἰς
τὴν ἀνατολὴν, καὶ ἕως τοῦ
τόπου γενόμενος ἔνθα ἐκηρύχθη
καὶ ἐπράχθη, καὶ ἀκριβῶς
μαθὼν τὰ τῆς Παλαῖς Διαθήκης
βιβλία, ὑποτάξας ἔπεμψά σοι·
ὧν ἐστι τὰ ὀνόματα·
Μωϋσέως πέντε,
   Γένεσις,
   Ἔξοδος,
   Ἀριθμοὶ,
   Λευϊτικὸν,
   Δευτερονόμιον·
Ἰησοῦς Ναυῆ,
Κριταὶ,
Ροὺθ·
Βασιλειῶν τέσσαρα
Παραλειπομένων δύο·
Ψαλμῶν Δαβίδ·
Σολομῶνος Παροιμίαι, ἢ καὶ
Σοφία,
Ἐκκλησιαστὴς,
Ἆσμα ἀσμάτων.
Ἰωβ·
Προφητῶν,
   Ἡσαΐου,
   Ἱερεμίου·
   τῶν δώδεκα ἐν μονοβίβλῳ·
   Δανιὴλ,
   Ἰεζεκιὴλ,
   Ἔσδρας.
Ἐξ ὧν καὶ τὰς ἐκλογὰς
ἐποιησάμην, εἰς ἓξ βιβλία
διελών.

vation. Therefore, when I traveled to the east and came to the place where all these things were proclaimed and done, I learned precisely the books of the Old Testament, made a list and am sending it to you. These are their names:

*Five books of Moses:*
   Genesis
   Exodus
   Numbers
   Leviticus
   Deuteronomy
Joshua son of Nun
Judges
Ruth
Kings (in four parts)
Chronicles (in two parts)
The Psalms of David
The Proverbs of Solomon
(Wisdom)
Ecclesiastes
Song of Songs
Job
*The Prophets*
   Isaiah
   Jeremiah
   The Twelve in one book
   Daniel
   Ezekiel
   Ezra
From these I have taken extracts and arranged them in six books.

Melito drew up this list and prepared extracts from the various OT books for his brother (fellow bishop?) Onesimus. He states that Onesimus wished to know the number and order of the books, which he lists by their Greek names. It is reasonable to assume that Melito is including Lamentations with Jeremiah and Nehemiah with Ezra. However, what exactly is meant by *order* is hard to determine. In his list of the Pentateuch Melito inverts Leviticus and Numbers (unless this was a copyist's error). Also, the order of the prophets is peculiar. The number is also peculiar, since Melito lists twenty-one books, not the more familiar twenty-two or twenty-four. However, he may have been attempting to list twenty-two books as Josephus did and as Origen and Jerome did after him. That he is concerned about the count is clear from his stipulation that the minor prophets make up one book, and because he splits Judges and Ruth (but keeps them together in his list) to make up for combining Samuel and Kings into one book. This might explain why Esther is missing. It would be the twenty-second book, but may have been omitted by oversight. Esther is often the last book in later canonical lists (e.g., Origen, Epiphanius, Amphilochis, Hilary, and one of Jerome's lists), and may have been accidentally left off the end of the list.

Thus, at the very least, Melito, the earliest Christian to list the OT canon, shows agreement with the contemporary Jewish canon with the possible exception of Esther. As we have already seen, Esther is the least well-attested member of the canon.

It is also interesting to note that Melito specifically divides the canon into two parts in his introduction (Law and Prophets) and that his list implies a threefold subdivision of the OT books outside the Pentateuch: the historical books (Joshua–Chronicles), the poetic/wisdom books (Psalms–Job) and the Prophets. It would seem that when he traveled to Palestine, he did not find there in the second century a twenty-four book tripartite canon. Moreover, Daniel and Ezra were among the prophets. This would confirm our suspicion that the rabbinic arrangement of the canon was Babylonian, not Palestinian. One feature of Melito's list is important for later Christian lists: the poetic/wisdom books are not last in canonical order, but precede the prophets, a feature that will become standard in Christian arrangements of the canon. However, we should not think of this as a Christian innovation, since Melito has stated that he got his list from Jewish sources. Instead, the earlier Jewish two-part canon attested at Qumran and in the NT (and perhaps by the introduction to Ben Sira ) was adopted by Christians, and Melito provides us with the first evidence of this.

## The Bryennios List

An ancient list of the OT canon was first published by Bryennios and later by Audet.[196] Audet dates this list to the second century.[197] Audet also demonstrated that the Bryennios List shared a common tradition with the later canonical lists of Epiphanius (d. AD 403).[198] The list preserves two names for each book: a Hebrew or Aramaic name in Greek transliteration and the Greek name. The list reads:[199]

| | |
|---|---|
| βρισίθ γένεσις | Genesis |
| ἐλσιμόθ ἔξοδος | Exodus |
| ὀδοικρά λευϊτικόν | Leviticus |
| διιησοῦ ἰησοῦ ναυή | Joshua son of Nun |
| ἐλεδεββαρί δευτερονόμιον | Deuteronomy |
| οὐιδαβίρ ἀριθμοί | Numbers |
| δαπούθ τῆς ῥούθ | Ruth |
| διώβ τοῦ ἰωβ | Job |
| δάσοφτιμ τῶν κριτῶν | Judges |
| σφερτελίμ ψαλτήτιον | Psalms |
| διεμμουήλ βασιλειῶν α´ | 1 Kingdoms [1 Samuel] |
| διαδδουδεμουήλ βασιλειῶν β´ | 2 Kingdoms [2 Samuel] |
| δαμαλαχήμ βασιλειῶν γ´ | 3 Kingdoms [1 Kings] |
| ἀμαλαχήμ βασιλειῶν δ´ | 4 Kingdoms [2 Kings] |
| δεβριιαμίν παραλειπομένων α´ | 1 Chronicles |
| δεριιαμίν παραλειπομένων β´ | 2 Chronicles |
| δαμαλεώθ παροιμιῶν | Proverbs |
| δακοέλεθ ἐκκλησιαστής | Ecclesiastes |
| σιρὰ σιρίμ ἆσμα ἀσμάτων | Song of Songs |
| διερέμ ἰερεμίας | Jeremiah [including Lamentations?] |
| δααθαρσιαρ δωδεκαπρόφητον | The Twelve Prophets |

---

[196] Jean-Paul Audet, "A Hebrew-Aramaic List of Books of the Old Testament in Greek Transcription," *JTS* 1 (1950) 135–54.

[197] Audet, "Hebrew-Aramaic List," 145.

[198] McDonald, *Formation*, 112 argues that the Bryennios List should be dated to the middle of the fourth century because of its similarity to the lists in Epiphanius. However, he ignores all of the other arguments used by Audet to date the Bryennios list. I fail to see why the Bryennios list has to be placed in the fourth century merely because Epiphanius was active then. Epiphanius could well have been drawing on an older tradition to produce his lists. Rather, it would seem that in order to argue for a very late date for the canonization of the OT, McDonald purposely pushes the evidence to the latest possible date to support his thesis.

[199] Audet, "Hebrew-Aramaic List," 136.

| δησαίου ἠσαίου | Isaiah |
| διεεζεκιήλ ιεζεκιήλ | Ezekiel |
| δαδανιήλ δανιήλ | Daniel |
| δέσδρα ἔσδρα α' | Ezra |
| δαδέσδρα ἔσδρα β' | Nehemiah |
| δεσθής ἐσθήρ | Esther |

The number and order of the books in this list is peculiar. The Pentateuch is interrupted by Joshua, and Numbers and Deuteronomy are inverted. Katz proposes that this was caused by an error in copying from a manuscript that was originally written in boustrophedon.[200] Thus, the second line was written "Joshua – Deuteronomy – Numbers" but was intended to be read "Numbers – Deuteronomy – Joshua." But the rest of the list is peculiar with only a few groups of books in familiar order: Samuel – Kings – Chronicles is common enough as is Proverbs – Ecclesiastes – Song of Songs. The order Ezekiel – Daniel – Ezra matches Melito's list and since it is followed by Esther, the Bryennios list may confirm that Eusebius' account of Melito's list may have been defective in omitting Esther.

The number of books in the list is twenty-seven. Clearly this list could not have been derived from the twenty-four book tripartite arrangement of the canon. The Writings are scattered too widely within this list for that to be possible. However, it is entirely possible that this list is related to the twenty-two book mode of arranging the canon. Samuel, Kings, Chronicles and Ezra-Nehemiah clearly are presented as two books each. If they were counted as one, the total would be reduced to twenty-three books. If Ruth was then united to Judges (though it is not next to it in the list) the count would be twenty-two. Therefore, this list has more in common with the twenty-two book mode of arranging the canon and probably is related to it.

## Origen

Origen was born about AD 185, probably in Alexandria. His travels took him to Rome, Palestine, Greece and Asia Minor. He is most often associated with the city of Caesarea in Palestine. He died in 254.

---

[200] Peter Katz, "The Old Testament Canon in Palestine and Alexandria," *ZNW* 47 (1956) 206. Boustrophedon was a form of writing in which the lines are written alternately right to left and left to right. (Like the plowing of furrows with an ox [Greek: *bous*].)

Eusebius records for us Origen's list of canonical books that was originally part of a commentary on Psalm 1. This commentary was written while Origen was still in Alexandria, making the latest possible date of composition 231. Origen wrote:[201]

Οὐκ ἀγνοητέον δ' εἶναι τὰς ἐνδιαθήκους βίβλους, ὡς Ἑβραῖοι παραδιδόασιν, δύο καὶ εἴκοσι ὅσος ὁ ἀριθμὸς τῶν παρ' αὐτοῖς στοɩχείων ἐστίν....Εἰσὶ δὲ αἱ εἴκοσι δύο βίβλοι καθ' Ἑβραίους αἵδε· ἡ παρ' ἡμῖν Γένεσις ἐπιγεγραμμένη, παρὰ δὲ Ἑβραίους ἀπο τῆς ἀρχῆς τῆς βίβλου, Βρησὶθ, ὅπερ ἐστιν ἐν ἀρχῇ, Ἔξοδος, Οὐαλεσμὼθ, ὅπερ ἐστὶ ταῦτα τὰ ὀνόματα· Λευϊτικὸν, Οὐϊκρὰ, καὶ ἐκάλεσεν·

Ἀριθμοὶ, Ἀμμεσφεκωδείμ· Δευτερονόμιον, Ἔλλε Ἀδδεβαρὶμ, οὗτοι οἱ λόγοι· Ἰησοῦς υἱὸς Ναυῆ· Ἰωσοῦε βὲν Νοῦν. Κριταὶ, Ῥοὺθ, παρ' αὐτοῖς ἐν ἑνι Σωφετίμ· Βασιλειῶν πρώτη, δευτέρα, παρ' αὐτοῖς ἓν Σαμουήλ, ὁ Θεό-κλητος· Βασιλειῶν τρίτη, τετάρτη, ἐν ἑνὶ Οὐαμμέλεχ Δαβίδ, ὅπερ ἐστὶ βασιλεία Δαβίδ. Παραλειπομένων πρώτη, δευτέρα, ἐν ἑνὶ Διβρὴ Ἀϊαμὶμ, ὅπερ ἐστὶ λόγοι ἡμερῶν· Ἔσδρας πρῶτος καὶ δεύτερος, ἐν ἑνὶ Ἐζρᾶ, ὅ ἐστι βοηθός. Βίβλος Ψαλμῶν, Σέφερ Θιλλίμ.

Σολομῶντος Παροιμίαι, Μισλώθ.

It should be noted that the canonical books as the Hebrews have handed them down are twenty-two, like the number of their letters....The twenty-two books according to the Hebrews are as follows:

Genesis, as we call it; the Hebrews call it *Bresith* from the book's first word which means *in the beginning*

Exodus; *Oualesmoth* (that is, *these are the names*)

Leviticus; *Ouikra* (*and he called*)

Numbers; *Ammesphekodeim*

Deuteronomy; *Elle Haddebarim* (*these are the words*)

Joshua son of Nun; *Joshua ben Nun*

Judges, Ruth (they consider it one book: *Sophetim)*

1 and 2 Kingdoms (they consider it one book: *Samuel [called by God]*)

3 and 4 Kingdoms (in one book: *Ouammelech David; that is, the kingdom of David*)

1 and 2 Chronicles (in one book: *Dibre Aiamim; that is, accounts of days*)

1 and 2 Esdras (in one book: *Ezra, that is, helper*)

The book of Psalms; *Sepher Tellim*

---

[201] Eusebius, *Church History* 6.25, *PG* 20.580–81.

Ἐκκλησιαστής, Κωέλεθ.

Ἆσμα ᾀσμάτων, οὐ γὰρ ὡς ὑπο-
λαμβάνουσί τινες Ἄσματα ᾀσμάτων, Σὶρ Ἀσιρίμ·

Ἡσαΐας, Ἰεσαϊά.

Ἱερεμίας σὺν Θρήνοις καὶ τῇ ἐπι-
στολῇ, ἐν ἑνὶ Ἱρμία·

Δανιήλ, Δανιήλ·

Ἰεζεκιὴλ Ἰεεζεκήλ·

Ἰώβ, Ἰώβ·

Ἐσθήρ, Ἐσθήρ.

Ἔξω δὲ τούτων ἐστὶ τὰ Μακ-
καβαϊκὰ, ἅπερ ἐπιγέγραπται Σαρβὴθ
Σαρβανὲ Ἔλ.

Solomon's Proverbs; *Misloth*

Ecclesiastes; *Koeleth*

Song of Songs (not as some suppose, Songs of Songs); *Sir Hasirim*

Isaiah; *Isaiah*

Jeremiah with Lamentations and the Letter (in one book: *Jeremiah*)

Daniel; *Daniel*

Ezekiel; *Ezekiel*

Job; *Job*

Esther; *Esther*

Apart from these is Maccabees entitled *Sarbeth Sarbane El*

Though Origen lists only twenty-one books, he numbers them as twenty-two. The Minor Prophets are missing from the list. Whether this was an oversight by Origen himself or an omission by a later copyist we cannot say. However, since the Minor Prophets as a group are included in all sources relating to the canon dating back to the second century BC and are included in all canonical lists after Origen's time, and since Origen's extant works contain references to the Minor Prophets as Scripture, we can hardly posit that they were omitted purposefully.

Origen's list makes explicit features contained in or implied in Melito's list. The number of books is reckoned at twenty-two, which also may have been Melito's enumeration (assuming that Esther was accidentally omitted from his list). Jeremiah includes all the works attributed to Jeremiah including Lamentations and the Letter of Jeremiah or Baruch.[202]

This last piece of information is instructive. It tells us that Origen is striving to align the Greek OT with its Hebrew counterpart. He is advocating a view common in the ancient church—that the Jews had altered parts of the Hebrew text for apologetic reasons. This he made plain in his *Letter to Africanus*:[203]

---

[202] Ellis, *Old Testament*, 14–15, argues that Baruch is more likely the meaning if the text as we have it is what Origin wrote. However, Ellis argues that the inclusion of "the letter" with Jeremiah and Lamentations is a later scribal gloss.

[203] *Letter to Africanus* 9, PG 11.65.

τί δήποτε οὐ φέρεται παρ᾽ αὐτοῖς ἐν τῷ Δανιὴλ ἡ
ἱστορία, εἰ, ὡς φῇς, τοιαῦτα περὶ αὐτῆς οἱ σοφοὶ αὐτῶν
παραδιδόασι. Λεκτέον δὲ πρὸς ταῦτα, ὅτι ὅσα δεδύνηνται
τῶν περιεχόντων κατηγορίαν πρεσβυτέρων, καὶ ἀρχόν-
των, καὶ κριτῶν, περιεῖλον ἀπὸ τῆς γνώσεως τοῦ λαοῦ,
ὧν τινὰ σώζεται ἐν ἀποκρύφοις.

Why then is the *History [of Susanna]* not contained in
their Daniel, if, as you say, their wise men handed down
such stories? The answer is that they concealed whatever
was able to bring accusations against the elders, rulers and
judges from the knowledge of the people. Some of these
have been preserved in apocryphal writings.

In this letter he notes several times that the holy books contain more
in their (Greek) Christian forms than in their (Hebrew) Jewish forms.[204]
In this letter he also clearly states that in controversies with the Jews he
quotes only passages found in their copies (ἀντιγράφοι) of the Scriptures, not passages found only in Christian copies:[205]

Ἀσκοῦμεν δὲ μὴ ἀγνοεῖν καὶ τὰς παρ᾽ ἐκείνος, ἵνα,
πρὸς Ἰουδαίος διαλεγόμενοι, μὴ προφέρωμεν αὐτοῖς τὰ
μὴ κείμενα ἐν τοῖς ἀντιγράφοις αὐτῶν, καὶ ἵνα συγ-
χρησώμεθα τοῖς φερομένοις παρ᾽ ἐκείνοις· εἰ καὶ ἐν τοῖς
ἡμετέροις οὐ κεῖται βιβλίος·

I make it a practice not to be ignorant of their various
readings so that in my controversies with the Jews I will
not quote to them something not found in their copies and
so that I make use of what is found in them, even if it is
not found in our copies.

Thus, he assumed that the Greek text reflected the original collection
of Hebrew works. This applies to the various works attached to Daniel
(Prayer of Azariah, Song of the Three, Susanna, Bel and The Dragon)
and the additions found in Greek Esther. It would appear that he accepts
both 1 Esdras (a Greek paraphrase of 2 Chronicles 35–36, Ezra and part
of Nehemiah) along with 2 Esdras (a Greek translation of Ezra-

---

[204] E.g., *Letter to Africanus* 3, *PG* 11.57

[205] *Letter to Africanus* 5, *PG*, 11.59–62, 65–66. Note that in this passage as in others he
speaks only of differences in the *contents* of the books. He does not claim that the Jews
excised entire books from the canon.

Nehemiah), unless he is simply identifying the Greek versions of Ezra and Nehemiah that were separated in some manuscripts. However, no matter which is the case, he equates them with the Hebrew Ezra-Nehemiah.

Therefore, Origen views the OT canon as normative in its *presumed* most ancient form in Hebrew. This is made clear in that he rejects 1(?) Maccabees, though he knows its Hebrew name. *For Origen the OT canon is the canon the church received from the Jews in earlier generations.* Note that he states at the beginning of his list that this is the canon as the Hebrews have handed it down and nowhere does he advocate that Christians view other books as canonical apart from these. His mention of 1 Maccabees was probably due to the popularity of this book in the church. Yet, though it was popular in the church, this was not determinative of its canonicity, nor does he anywhere argue that it should be canonical in the church. Indeed, Origen knew of other books that were used in the church, but not canonical. In his letter to Africanus he knows that Judith and Tobit are used in the church, but are not used by the Jews or even found among their "hidden books."[206]

However, Sundberg argues that Origen was only stating the contents of the Jewish OT canon, not the Christian canon.[207] Sundberg argues from the fact that Origen recognized different *readings* between the Hebrew OT text and the Greek text. This is pushing the evidence too far. Origen never states that he accepts *books* into the OT canon that the Jews do not accept. He only states that he accepts certain *contents within the books* in the canonical collection that the Jews did not. Origen *is* a witness to the popularity of books in the church which were not heretofore considered canonical. He *is not* an advocate for inclusion of books in the canon that the Jews do not accept. Ellis agrees, stating,[208]

> His defense of the Septuagint additions to Daniel, i.e. Susanna, does not represent a different judgement (sic) about *the books* that belong in the canon. Rather, as the context makes evident, it concerns *variant readings and diverse content* within a commonly received book of the Hebrew canon. Like Justin (*Dial.* 71–73), Origen suspects that the texts of the rabbis may have been tampered with.

---

[206] *Letter to Africanus, PG,* 79–80.

[207] Sundberg, *Old Testament,* 134–38.

[208] Ellis, *Old Testament,* 16.

We should note one other feature of Origen's list: he equates the number of books with the number of letters in the Hebrew alphabet. Origen is the earliest to do this. Though Josephus enumerated the books as twenty-two, he never connected it with the Hebrew alphabet. Thus, we do not know of the significance of the twenty-two book canon. Were the books deliberately arranged so as to produce the same number of books as Hebrew letters? Or was the correspondence noted later and used as a mnemonic device?[209]

### Summary: The Christian OT in the Second and Third Centuries

The earliest lists of canonical books we have in the church continue the tradition received from the first century. Melito connects the canon with Palestine and, therefore, probably with the traditional Jewish canon. The Bryennios List preserves the Hebrew names for the books, again emphasizing that the church received its first canon from the Jews. Origen continues this tradition, but also witnesses to the popularity of certain other Jewish books. Thus, in the first three centuries the church began to use the OT canon as recognized by Jews, and it also used other Jewish books. It even began to value these other books and some viewed them as authoritative. But some members of the church did not simply presume that Jewish books that were popular in the church were part of the OT canon. When they actually took the time to take a sober look at the books the church received from the first century as canonical, the lists produced corresponded to the Hebrew OT canon.

The church also is a witness to the fact that this canon was enumerated as twenty-two books not only by Christians but also by Palestinian Jews (not twenty-four as in rabbinic Judaism). Melito obtained a list that, if not a twenty-two book canon, certainly was akin to it and he states that he obtained this list in Palestine. Origen, who lived in Egypt and later in Palestine, clearly states that the Jews had a twenty-two book canon. Moreover, no Christian source in the second or third century demonstrates any knowledge of the tripartite division of the canon. Therefore, this evidence confirms that the development of the canon into

---

[209] This is not entirely out of the realm of possibility. As a child I was taught to remember the number of books in the OT as 39 by noting that the word *Old* had 3 letters and the word *Testament* had 9 letters. Yet no one would argue that the list of books in English Bibles was deliberately organized to correspond to the English title *Old Testament*.

twenty-four books was a later rabbinic development, most likely of Babylonian origin.

Another difference between the Jewish Talmudic and the Jewish Palestinian/Christian canons in the second and third centuries is in the groupings of certain books. Both continue the tradition of grouping together the twelve Minor Prophets. Both also seem to place Psalms, Proverbs, Ecclesiastes and Song of Songs together in a group, a tradition that seems at least as old as Josephus (see above page 116).[210] The grouping together of Judges and Ruth and Jeremiah and Lamentations appears to reach back at least to Josephus, as does the twenty-two book reckoning of the OT canon. Moreover, we can discern in all the Christian lists a tendency to group the books outside the Pentateuch into three subgroups: history (Joshua, Judges, Ruth, Samuel, Kings, Chronicles), poetry/wisdom (Psalms, Proverbs, Ecclesiastes, Song of Songs) and prophets (Isaiah, Jeremiah, Ezekiel, Daniel, The Minor Prophets). This can even been seen in the Bryennios list, despite its eccentric order. Some books are still finding their spots in the list (Job, Ezra-Nehemiah, Esther). Thus, we cannot say that the order common in Christian Bibles is older than that found in Jewish Bibles. Both were still developing in this period. We can state, however, that the order found in Christian Bibles has its roots in an arrangement that is documented as early as the late first century (Josephus) except that the poetic/wisdom books are placed before the prophets. The order found in Jewish Bibles is not documented until the late second century (the Talmud), but does preserve the general arrangement that places the poetic/wisdom books last (along with books not formerly grouped with them).

The church's earliest witness to the OT canon, therefore, is to the same canon as accepted by Jews and in an arrangement that was used by Jews in Palestine. *No writer of the first three Christian centuries when setting out to define the canon includes any books outside the Hebrew OT canon.* The acceptance of additional books came in later centuries. It is to these centuries we now turn in order to complete the picture of the OT canon. However, we will cover this evidence in a more summary fashion.

---

[210] Note that even the Bryennios List, despite its peculiar order, groups together Proverbs, Ecclesiastes, and Song of Songs.

## *After the Third Century*

### Christians in the East

With the developing interest in defining the NT canon and the production of lists of canonical books, the church began to produce lists of OT canonical books. In the East where Greek remained the language of the church we find a number of Fathers from the fourth century who write about their view of the canon. The Council of Laodicea, held in the middle of the fourth century became the first council to adopt an official list of canonical books.

### Eusebius, Bishop of Caesarea (ca. 260–ca. 339)

Known as the Father of Church History, Eusebius not only preserves for us the canonical lists of Melito and Origen, but he also included in his *Church History* (completed in 317) the canonical statement of Josephus. Thus, at the beginning of the fourth century Eusebius continues the tradition from the second and third centuries.

### Athanasius, Bishop of Alexandria (328–373)

Known best for his defense of the Nicene formulations on the person of Christ against Arian doctrine, as well as for his contributions that led to the formulation of trinitarian doctrine, Athanasius was given the title the Father of Orthodoxy. In his *Easter Letter 39* of 367 Athanasius lists the canonical books of the OT and the NT.[211] He counts the OT canon as twenty-two books and connects this number with the number of letters in the Hebrew alphabet. He obtains his count by omitting Esther and counting Judges and Ruth as two books (though listing Ruth immediately after Judges). He counts Jeremiah, Lamentations, Baruch and the Letter of Jeremiah as one book, continuing the tradition of assuming that these books are genuine writings of the prophet. Although not making the subdivisions of the canon explicit, he groups together the Pentateuch, the Historical books (Joshua, Judges, Ruth, 1–4 Kingdoms, 1–2 Chronicles, 1–2 Ezra), the Poetic/Wisdom books (Psalms, Proverbs, Ecclesiastes, Song of Songs, Job) and the Prophets (The Twelve, Jeremiah, Ezekiel, Daniel).

---

[211] *PG* 26.1435–40.

Athanasius also recognizes other books outside the canon as appointed to be read in the church by the Fathers. These are the Wisdom of Solomon, Sirach, Esther, Judith and Tobit as well as the Didache and the Shepherd of Hermas. Beyond these he also notes that there are heretical books.

## Cyril, Bishop of Jerusalem (315–386)

Cyril became bishop of Jerusalem around 350. However, this Church Father suffered persecution for his beliefs and was deposed from his position and exiled several times. In his *Catechetical Lectures* Cyril sets forth his view of the OT and NT canons.[212] The OT canon is divided into two sections: Law and Prophets. Like Athanasius he lists twenty-two books. What Athanasius left implicit Cyril makes explicit: he divides the Prophets into three sections: Seven historical books (Joshua, Judges-Ruth, 1–2 Kingdoms, 3–4 Kingdoms, 1–2 Chronicles, 1–2 Esdras, Esther); Five poetic books (Job, Psalms, Proverbs, Ecclesiastes, Song of Songs); Five prophetic books (the Twelve Prophets, Isaiah, Jeremiah-Baruch-Lamentations-Letter, Ezekiel, Daniel). It is not clear whether 1–2 Esdras refers to Ezra-Nehemiah or includes the Greek 1 Esdras. After listing the NT books Cyril concludes his canonical list by noting that the church also has books of "second rank" that are outside the canon but read or cited in the church, and he warns catechumens about reading heretical books. Therefore, he would seem to agree with Athanasius in his view of the canon and of church books that are used but not considered canonical.

## Epiphanius, Bishop of Salamis (ca. 310–404)

Epiphanius was born near Eleutheropolis in Palestine and became bishop of Salamis on Cyprus in 367. He was known for his learning and piety as well for his zeal for orthodoxy. Epiphanius' writings contain three canonical lists that do not completely agree. Two of his lists appear in *Weights and Measures*.

In the earlier list in *Weights and Measures* Epiphanius lists twenty one books (Judges-Ruth, 1–2 Chronicles, 1–2 Kingdoms, 3–4 Kingdoms are counted as one each).[213] He omits Job, perhaps by accident since it appears in his other lists. Jeremiah is listed without any reference to

---

[212] Catechetical Lectures IV, *PG* 33.497–500

[213] *Weights and Measures* 4, *PG* 43.244.

Lamentations or other books in the Greek Jeremiah corpus. He also divides the canon into four parts: Law, Poets, Holy Writings, Prophets, plus Ezra and Esther. With this list he also states the distinction between canonical and apocryphal books: unlike canonical books apocryphal books are not authoritative even though they are read in the church.

In his second list compares the twenty-two books of the canon with twenty-two works of God during the six days of creation, with the twenty-two letters of the Hebrew alphabet, and with the twenty-two sextarii in a modius.[214] In this list he first gives the Hebrew name of each book transliterated in Greek letters followed by the Greek name for the book. His list appears to be related to the Bryennios List.[215] The list actually contains twenty-seven names with Lamentations missing (but added at the end as an additional book), but Baruch included. Judges and Ruth are counted as one book. The list reduces to twenty-two books if 1–4 Kingdoms, 1–2 Chronicles and 1–2 Esdras are counted as one.

A third list appears in Epiphanius' *Against Heresies*.[216] Here he claims to be giving the Jewish canon, but gives the tally of books as twenty-seven. This list can easily be seen to be derived from the twenty-two book count since Judges is immediately followed by Ruth, 1–4 Kingdoms are counted as four books, not two, and 1–2 Chronicles are counted as two books as are 1–2 Esdras. Jeremiah, Lamentations, Baruch and the Letter of Jeremiah are counted as one.

In his *Panarion* or *Heresies* he also included a few comments on the OT canon.[217] He notes that twenty-seven books were given by God to the Jews, but that they are to be counted twenty-two since ten of the books are doubled and counted as only five. After giving a list of the NT canon he notes the existence of other apocryphal books that are near to the OT in substance, specifically listing Sirach and the Wisdom of Solomon.

Ellis summaries Epiphanius' approach to the OT canon:[218]

---

[214] *Weights and Measures* 23, *PG* 43.277–80.

[215] Audet, "Hebrew-Aramaic List," 135–54.

[216] *Against Heresies* 1.1.8, *PG* 41.213.

[217] *Panarion* 76, *PG* 41.213.

[218] Ellis, *Old Testament*, 23.

In these passages Epiphanius, a disciple of Athanasius, agrees with the Alexandrian in identifying two classes of books that are read in the church. Unlike Athanasius, he names the second class "apocrypha" and, similar to Augustine (*De Doct. Christ.* 2,12f.), can regard both as "holy books" or "divine writings" (*Haer.* 76,1). That the "apocrypha" have no special connection with the Old Testament is evident also from the fact that he (again like Athanasius) can mention them, *viz.* Wisdom and Ben Sira, after the New Testament books.

## Gregory of Nazianzus, Bishop of Constantinople (329–389)

Gregory of Nazianzus was one of the leaders of the orthodox movement and, along with fellow Cappadocian Theologians Basil the Great and Gregory of Nyssa, was responsible for the virtual defeat of Arianism at the Council of Constantinople in 381.

In *Carmen* Gregory records a list of twenty-two books and notes the analogy to the number of books in the Hebrew alphabet.[219] The books outside the Pentateuch are divided into three sections of seven historical, five poetic and five prophetic books, as in Cyril. However, Gregory omits Esther and counts Judges and Ruth separately. He does not mention any books appended to Jeremiah.

## Amphilochius, Bishop of Iconium (ca. 340–ca. 395)

Gregory of Nazianzus preserved a list of the OT canon drawn up by Amphilochius, who was a friend of the Cappodocian Theologians.[220] Like others, Amphilocius' list groups together the Pentateuch, Historical, Poetical and Prophetic books. He lists the books individually, giving a total of twenty-six (the Minor Prophets are listed as one book). He notes at the end of his list that some add Esther.

## The Council of Laodicea (ca. 360)

The Council of Laodicea, which met sometime between 343 and 381, is the first ecclesiastical body to rule on the canonical books of both the OT and the NT. Canon 59 restricted reading in the church to the OT and NT canons. In canon 60 the council adopted a list of books identical to the list of Cyril with the exceptions of the positions of Esther and Job (though Esther was kept among the historical books and Job among the

---

[219] *Carmen* 1.12.5, *PG* 37.472–74.
[220] *Carmen* 2.2.8, *PG* 37.1593–96.

poetic books).[221] However, canon 60's authenticity is doubted by some because Dionysius Exiguus does not have this canon in his translation of the Laodicean decrees, nor did Martin of Braga in the sixth century include it in his collection of the council's decrees.

### The Muratorian Canon (Mid-to-Late Fourth Century)

The Muratorian Canon is a list of NT books that was found by Ludovico Antonio Muratori in the Ambrosian Library at Milan in the eighteenth century. The canon is contained in a codex from the seventh or eighth century. Traditionally dated to the second century and placed in the West, Sundberg and more recently McDonald have presented persuasive arguments that it actually was composed in the East in the fourth century.[222] An interesting feature of this canon is that it lists the Wisdom of Solomon as a NT book.

This is a very curious inclusion since the canon attributes this book to the friends of Solomon who wrote it in his honor—definitely out of place in the NT canon, but at home in the OT canon. The Muratorian Canon, therefore, alerts us to the interrelationship of the parallel developments in the views of the OT and NT canons during this period. The church was in the process of defining the NT canon. Questions of the OT and NT canons are often treated at the same time in the Fathers. The author of the Muratorian Canon obviously recognized that the tradition for the inclusion of the Wisdom of Solomon in the OT was weak. As we have seen, Athanasius and Epiphanius specifically excluded the Wisdom of Solomon from the OT canon but noted that it was read in the church. The author of the Muratorian Canon attempted to give it canonical status in the NT canon instead.

### Summary: The OT Canon of Fourth-Century Eastern Christians

Almost without exception we can see several general approaches to the OT canon in the East during the fourth century:

**The acceptance of earlier tradition concerning the canon.** In general, the eastern Fathers of the fourth century follow the trajectory established among Christians in the second and third centuries.

---

[221] G. D. Mansi, *Sacrorum conciliorum nova et amplissima collectio.* (Florentiae, 1759–92), 2, 573f according to Sundberg, *Old Testament*, 58. [I have been unable to verify this reference.]

[222] Albert C. Sundberg, Jr., "Canon Muratori: A Fourth-Century List," *HTR* 66 (1–41); McDonald, "Integrity," 121–26 and *Formation*, 209–20.

**The number of books in the canon.** With two exceptions (Amphilochius and one list by Epiphanius), the number of books in the canon is reckoned as twenty-two. This is often connected with the number of letters in the Hebrew alphabet. The number of books is either counted as twenty-two by considering Judges and Ruth as one book or by counting them as two books and omitting Esther.

**The status of Esther as a canonical book.** As we have seen from the beginning of this study, Esther is the one book about which there is some doubt as to its canonical status even as late as the fourth century.

**The status of ancient Jewish books read in the church.** The Eastern Fathers of the fourth century begin to make a distinction between the canonical books and other books of Jewish origin that are read in the church, but are not canonical. At the same time, they continue the practice of including the Greek additions to the canonical books, especially the additional works credited to Jeremiah.

**Subdividing the canon.** Subdivisions of the books outside the Pentateuch are developed based on groups that were beginning to form in the second and third centuries. By the beginning of the fifth century Christians had organized the OT canon into four groups: Pentateuch, History, Poetry and Prophets, an organization that is found in Christian Bibles today. This is a uniquely Christian order.

**The effect of the formation of the NT canon on the OT canon.** The question of the extent of the OT canon was influenced by the church's struggle to define the NT canon during this period.

Christians in the West

No writer in the Christian west produced a list of the OT canonical books before the fourth century. The early lack of concern for defining the canon allowed popular usage within the church to assert a powerful influence on the contents of the western church's canonical lists. Because popular opinion had become so entrenched, the opinions of some Church Fathers who drew up canonical lists were shaped by it. Books that heretofore were not considered part of the canon by Jews or by Christians who had carefully written on the matter would increasingly become part of canonical lists. Church Fathers, with the notable exception of Jerome, would be loathe to challenge the tradition of usage that had developed in the church and in some cases even accepted this tradition themselves.

This reluctance to accept change to what had become popular usage is noted in Augustine's *Letters* where he remarks that a North African congregation loudly corrected its bishop when he read Jerome's translation of Jonah 4:6 and it differed from the traditional wording.[223] Therefore, we should not be surprised if the canonical lists of the Western church reflect what Ellis characterizes as the triumph of popular custom over carefully considered judgment.[224]

### Hilary, Bishop of Poitiers (ca. 315–367)

Hilary was born in Poitiers in Gaul to pagan parents. He was an ardent opponent of Arianism, which led to his banishment to Phrygia in Asia Minor in 356. In 361 he returned to Poitiers and purged Gaul of Arianism.

In his commentary on the Psalms, Hilary lists the canonical books of the OT.[225] He lists twenty-two books of the OT, including Esther. Jeremiah probably includes the Letter of Jeremiah. At the end of his list Hilary notes that some count twenty-four books by the addition of Judith and Tobit. While it would be tempting to connect the twenty-four book count with the rabbinic reckoning of the OT, this appears unlikely since Hilary counts Ruth with Judges and Lamentations with Jeremiah and compares the number of books to the number of letters in the Greek alphabet. More likely, the count of twenty-four books was either borrowed from Judaism without borrowing the rabbinic arrangement of the canon, or it was adopted under the influence of 4 Ezra, which was known and read in the West.

### The Mommsen Catalogue (359–365)

The Mommsen Catalogue, also known as the Cheltenham List, is a Latin list of the OT and NT drawn up in North Africa. It contains references to the consulships of Valentinian and Valens, which indicate that it was drawn up between 359 and 365. The Catalogue's OT canon is: Genesis, Exodus, Leviticus, Numbers, Deuteronomy, Joshua, Judges, Ruth, 1 Kingdoms, 2 Kingdoms, 3 Kingdoms, 4 Kingdoms, (1–2) Chronicles, (1–2) Maccabees, Job, Tobit, Esther, Judith, Psalms, Solomon, Isaiah, Jeremiah, Daniel, Ezekiel and the Twelve Prophets. At the end it compares the twenty-four canonical books with the twenty-four elders of

---

[223] Augustine, *Letters* 71.5.
[224] Ellis, *Old Testament*, 19–36.
[225] *Comm. In Pss.* Preface 15; *PL* 9.241.

the book of Revelation. However, the list itself contains twenty-five names. Perhaps it assumes that Judges and Ruth are to be counted as one book. It achieves room for Tobit, Judith and Maccabees by combining Proverbs, Ecclesiastes and Song of Songs (and perhaps Wisdom and Sirach) under one title.

Heretofore no list has ever counted the Solomonic books as one nor to my knowledge does any other canonical list of this period. In addition, this list appears to count 1–4 Kingdoms as four books, but Chronicles as only one book, another unique feature. This list appears to be a concession to popular usage in the way it attempts to list twenty-four books so as to include Tobit, Judith and Maccabees.

Despite its concession to popular usage, this list seems to follow the groupings of the non-Mosaic books common in Christian circles. Maccabees, Tobit, Esther and Judith, along with Job are grouped with the historical books. The poetical books (Psalms and Solomon) and the prophetic books follow this. Thus, the Mommsen Catalogue shows not only a tendency to include the books of the wider canon that was developing in the Latin west but also to include the extra books within appropriate categories.

## Rufinus (ca. 345 – ca. 410)

Tyrannius Rufinus was born near Aquileia, Italy. He lived as a monk in Egypt and on the Mount of Olives, where he helped found a monastery. Later he returned to Aquileia where he served as presbyter. He was a friend of Jerome, but later had a bitter dispute with him over some of the doctrines propounded by Origen.

In his *Commentary on the Apostles' Creed* he lists the books of the OT.[226] His list may be influenced by Hilary's, since he had a copy of Hilary's *Commentary on Psalms* copied for him by Jerome.[227] However, the order of the books in Rufinus' list is not the same as Hilary's nor does he mention that some include Tobit and Judith in the canon.

Rufinus lists twenty-two books of the canon, but divides them into five books of the Law, thirteen of the Prophets and four containing hymns and precepts. His prophetic section lists the historical books, including Esther, before the prophetic books. Thus, Rufinus also confirms the developing consensus on the organization of the canonical books, though instead of listing the poetic books between the historical

---

[226] *Commentary on the Apostles' Creed* 37; PL 21.373–75.

[227] Jerome, *Letters* 5.2

books and the prophetic books, he places them at the end of his list. Thus, his list is the only Christian list to place the poetic books at the end of the canon as in first century arrangements and the later Jewish arrangement.

Rufinus also recognized three categories of religious books: canonical, ecclesiastical and apocrypha. He lists the ecclesiastical books after his lists of OT and NT canons. They are Wisdom, Sirach, Tobit, Judith and Maccabees. In addition, Rufinus states that they were not to be used for the confirmation of doctrine. The apocrypha were, according to Rufinus, books that were not to be used in the church.

Ellis makes these comments on Rufinus' method for determining the canon:

> His repeated references to "the fathers" or "the ancients" as the transmitters of the canon show that he derived his understanding of the matter not from popular usage but from traditional authorities such as Cyril (whom he must have met in Jerusalem), Origen and other Fathers whose writings he had read. Rufinus gives us the impression that he was not so much opposing a differing canon currently advocated in Italy as clarifying uncertain distinctions between canonical and uncanonical books, distinctions that had been preserved among the Greek theologians but were less clearly perceived among the churches of the West.

## Augustine, Bishop of Hippo (354–430)

Augustine, the greatest Father of the Latin church, was born in North Africa to a non-Christian father (who did convert to Christianity and was baptized shortly before his death in 371) and a Christian mother. Although he was enrolled as a catechumen, when he went to Carthage for formal education he was drawn into its cosmopolitan atmosphere. For nine years he was under the influence of Manichaeism, though he never formally converted. He taught grammar at Carthage and later at Milan, where he came under the influence of its Christian bishop Ambrose and was eventually baptized. He later returned to North Africa and became bishop of Hippo. For over thirty years Augustine was the most prominent African Christian theologian, defending the catholic faith against Donatists and Pelagians. His influence was decisive for several church councils in North Africa.

Unlike the other Latin Church Fathers who left us with canonical lists, he never spent a significant portion of his life in the Christian east. Therefore, his views of the canon reflect popular piety in the western Christian church, which he seemed rather reluctant to contradict. For instance, he wrote Jerome twice (in 394/395 and 403) requesting that the basis for his new Latin Bible be the Septuagint, not the Hebrew text.[228]

Augustine's list of the OT canon is contained in his work *On Christian Doctrine*.[229] He numbers the books as forty-four.[230] To achieve this count he reckons 1–4 Kingdoms as four books, 1–2 Chronicles as two books, 1–2 Ezra as two books, the Minor Prophets as twelve books and includes Tobit, Judith, 1–2 Maccabees (two books) among the historical books, and Wisdom and Sirach along with the poetic books. However, he does not recognize a separate grouping of poetic books. Instead, he includes them as part of the prophetic books, though the other books of the prophets are said to be the prophetic books in the strict sense.

Augustine's list shows several peculiarities. He considers Ruth as a preface to 1 Kingdoms (1 Samuel) instead of a part of Judges. His list recognizes the Pentateuch and three groups within the remaining books, as in the eastern Fathers. However, his three groups are unique to him: historical books (Joshua, Judges, Ruth, Kingdoms, Chronicles); miscellaneous books (Job, Tobit, Esther, Judith, Maccabees, Ezra); and prophetic books (Psalms, Proverbs, Song of Songs, Ecclesiastes, Wisdom, Sirach, the Minor Prophets, Isaiah, Jeremiah, Daniel and Ezekiel). Although he counts the Minor Prophets as twelve books, he acknowledges that they are normally counted as one book.

Augustine acknowledges only three books by Solomon: Proverbs, Song of Songs, and Ecclesiastes. He notes that Wisdom and Sirach are ascribed to Solomon, but he offers the opinion that they were both authored by Jesus, son of Sirach. Since they are not by Solomon, he finds another reason for their authority—that they have attained (popular?) recognition in the western church as authoritative. He states this

---

[228] Augustine, *Letters*, 28 and 71; especially *Letters* 71.5 where he writes to Jerome that a riot broke out in one North African church when a bishop read Jerome's new translation of Jonah 4:6 which called the plant which shaded Jonah *ivy* instead of the Septuagint's traditional *gourd*.

[229] *On Christian Doctrine* 2.13; *PL* 34.41

[230] The significance of this number (double the traditional 22) is not explained by Augustine.

explicitly in his *City of God*.[231] Later in the *City of God* he makes a similar claim for 1–2 Maccabees.[232] It is interesting to note that he also considered 1 Enoch to be divinely inspired, but not canonical.[233] Its inspiration was attested by Jude's quotation of it (see discussion on page 108). However, according to Augustine 1 Enoch was not included in the canon of Scripture preserved in the ancient collection in the Temple by the Jewish priests.

These statements on the canon by Augustine mark a different attitude than seen in the eastern Fathers. For the eastern Fathers the canon received from the Jews was normative also for Christians. They may have believed that the Jews later omitted certain portions of the canonical books from their Hebrew copies (i.e., variants in many OT books as well as additional material in Esther, Daniel, and Jeremiah) but they did not assert that the church could add to the OT canon that it received from the Jews.[234] Augustine, however, views the church's opinion as decisive in the determination of the canon. By its authority and tradition the church can include books in the OT canon that Jews in Jesus' day had never included. Thus, he explicitly includes 1–2 Maccabees, Wisdom, and Sirach as books ordained as canonical by the church. Perhaps he would have included Tobit and Judith in this category, though he made no statement to that effect.

Thus, among the Church Fathers of the fourth and fifth centuries who have left us canonical lists of the OT, Augustine is the first to articulate a doctrine of the canon that elevates the church's later practice over the canon received from the synagogue in the first century. Moreover, Augustine claims the right of Western churches to do this even if the eastern churches do not.[235]

## Jerome (ca. 340–420)

Sophronius Eusebius Hieronymus was born in Dalmatia to Christian parents. At the age of 19 he was baptized in Rome, where he had gone to study. His travels took him to Constantinople, Antioch, Palestine and

---

[231] *City of God*, 17.20.

[232] *City of God*, 18.36.

[233] *City of God*, 15.23.

[234] Like other church Fathers, Augustine argued that God inspired the Septuagint translators and, therefore, the Septuagint was as authoritative as, if not more authoritative than, the Hebrew text. Cf. *City of God*, 43.

[235] See especially *City of God*, 17.20.

Egypt, though he finally settled in Bethlehem in 386. He was present at the Council of Constantinople in 381 and, as secretary to Pope Damasus I, was in attendance at the Council of Rome in 382. Jerome was one of the few in the church to learn Hebrew. His work of translating the Bible into Latin was, for the OT, based on the Hebrew text.

Jerome, who had copied Hilary's canonical list for Rufinus and who began his study of Hebrew during his first visit to Antioch a number of years before, later sharpened his acceptance of the Hebrew OT canon as the normative list of canonical books. Because of his knowledge of Hebrew he not only rejected books he called *apocrypha* (Wisdom, Sirach, Judith, Tobit, the Shepherd of Hermas), but he also rejected Maccabees and the additions to Daniel and Esther. [236] He did not accept Baruch as a part of Jeremiah. Except for a quickly produced translation of Tobit and Judith made at the request of his friends and the inclusion of the additions to Esther in his Latin Bible, Jerome did not translate these books.

Jerome left two canonical lists. One appears in a letter to Paulinus.[237] The more important list is in his preface to his translation of Samuel and Kings. This preface he entitled the *Helmeted Preface*, intending it to be a defense of the criticism he knew he would face, especially from the western Christian churches. In this preface he lists the books according to the rabbinic system of Law (5 books), Prophets (8), and Writings (9). The number of books is twenty-two, corresponding, as Jerome notes, to the number of letters in the Hebrew alphabet. He also notes that some Jews reckon the books as twenty-four and comments that this is achieved by separating Ruth from Judges and Lamentations from Jeremiah. He compares the reckoning of twenty-four books to the number of elders in the book of Revelation. He even notes that the canon could be reckoned as twenty-seven books (the number of Hebrew letters if one also counts the five letters that have special final forms) by splitting the double books (Samuel, Kings, Chronicles, Ezra-Nehemiah, Jeremiah-Lamentations).

Jerome's attitude toward the canon is the polar opposite of Augustine's. He recognizes only the books contained in the Hebrew canon and only in their Hebrew form. He does not recognize the right of

---

[236] *Prologue to the Books of Samuel Kings; Prologue to the Books of Solomon.* Jerome's use of the term *apocrypha* corresponds to that of Epiphanius, whom Jerome had known for some time.

[237] *Letters* 53.8; *PL* 22.545–48.

the church to define the canon based on its traditions, but defends the canon received from the synagogue as the true canon. That does not mean, however, that Jerome would banish the books he called *apocrypha* from the church. He notes that the church reads these books for edification, but that they are not used to confirm doctrine.[238] Therefore, for Jerome the term *apocrypha* does not have the pejorative connotation that later became attached to it.

## The Council of Rome (392) and The Council of Hippo (393)

The fourth century Latin church produced two canonical lists at church councils. The first of these held at Rome under Pope Damasus I adopted a list that included not only the books in the Hebrew canon, but also the books of Wisdom and Sirach (as part of the Solomonic books) and Tobit, Judith, and 1–2 Maccabees.[239] This canon is identical to the Roman Catholic canon later endorsed by the Council of Trent. The Council of Hippo, which was under Augustine's influence, also adopted this canon and classified Sirach and Wisdom along with Proverbs, Ecclesiastes and Song of Songs as books of Solomon.[240]

## The Great Septuagint Codices

The OT books found in the great Septuagint codices are of little help in compiling a list of canonical books. In fact, in some cases they contain books that no Church Father of the East or West endorsed as canonical. Table 8 lists the books outside the Hebrew canon contained in Codex Vaticanus, Codex Sinaiticus, and Codex Alexandrinus.

---

[238] *Prologue to the Books of Solomon.*

[239] C. H. Turner, "Latin Lists of the Canonical Books," *JTS* 1 (1900), 554–60.

[240] Mansi, *Sacrorum conciliorum*, 3, 850 according to Sundberg, *Old Testament*, 59.

## Table 8
## Books Outside the Hebrew Canon in the Great Septuagint Codices

|                     | Codex Vaticanus | Codex Sinaiticus | Codex Alexandrinus |
|---------------------|:---------------:|:----------------:|:------------------:|
| Tobit               | X               | X                | X                  |
| Judith              | X               | X                | X                  |
| Wisdom              | X               | X                | X                  |
| Sirach              | X               | X                | X                  |
| Baruch              | X               | ?                | X                  |
| Epistle of Jeremiah | X               | ?                | X                  |
| 1–2 Maccabees       |                 | X                | X                  |
| 3–4 Maccabees       |                 |                  | X                  |
| Psalms of Solomon   |                 |                  | X                  |

Note: Codex Sinaiticus is missing leaves containing all or part of some books. Of the Pentateuch only Genesis and Numbers survive. Lamentations (which follows Jeremiah) is incomplete. It is followed by the Minor Prophets, of which only Joel-Malachi are present. Therefore, this codex could have included Baruch and the Epistle of Jeremiah following Lamentations. Codex Vaticanus and Codex Alexandrinus contain the Septuagint versions of all of the books of the Hebrew OT.

As this table demonstrates, no agreement exists as to the number of books that were included with the Greek version of books from the Hebrew OT canon. However, the books found in the Hebrew OT are included in all of them. Therefore, one cannot draw any conclusion about the alleged Septuagint canon from the books bound together in these codices except that the books corresponding to the OT Hebrew canon were always included. In fact, they more likely reflect the whims of the book's manufacturer or the manufacturer's client as to which books (whether canonical or not) to include. These codices probably represent a mixture of canonical and noncanonical books that were popular in the church.

### Summary: The OT Canon of Fourth Century Western Christians

From this survey of fourth century canonical lists of the Latin church we can discern the following trends:

**The number of canonical books.** The number of books in the canon is reckoned in several ways. The count of twenty-two books, common in the East, is also found in the West (Hilary, Rufinus, Jerome). Jerome explicitly attributes this number to the reckoning of the Jews whom he knew in Palestine, confirming that this method of counting the books persisted among Palestinian Jews up to the end of the fourth century.

However, the reckoning of twenty-four books is also used in the West and in some cases is connected with the number of elders in the book of Revelation (Hilary, the Mommsen Catalogue, Jerome). The origin of the twenty-four book enumeration among western Christians is unknown. Jerome mentions that the books could be reckoned as twenty-seven and Augustine has a unique enumeration of forty-four books. In some cases the number of books appears to be manipulated in order to include some books not recognized in the Hebrew canon (Hilary, the Mommsen Catalogue).

**The content of the canon.** Those Fathers who had spent a significant amount of time in the East adopted the attitudes prevalent in the East concerning the canon. (However, Esther is always included in canonical lists from the West.) Thus, Hilary, Rufinus and Jerome to varying degrees reject books that were commonly included in the canon in western popular opinion. Hilary does concede that some include Judith and Tobit in the canon (but he does not mention Wisdom, Sirach or Maccabees). Rufinus does not include Wisdom, Sirach, Tobit, Judith or Maccabees in the OT canon, but classifies them as ecclesiastical books. Jerome goes even further than Rufinus, rejecting as canonical parts of the Septuagint that others in both the East and the West assumed were genuine writings of the prophets: the additions to Esther, the supplements to Daniel and Baruch and the Letter of Jeremiah. However, even Jerome recognizes books such as Judith and Sirach (which he labeled *apocrypha*) as books respected in the church and useful for some purposes.

**The western church's adoption of a wider canon.** Augustine, who spent no significant time in the East, is the only Father to accept the popular practice of the church in the West and include in his canon books rejected both in the East and in Judaism. Augustine defends the church's right to define the OT canon, even as he acknowledges that some books were not part of the ancient Jewish canon that the church received. Augustine's influence and the entrenched nature of public opinion in the West prevailed in the Latin church, so that the wider canon was accepted there despite the strenuous objections of Jerome.

### *Summary*

This chapter has presented evidence for the OT canon from the second and third centuries in both Jewish and Christian sources. In addition, the evidence from Christians in the fourth century has been summarized. Figure 3 gives a synopsis of the evidence from the second and third centuries. Figure 4 presents a synopsis of the evidence from the fourth century.

## Figure 3
## Jewish and Christian Evidence for the Canon in the Second and Third Centuries

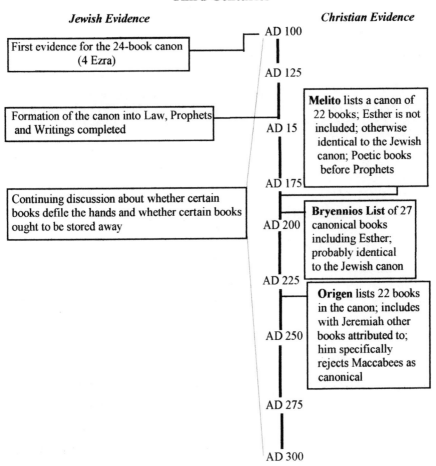

*Jewish Evidence*                                    *Christian Evidence*

AD 100

First evidence for the 24-book canon
(4 Ezra)

AD 125

**Melito** lists a canon of 22 books; Esther is not included; otherwise identical to the Jewish canon; Poetic books before Prophets

Formation of the canon into Law, Prophets and Writings completed

AD 15

AD 175

Continuing discussion about whether certain books defile the hands and whether certain books ought to be stored away

**Bryennios List** of 27 canonical books including Esther; probably identical to the Jewish canon

AD 200

AD 225

**Origen** lists 22 books in the canon; includes with Jeremiah other books attributed to; him specifically rejects Maccabees as canonical

AD 250

AD 275

AD 300

**Figure 4**
**Christian Evidence for the Canon in the Fourth Century**

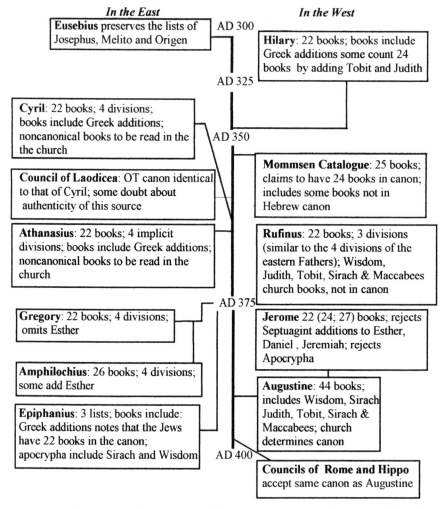

*In the East*                                    *In the West*

| | AD 300 | |
|---|---|---|
| **Eusebius** preserves the lists of Josephus, Melito and Origen | | |
| | | **Hilary**: 22 books; books include Greek additions some count 24 books by adding Tobit and Judith |
| | AD 325 | |
| **Cyril**: 22 books; 4 divisions; books include Greek additions; noncanonical books to be read in the the church | AD 350 | |
| | | **Mommsen Catalogue**: 25 books; claims to have 24 books in canon; includes some books not in Hebrew canon |
| **Council of Laodicea**: OT canon identical to that of Cyril; some doubt about authenticity of this source | | |
| **Athanasius**: 22 books; 4 implicit divisions; books include Greek additions; noncanonical books to be read in the church | | **Rufinus**: 22 books; 3 divisions (similar to the 4 divisions of the eastern Fathers); Wisdom, Judith, Tobit, Sirach & Maccabees church books, not in canon |
| | AD 375 | |
| **Gregory**: 22 books; 4 divisions; omits Esther | | **Jerome** 22 (24; 27) books; rejects Septuagint additions to Esther, Daniel , Jeremiah; rejects Apocrypha |
| **Amphilochius**: 26 books; 4 divisions; some add Esther | | |
| | | **Augustine**: 44 books; includes Wisdom, Sirach Judith, Tobit, Sirach & Maccabees; church determines canon |
| **Epiphanius**: 3 lists; books include: Greek additions notes that the Jews have 22 books in the canon; apocrypha include Sirach and Wisdom | AD 400 | |
| | | **Councils of Rome and Hippo** accept same canon as Augustine |

Based on the evidence from this chapter we can draw the following conclusions:

**The number of books in the canon.** Though the number of books in the canon is reckoned in various ways, the two most prominent systems number the books as twenty-two or twenty-four books.

**The Canon as Twenty-Two Books.** The twenty-two book system has slightly earlier attestation from the first century (Josephus). This is originally a Jewish reckoning of the books that was popular in Palestine. However, the Church Fathers adopted it, and it became the main method of counting the canonical books. It is used by Origen, Athanasius, Cyril, Epiphanius, Gregory, Amphilochius, Hilary, Rufinus, Jerome and, perhaps, the Council of Laodicea. Both Origen and Jerome state that this was the method of reckoning the canon among (Palestinian) Jews in their day. Melito, though he does not explicitly state that he got his canonical list from Jews, does state that he discovered the method of counting the canonical books in Palestine. Thus, we have attestation from the first century through the fourth century of this method of counting the books. Moreover, the Christian canonical lists that do not count the books as twenty-two are dependent on the twenty-two book canon. This is certainly true of the Bryennios List and Epiphanius' list of twenty-seven books. But it is also true of Augustine's forty-four book list that supplements the canon with the Apocrypha/Deuterocanonical books, arranges them in an order similar to that found in most twenty-two book lists and arrives at a number of books precisely double that of most of the other Church Fathers.

**The Canon of Twenty-Four Books.** The twenty-four book canon is first attested at the end of the first century and is mainly a Talmudic reckoning of the canon. Apart from the Mommsen Catalogue (whose order is more akin to the twenty-two book lists) and Hilary's note that some Christians add Tobit and Judith to the twenty-two book canon to produce a twenty-four book canon, no Christian list reckons the books as twenty-four. Jerome mentions that some Jews produce a list of twenty-four books by separating Ruth from Judges and Lamentations from Jeremiah. In fact, this is precisely the first step that had to be taken to leap from Josephus' reckoning of the canon to the Talmudic canon. Therefore, it would appear that the Jewish canon reckoned at twenty-four books is slightly younger than the Jewish/Christian canon reckoned at twenty-two books. The Talmudic canon is probably of Babylonian origin, since the twenty-two book reckoning is attested among Palestinian Jews down to the end of the fourth century.

**The Organization of the Canon.** The organization of the canon and the order of its books are later developments. The twenty-two book canon eventually leads to the Christian fourfold topical division of the canon into Pentateuch, History, Poetry, and Prophets. This arrangement served well the Christian message that Jesus (as depicted in the Gospels at the beginning of the NT) fulfilled the prophets' words. The twenty-four book canon eventually leads to the Jewish tripartite division into Law, Prophets, and Writings that probably developed because of Jewish liturgical considerations. However, neither of these is the oldest way of dividing the canon. Both developed from a simple two-part canon of Law and Prophets. The twenty-two book and twenty-four book lists display common ancestry as evidenced by the way they contain similar groupings of books. Both group together the books of Moses. Both count the Minor Prophets as one book. Like the Talmudic order, Christian lists usually keep the Solomonic books (Proverbs, Ecclesiastes, and Song of Songs) together. Again, like the Talmudic order, the books of Israel's history tend to follow the order Joshua, Judges, Samuel, and Kings (Christian lists often add Chronicles and Ezra). Beginning with Josephus, the twenty-two book lists fairly consistently group together Psalms, Proverbs, Ecclesiastes, and Song of Songs as poetical/wisdom books. This is found not only in Josephus, but also *every* Christian list except the Bryennios List and one of Epiphanius' three lists. Often Job is included in this group at the beginning (Cyril, once in Epiphanius, Gregory, Amphilocius, Jerome) or the end (Melito, Athanasius). The Bryennios List, Origen, Hilary and Rufinus do not group Job with the other poetic/wisdom books, although in Rufinus' list it does occur immediately before the poetic books.

**The Contents of the Canon.** Two questions about the contents of the canon are raised by the evidence after the first century. One is a question that survives from previous centuries: the status of Esther. The other is a question that is raised by the Christian church: the status of additional books or portions of books not found in the Hebrew canon.

**The Status of Esther.** Esther is not included in the lists of Melito, Athanasius and Gregory. Athanasius explicitly excludes Esther from the canon by including it with books read in the church for edification. Gregory, who certainly was influenced by Athanasius, also omits Esther from his list. Amphilochius equivocates, noting that some add Esther to the canon. Esther, therefore, is the book of the Hebrew OT canon with the least claim to canonical status. It is perhaps not used by Ben Sira (see page 42), not present among the Qumran manuscripts and missing from the lists of three Church Fathers. On the other hand, there is no attestation for Ruth in Ben Sira, yet its canonical status is unquestioned. The Qumran sectarians had calendrical and theological reasons for neglecting Esther. Melito's omission may be accidental, since his list contains the peculiar total of twenty-one books. Perhaps he meant to list twenty-two, especially since his list derives from Palestine. Therefore, the only clear objections to Esther would be that of Athanasius and Gregory and, perhaps, Amphilochius. These three Fathers are acquaintances of each other and of the same general theological mindset. Therefore, the weight of evidence is in favor of the inclusion of Esther in the canon from the beginning.

**Additions to the Canon in Greek Bibles in the East.** The Church Fathers defend at least some additional material in the Greek (or Latin) Bible's OT canon. For those in the East this defense was confined to those parts of the OT that were presumed to be originally part of the Hebrew text, but omitted by the Jews: the additions to Esther, the additional Daniel material and the books associated with Jeremiah (Baruch and the Letter of Jeremiah). *For the eastern Church Fathers this was not a matter of adding books to the canon or indications that the canon was still open.* Instead, it was based on the mistaken premise that the Jews tampered with certain books. Some other books, such as Wisdom and Sirach were accepted in the church as useful reading, but not canonical. The eastern church consistently held this distinction between canonical books received from the Jews and other Jewish literature.

**Additions to the Canon in Greek Bibles in the West.** In the West the situation was somewhat different. Because western theologians did not begin to define the canon until the fourth century, popular usage among the churches in the West exerted much more pressure than it did in the East. In the East already in the second century Melito had begun to define the canon and later Fathers distinguished between the OT canonical books and other books received from Jewish sources and read in the church. This distinction was not as sharply defined in the West so that when the contents of the OT canon were looked at more closely, public opinion tended to override sober judgment. This can be seen in Hilary's comment that some include Judith and Tobit in the canon and is certainly true for the Mommsen Catalogue. Augustine, the only Church Father of the fourth century who wrote on the canon and spent no time appreciable time in the East reinforced the popular opinion in the West. The western councils of the fourth century agreed. Despite the efforts of Jerome, the only western Father to study the matter and investigate the OT canon in its original language, the church in the West would follow the lead of Augustine. However, it should be carefully noted that Augustine did not argue that the OT canon he recognized was the one received from the Jews in the first century. To the contrary, he recognized that it was not the Jewish canon that was from the Temple archives. Instead, he asserted the (western) church's right to add to the canon. For Augustine, the canon was not closed until the church said it was closed, even if it was considered closed by others at a much earlier date.

Thus, for Christian churches in the West and, later some in the East, the canon was expanded. Some churches, notably the Ethiopian church, would include books not recognized elsewhere in Christendom. However, of the books received into the wider canon and called *Deuterocanonical* by Roman Catholics or *Apocrypha* by Protestants, we can find two different reasons for their acceptance by the church, as presented in Table 9.

## Table 9
## The Reason for the Acceptance of Additional Books in Christian OT Canons

| *Compositions Mistakenly Considered Part of the Original Prophetic Corpus (by both Eastern and western Church Fathers)* | *Compositions Received Under the Authority of the Church (especially in the West)* |
|---|---|
| Additions to Esther | Tobit |
| Additions to Daniel: | Judith |
|    The Prayer of Azariah | Wisdom of Solomon[*] |
|    The Song of the Three | Sirach[*] |
|    Susanna | 1 Maccabees |
|    Bel | 2 Maccabees |
|    The Dragon | |
| Works Attributed to Jeremiah: | |
|    Baruch | |
|    The Letter of Jeremiah | |
| 2 Esdras (4 Ezra) | |
| Wisdom of Solomon[*] | |
| Sirach[*] | |

Note: Some in the church included the Wisdom of Solomon and Sirach as works by Solomon or by Solomon's companions. Others did not, but considered them books honored and read in the church.

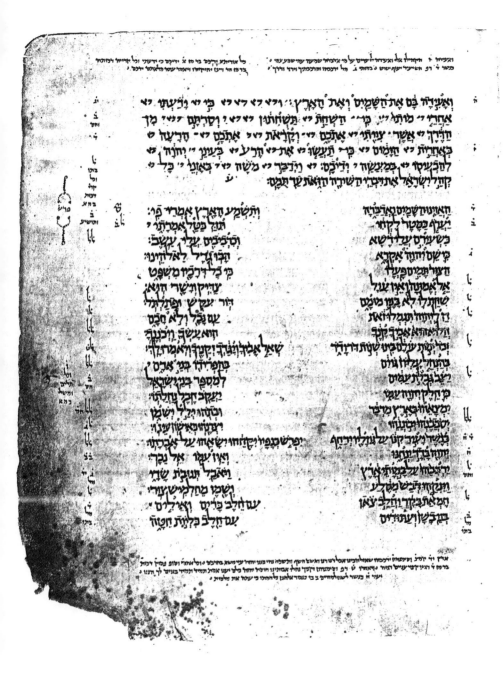

*The Aleppo Codex: Provided with Masoretic Notes and Pointed by Aaron Ben Asher.*
Jerusalem: The Magnes Press, the Hebrew University, 1976.

# 5

# Summary and Conclusions

At the beginning of this study we surveyed older attempts to explain the formation of the OT canon. The Triple Canon Theory was the dominant explanation for the formation of the OT from the end of the nineteenth century to the middle of the twentieth century. However, since its demise several competing theories that divide roughly into two types—early date theories and late date theories—have vied to replace it. None of these has gained widespread recognition. Now that we have examined the evidence over six centuries, the time has come to evaluate the reasons why no current theory has gained widespread acceptance.

## *Methodological Problems with Current Theories on the OT Canon*

### Imposition of Later Evidence on Earlier Evidence

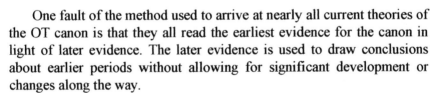

One fault of the method used to arrive at nearly all current theories of the OT canon is that they all read the earliest evidence for the canon in light of later evidence. The later evidence is used to draw conclusions about earlier periods without allowing for significant development or changes along the way.

This is especially true of the way that early date theories assume the second- and third-century AD evidence for the tripartite Hebrew canon ought to be imposed on earlier evidence. Thus, the Prologue to Sirach, Philo and Luke 24:44 are read as if they offer evidence for a three-part canon. For the Prologue this means misreading its evidence. Its mention of the books that Ben Sira studied does not require that the three categories be equated with the three sections of the Hebrew OT attested by later evidence. The phrase "the Law, the Prophets and the Psalms" as used in Philo and Luke is interpreted to be equivalent to the later-attested three-part canon despite the fact that in neither Philo or the NT is *Psalms* ever used as a synonym for the Writings and that shortly afterward Philo defines what he means by the Psalms. In addition, the evidence from 4QMMT demonstrates that this phrase probably should be understood as a variation of a twofold arrangement of the canon as Law and Prophets with *Psalms* meaning the book of Psalms alone.

Moreover, the first clear evidence of a three-part canon from Josephus is often dismissed as idiosyncratic since it does not match the later three-part canon. Indeed, a close look at the evidence *in chronological order* reveals the arrangement found in Josephus to be a step in the development towards both the three-part Jewish canon and the four-part Christian canon. This would have been more obvious had attention been paid to the chronological order of the evidence.

However, late-date theories of the canon suffer from the same problem in a different way. While they are less likely to impose the tripartite canon on earlier evidence, they demand something that the earlier evidence does not provide: a definitive list of books that comprise the canon. Since later evidence does provide this, the date of the closing of the canon is placed among this evidence in the late first century or later. Therefore, earlier evidence from Ben Sira through Josephus is discounted because it is less specific in its details. This is despite the fact that Josephus clearly and forcefully states that Jews long before his day possessed a definitive collection of Scriptures. It is contrary to the clear assumption of a canon in a number of places in the NT and the weight of the evidence as early as Ben Sira.

In essence, those who hold to late-date theories of the OT canon demand that the canon cannot have been accepted and acknowledged until its contents were listed. This is imposing a later view of the canon (i.e., that of a well-defined list) on the earlier evidence. However, some early evidence points to the canon as defined by an official Temple archive and not as a list (e.g., 2 Maccabees and Josephus). Thus, the late-date theories are also guilty of imposing conclusions from later evidence on the earlier evidence.

Moreover, these late-date theories purposely discount all evidence that present less than the maximum threshold for defining a canon. This is somewhat akin to a prosecuting attorney refusing to try a murder case without videotape of the murder clearly showing the perpetrator, the victim and the weapon. However, circumstantial evidence *is* relevant in proving the guilt of an accused lawbreaker beyond a reasonable doubt. In the same way, the evidence from times before the canon was explicitly defined as a list of books is relevant. When this evidence is properly examined, we can draw conclusions from it that leave no reasonable doubt about the existence of a canon and little doubt about its contents.

### Using Post-Second Temple Definitions of Canon to Define the Canon During the Second Temple Period

This leads to the second problem with nearly all current theories: They attempt to use a later definition of canon as a *list* of accepted authoritative books as a part of their investigation of the canon. However, the concept of the canon as a list may be only a later development due to historical circumstances. Given the evidence, I would propose that the canon came to be a list as a result of one extremely important event: the fall of Jerusalem and its Temple to the Romans in AD 70. Before this time there was little need for lists to define the canon. The canon was the collection of holy, inspired, authoritative books in the Temple. The canon could be *assumed* to be known and acknowledged by most Jews because of this normative archive. (This explains the references in the NT which assume the existence of a commonly agreed upon Scripture.) Only with the destruction of the Temple did there arise a need to define the canon as a list that could gain common acceptance. Moreover, this need was addressed in two different ways by the two religious communities that valued it: Judaism and Christianity.

The problem arises when we insist that there was no canon until it was defined the way we presently define it. We could draw an analogy to the definition of the unit of length called a *meter*. Originally a meter was to be one ten-millionth of the distance from the equator to the North Pole along the meridian that runs through Paris. French scientists estimated this distance and divided it into ten-millionths. Later, when it was discovered that the earth was not perfectly spherical, the meter was redefined as the distance between two lines inscribed on a platinum-iridium bar kept in Paris. Later, when more precision and reproducibility was needed, the meter was redefined as a certain number of wavelengths of red light from a krypton-86 source. Finally, in 1983 when scientists needed even more precision, the meter was redefined as the distance light travels through a vacuum in a certain period of time. We certainly would be in error if we held that no meter existed in the nineteenth century or most of the twentieth century because it was not defined the way we have defined it since 1983. In the same way, it would be an error to insist that no canon existed simply because it was not defined as a list—a definition which did not exist until the late first century at the earliest. Yet this is what most theories of the canon do. This is especially true of the late date theories, but it is also implicit in the attempts by those who hold to early-date theories when they attempt to impose later canonical organizations and lists on earlier evidence. However, the evidence from before AD 70 indicates that the canon, though it existed, was not conceived of as a list at this time.

### Looking for Evidence for the Formation of the Canon Instead of Evidence for Its History Subsequent to Its Formation

A final methodological fault that is highlighted when the evidence is considered in chronological order is that scholars have often been looking for the wrong thing. The search has been for evidence of the formation of the canon or at least of the closing of the canon. However, none of the evidence appears to point in that direction. Instead, the evidence appears to present the history of the canon subsequent to its formation. As Schechter noted a century ago, Ben Sira appears to be a post-canonical book that makes extensive use of the canon.[241] With the exceptions of Ruth and Esther (and possibly Daniel, if its composition is placed after Ben Sira), Ben Sira knows and uses all the books of the OT canon. As we have seen, the finds from Qumran reinforce this. From at least the last third of the first century BC this canon can be referred to as "the Law and the Prophets" or "the Law, Prophets and Psalms." Therefore, it is more likely that subsequent developments are not evidence of the *formation* of the canon, but of its *history subsequent to its formation.*

### *A New Theory of the History of the Canon*

What is needed, then, is a theory of the OT canon that explains the evidence and accounts for the developments that are seen when the evidence is examined in chronological order. The theory I propose rests on three conclusions drawn from the evidence:

1. The OT canon was formed before the second century BC. The only possible exceptions are the inclusion of Esther and possibly Daniel (if a date of approximately 164 BC is accepted for its final form in Hebrew. Note that evangelical

---

[241] Schechter and Taylor, *Ben Sira*, 26.

scholars would date Daniel much earlier and would, therefore likely argue that Daniel should not be considered a possible exception). However, it would appear that the evidence for excluding Esther is mostly accidental except for later statements by some Christian Church Fathers.

2. Before the fall of Jerusalem to the Romans in AD 70 the canon was understood to be a set of holy books accepted as normative by all Jews. These books were collected in an official archive in the Temple.

3. After the fall of Jerusalem the Temple archives ceased to exist. During the following centuries the canon made a transition to a list of holy books accepted as normative. This transition took place in different ways among Jews than among Christians.

Figures 5 and 6 outline this theory in more detail.

### Figure 5
### The History of the OT Canon from 200 BC to AD 500

The canon is collected in the Temple archives and become accepted by Jews sometime in the late Persian period. The canon is in theory open, if another prophet should arise. However, in practice it is closed. It is probably in this period that the canon is divided into two parts: Law and Prophets.

Subsequent authors such as Ben Sira and Philo study the canonical books and base their writings on them. Some write pseudonymous books whose putative authors are mentioned in canonical books, especially the Pentateuch. Though valued by some Jewish groups, none of these are generally accepted by Jews as canonical and none is ever referred to as among the Law and the Prophets.

If Daniel was composed ca. 164 BC, it is accepted into the canon among the Prophets almost immediately. (A manuscript of Daniel from the late first century BC was found at Qumran; Daniel is accepted as a prophetic book at Qumran.)

During the first century BC some begin to separate the Psalms from the Prophets and refer to "the Law, the Prophets and the Psalms" as a designation of the canon.

By the time of Josephus in the mid-to-late first century AD the canon can be divided into three sections of Law, Prophets and Poetic/Wisdom books. The canon consists of 22 books.

Christians adopt the 22-book OT 2-part canon. However, they use the Greek text and accept some of the Greek additions to Jeremiah, Daniel and Esther; other books of Jewish origin are read and esteemed in the church.

In the late first century Jews begin to number the canon as 24 books by separating Ruth from Judges and Lamentations from Jeremiah.

**Among Babylonian Jews:** By the third century the Hebrew OT canon is divided into Law, Prophets and Writings; the Writings are separated from the Prophets on the basis of liturgical use; **Palestinian Jews** continued to organize the canon into 22 books

By the fourth century the OT generally divided into four sections Law; History; Poetry/Wisdom; Prophets

In the East, a careful distinction is maintained between canonical books and books read and esteemed in the church

In the West, popular usage leads to the inclusion of additional books read and esteemed in the church within the canon

**Figure 6**
**History of the Organization of the Canon**

```
                    ┌──────────────────────────┐
                    │    Probable oldest        │
                    │ organization of the canon │
                    │    Law and Prophets       │
                    └──────────────────────────┘
```

| 2nd century BC – mid 1st century AD | 2nd century BC – Mid 1st century AD |
|---|---|
| *Law and Prophets* two-part canon is most common way of referring to the canon (Qumran, Philo, NT, 2 Maccabees, 4 Maccabees) | *Law, Prophets and Psalms* occasionally the canon is divided into three parts by separating the Psalms from the Prophets (4QMMT, Philo, Luke) |

| 2nd century – 4th century Christians | mid-to-late 1st century AD Jews |
|---|---|
| *Law, History, Poetic/Wisdom, Prophets* Christians adopt the two-part organization of the canon of 22-book and eventually organize it into four parts by subdividing the Prophets into three parts | *Law, Prophets, Poetic/Wisdom Books* the Solomonic books are removed from the Prophets and added to the third section of a 22-book canon |

| Late 4th century | Late 1st century – early 3rd century Rabbinic Jews |
|---|---|
| *OT and Deuterocanonicals* The church in the West begins to formally acknowledge additional books as canonical | *Law, Prophets, Writings* other books that are not included in the Jewish lectionary readings are moved from the Prophets to the third section of the canon of 24 books |

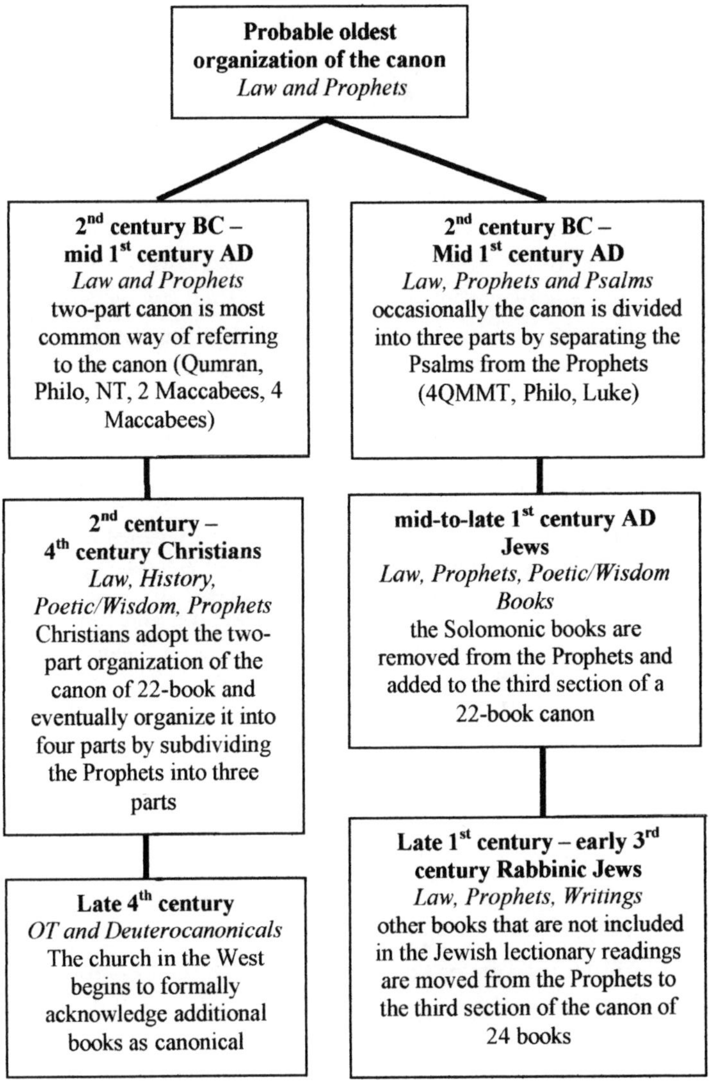

ↄ

## The Canon Was Formed Before the Second Century BC

While some have sought to place the formation of the canon as late as the third century AD and others as early as the mid-second century BC, nearly every source from Ben Sira onwards appears to presume the existence of a canon. Moreover, there appears to be broad agreement on the general contents of this canon. Some doubt can be raised about one or two books, but the existence of the general designation "the Law and the Prophets," a common phrase used by writers from diverse theological viewpoints, would appear to argue that a widespread consensus existed as to the contents of the Prophets as well as the Law. Moreover, the view that inspired prophecy in some sense ceased in the Persian period enjoys a long tradition from the second century BC to second or third century AD. Table 10 summaries the evidence:

### Table 10
### Witnesses to the Cessation of Inspired Prophecy

| Witness | Type of Evidence |
|---|---|
| Ben Sira | *implicit* (Ben Sira's Praise of Ancestors) |
| 1 Maccabees | *implicit* (prophecy had ceased) |
| New Testament | *implicit* (perhaps Matt 23:34–36; Luke 11:49–51; the written prophetic revelation seen as distinct from apostolic revelation and continuing prophecy, e.g., 2 Pet 3:1–2, 15–16) |
| Josephus | *explicit* (Against Apion 37–43) |
| 2 Esdras | *implicit* (canon as 24 book collection from Ezra) |
| Rabbinic Writings | *explicit* (t. Sota 13:2) |

Many of the items in Table 10 are implicit testimony to the writing of the last books of the canon in the Persian period. In and of themselves they would not provide much evidence. However, the weight of the several implicit references combined with explicit statements, especially of Josephus in the first century, tips the scales in favor of this long-standing tradition.

This evidence for the formation of the canon during the Persian period agrees with the conclusion of David Noel Freedman mentioned in chapter 1, although Freedman does not cite any of this evidence. Yet, Freedman's instincts appear to agree with the evidence. The only exception is the book of Daniel which, like a large number of scholars, Freedman dates to about 164 BC.

If Daniel was written about this date, it was quickly accepted into the canon apparently *without controversy* as a genuine book from the early Persian period. A copy of Daniel only about thirty years removed from 164 BC was found at Qumran. A large number of Jewish writings, including those from Qumran and Josephus as well as the NT accept Daniel as a genuine prophetic book written by Daniel the prophet in Babylon. Collins notes, "The Book of Daniel was widely accepted as a reliable and authoritative document by the end of the second century BCE."[242]

If Daniel dates from as late as 164 BC and gained swift acceptance as a holy book, a number of difficult, but ultimately unanswerable questions about its near-immediate acceptance by all Jewish groups need to be addressed. Unfortunately, exploring these questions is beyond the scope of this study. These include:

- Why did no Jewish sect—Pharisees, Sadducees, Essenes or others—dispute its inclusion in the canon? (Daniel would have received general acceptance about the time these groups were forming. Yet, as far as we know, no one disputed its prophetic credentials and it was given a place among the Prophets, unlike many pseudepigraphal books.)
- If Daniel 11 accurately portrays the career of Antiochus Epiphanes up to 11:39 but fails to accurately predict the Antiochus' death in the ensuing verses, why was it immediately received as prophecy and not quickly rejected as false prophecy soon after 164 BC when it became apparent that Antiochus did not die the way the book predicts?
- How was Daniel placed among the Prophets when other books of similar vintage claiming prophetic origins were not? How did a well-respected book like Ben Sira escape being placed among the Prophets? (I know of no Jewish source that treats Ben Sira as a prophetic book.)
- How are the apparent uses of Daniel in Ben Sira to be explained?

---

[242] John J. Collins, *Daniel: A Commentary on the Book of Daniel.* Hermenia. (Minneapolis: Fortress, 1993) 72. Since Collins does not believe that the canon was formed and accepted until the late first century he parenthetically adds, "The term 'canonical' is anachronistic for this period."

- How is it that material attributed to Daniel (much of it in Hebrew, to judge from Qumran) was not included in the Hebrew book? Were these written after 164 BC? If Daniel as we have it in Hebrew is a composite work, when did the addition of newer material end, and why did it end?

However, evangelical scholars will have no problem with holding that Daniel was part of the canon from an early date, since they advocate a date of composition in the Persian period. A Persian provenance is the clear claim of the text of Daniel. Compelling evidence supports that assertion, especially for readers who regard the text's claim as superior to post-enlightenment construals and theories of origin.

Nothing in this study resolves the question of the book of Daniel, though the evidence from Ben Sira suggests that Daniel may have been written earlier than 164 BC. However, only two alternatives exist for its inclusion in the canon:

1. It is earlier than supposed by many scholars, perhaps as early as the Persian period if evangelical scholars are correct.
2. Its final form dates from the second century and in this form it was swiftly accepted as a book from a genuine prophet of the late Babylonian and early Persian period without any known objections from any Jewish group or sect.

Thus, the canon was closed for all practical purposes in the Persian period. If Daniel was a later composition accepted into the canon, it was because it was understood to be a genuine work from that time. However, the absolute closing of the canon took place with the fall of Jerusalem and the accompanying loss of the Temple's archives. While the canon had been closed in practice before this, no books could possibly be added to the archives of holy books after this time.

It is interesting to note with Barton, that with the exception of Sirach, no book of the Hebrew canon or the wider Greek canon has as its putative author anyone living later than Ezra.[243] Barton adds, "There are no recent upstarts among the authors of books that were taken seriously as prophecy in the years around the turn of the era. *And so far as I know there is no case before about the third century AD of a Jewish work pseudonymously attributed to anyone later than Ezra.*"[244] Therefore, although much of the evidence for the effective closing of the canon is implicit (though some is explicit), there can be no doubt about the

---

[243] Barton, *Oracles of God*, 60.

[244] Barton, *Oracles of God*, 61. [emphasis mine]

tradition that the canon was first assembled and recognized in the Persian period. This tradition is as old as our evidence, is long-standing, and is persistent.

### Before AD 70: The Canon as an Official Archive in the Temple

Both 2 Maccabees and Josephus speak of books stored in the Temple. However, it is not until after the fall of the Temple that we have the first evidence for the number of books in the canon or for its subdivisions (Josephus, 4 Ezra) or of a list of books in the canon (the Talmud, Melito). This fact has been used by many who would date the final acceptance of the canon to the late first century or later to argue that no canon existed prior to the times of these lists, even though something very much like the present Hebrew OT is called "the Law and the Prophets" in earlier times.

What has not been noted heretofore is the significance of the Temple archives in shaping how explicitly the canon was defined. As long as the Temple archives existed, phrases such as "the Law and the Prophets" or "the Law, the Prophets and the Psalms" were adequate. It is likely that no one felt a pressing need for further definition. Only after the fall of the Temple, when an official archive could no longer be maintained, was the need for such a definition pressed upon Jews and Christians.

Many, especially among those who view the acceptance of the canon as a late development, argue that the Prophets was not a well-defined collection, but a fluid category that may have included books for some that others rejected (e.g., Jubilees, 1 Enoch). This position is maintained because we do not possess a *list* of the books belonging to the Prophets. However, we should note that in most of our sources we do not have a list of the books of the Law, yet no one has serious doubts about its contents. The Law is not defined by Ben Sira, 1 Maccabees, 2 Maccabees, 4 Maccabees, the NT, or any Qumran document. Nevertheless, almost all scholars are comfortable with understanding references to the Law in these documents as the five books of Moses, Genesis through Deuteronomy.

### After AD 70: The Canon as a List

The situation after the Roman capture of Jerusalem required a shift in thinking about the canon. No longer a collection in the Temple archives, the canon was more susceptible to sectarian tinkering—both additions

and subtractions could have been foisted upon Jews or Christians.
Therefore, the canon needed to be more tightly defined. By the end of the
first century it was beginning to be defined according to the number of
books it contained—either twenty-two or twenty-four books, depending
on how some books were combined. In the second century the books
were not only numbered but also listed.

From this perspective, it makes little sense to argue about which way
of listing and organizing the books is older—the Christian twenty-two
books in four divisions or the Jewish twenty-four books in three
divisions. While the roots of the Christian twenty-two book enumeration
appears to be slightly older (Josephus and Palestinian Jews), so do the
roots of the three-division scheme followed by Jews. However, the final
products of the differing Christian and Jewish organization of canon
appear to be the results of parallel developments. In fact, from the
common groupings of books in each, it would appear that they are both
children of a common heritage of canonical organization that may be
much older. Note the groups that they have in common as presented in
Table 11.

**Table 11**
**Groupings of Books in the Jewish and Christian Canons**

| Group | Place in Jewish Bible according to the Talmud | Place in Christian OT |
|---|---|---|
| Genesis – Deuteronomy | Torah | Pentateuch |
| Joshua – Kings | Early Prophets | Historical Books |
| Isaiah, Jeremiah, Ezekiel, the Twelve | Latter Prophets | Prophetic Books (placed after the Poetic/Wisdom Books) |
| Job, Psalms, Proverbs, Ecclesiastes, Song of Songs | Writings | Poetic/Wisdom Books (placed before the Prophetic books) |

Note: The Jewish Bible does not include Ruth in the Joshua-Kings group, the
Christian OT does. The Christian OT includes Lamentations with Jeremiah. In
the Talmud the order of the first two Poetic books is reversed (i.e., Psalms then
Job). As noted above in chapter 4, Job was one of the last books to find its place
in Christian lists.

Most of the books of the Hebrew canon are included in Table 11.
Only Ruth, Chronicles, Ezra-Nehemiah, Esther and Lamentations are
grouped differently. Of these, it would appear that the Christian order has
the slightly older claim that Ruth is to be grouped with Judges and
Jeremiah with Lamentations. The other books are placed differently in

the two canonical arrangements because of different views of how the canon ought to be organized. The Christian canon considers Chronicles, Ezra-Nehemiah, and Esther historical books whereas these are placed in the Writings in the Jewish canon because they were not part of the Sabbath liturgical readings.

Thus, even the order of the books in present-day Christian and Jewish canons points to an incipient organization of the canon that appears to be older than either one and perhaps antedates the fall of the Temple. Josephus' testimony could perhaps be seen as evidence that this ordering of the canon was already in progress in his day.

Finally, the wider Christian canon is a development that is due both to the shift in the canon from archival collection to list and to popular usage in the church. Even at this, there is no evidence that predates Origin in the late second century for including *any* material not found in the Hebrew canon and no evidence until the fourth century in the West for including books not somehow considered part of the canonical books of Jeremiah, Daniel, or Esther.

### Which Canon?

From this survey we are left with one question. Which OT canon is *the* OT canon? This, of course, was not a question that this study was designed to explore at the outset, but it is, nevertheless, one which ought to be briefly addressed. For Jews there is no question. No conclusive evidence exists that Jewish traditions ever accepted any books as canonical outside the twenty-four books of the Hebrew Bible.

For Christians, however, the question is more complicated. For those Christians who view the canon as an inheritance from the Jews of Jesus' day, for whom the view of the canon could be expressed by Paul's words that "they were entrusted with the oracles of God" (Rom 3:2), the answer is the shorter Christian canon that corresponds to the Hebrew Bible of Judaism. This, of course, is the attitude of Jerome and the Eastern Fathers and, later, of the Reformers, for whom Scripture was the source of theological truth. This is consistent with their principle for authority in the church. But for Christians who value the church's continuing traditions as a source of truth alongside Scripture, the answer is not so simple. Here Augustine's attitude will prevail as it did in the West, so that Roman Catholics and others will hold to a larger canon based on the church's prerogative to define its own canon even if this cannot be demonstrated to be the canon of the Jews in Jesus' day. Indeed, for

Christians who value the continued witness of the church or its traditions during the past twenty centuries as an equally important source of truth, this is a consistent position also.

Thus, for Christians the question of the extent of the OT canon will never be a purely historical question, but is bound up with the question of the source of teaching authority in the church. If teaching authority depends solely upon the prophets and Jesus and his apostles, only one canon is possible. If teaching authority extends beyond Scripture to tradition, then the canon is defined by the tradition one accepts.

# Bibliography

Ackroyd, P. R. "The Open Canon," Colloquium, Australian and New *Zealand Theological Review* 3 (1970) 279–91.

Allegro John M. *Qumrân Cave 4*. DJD V. Oxford: Clarendon, 1968.

Amir, Yehoshua. "Philo and the Bible," *Studia Philonica* 2 (1973) 1–8.

Anderson, G. W. "Canonical and Non-canonical" in P. R. Ackroyd and C. F. Evans, eds. *The Cambridge History of the Bible.* (Cambridge: Cambridge, 1970), 113–58.

Audet, Jean-Paul. "A Hebrew-Aramaic List of Books of the Old Testament in Greek Transcription," *JTS* 1 (1950) 135–54.

Aune, David E. "On the Origins of the 'Council of Javneh' Myth," *JBL* 110 (1991) 491–93.

Barr, James. *Holy Scripture: Canon, Authority, Criticism.* Philadelphia: Westminster, 1983.

Bathélemy, Dominque, "L'Etat de la Bible juive depuis le début de notre ère jusqu'à la deuxième révolte contre Rome (131–135)," in J. D. Kaestli and O. Wermelinger, eds., *Le Canon de l'Ancien Testament: Sa formation et son histoire* (Geneva: Labor et Fides, 1984), 10–11.

Barton, John. "The Law and the Prophets: Who are the Prophets," *OTS* 23 (1984) 1–18.

_____. Oracles of God: Perceptions of Ancient Prophecy in Israel after the Exile. New York: Oxford, 1986.

Baumgarten, Joseph. *Qumran Cave 4. XIII. The Damascus Document (4Q266–273).* DJD 18. Oxford: Clarendon, 1966.

Beckwith, Roger T. "Canon of the Hebrew Bible and the Old Testament." in *The Oxford Companion to the Bible.* Bruce M. Metzger and M. D. Coogan, eds. New York: Oxford, 1993, 102–4.

_____. "The Courses of the Levites and the Eccentric Psalms Scrolls from Qumran," *RevQ* 11 (1984) 499–524.

_____. "Formation of the Hebrew Bible." In *Mikra: Text, Translation, Reading and Interpretation of the Hebrew Bible in Ancient Judaism and Early Christianity*. CRINT. M. J. Mulder, ed. Minneapolis: Fortress, 1990, 39–86.

_____."A Modern Theory of the Old Testament Canon," *VT* 41 (1991) 385–95.

_____. *The Old Testament Canon of the New Testament Church.* Grand Rapids, MI: Eerdmans, 1986.

_____. "The Pre-History and Relationships of the Pharisees, Sadducees and Essenes," *RevQ* 11 (1982) 3–40

_____. "St. Luke, the Date of Christmas and the Priestly Courses at Qumran," *RevQ* 9 (1977) 73–94.

Beecher, Willis J. "The Alleged Triple Canon of the Old Testament," *JBL* 15 (1896) 118–28.

Ben-Hayyim, Z., ed. *The Book of Ben Sira: Text, Concordance and an Analysis of the Vocabulary.* Jerusalem: Academy of the Hebrew Language and the Shrine of the Book, 1973.

Bentzen, A. "Remarks on the Canonization of the Song of Solomon," *Studia Orientalia Ioanni Pedersen Dicata.* Denmark, 1953, 41–47.

Betz, Otto. "The Qumran Halakhah Text Miqsat Maʿasê Ha-Torah (4QMMT) and Sadducean, Essene, and Early Pharisaic Tradition," in D. R. G. Beattie and M. J. McNamara, eds., *The Aramaic Bible: Targums in Their Historical Context* (JSOTSup 166; JSOT, 1994), 176–202.

Beyer, Hermann Wolfgang. κανών in G. Kittel, ed. *TDNT*, vol. 3, 596–602.

Blenkensopp, Joseph. *Prophecy and Canon: A Contribution to the Study of Jewish Origins.* Notre Dame, IN: Notre Dame, 1977.

Broyde, Michael, "Defilement of the Hands, Canonization of the Bible, and the Special Status of Esther, Ecclesiastes, and Song of Songs." *Judaism* 44 (1995) 65–79.

Bruce, F. F. *The Canon of Scripture.* Downers Grove, IL: InterVarsity, 1988.

Brunswick, Sheldon R. "The Order of the Books" in Mishael M. Caspi, ed., *Jewish Tradition in the Diaspora: Studies in Memory of Professor Walter J. Fischel.* Berkeley: Judah L. Magnes Memorial Museum 1981, 91.

Burrows, Millar ed. *The Dead Sea Scrolls of St. Mark's Monastery.* vol. 2 fasc. 2: *The Manual of Discipline.* New Haven: American Schools of Oriental Research, 1951.

Cadbury, Henry J. "The Grandson of Ben Sira," *HTR* 48 (1955) 219–25.

Callaway, Philip R. "The Temple Scroll and the Canonization of Jewish Law," *RevQ* 49–52 (1988) 73–78.

Campbell Jonathan G. *The Use of Scripture in the Damascus Document 1–8, 19–20.* BZAW 228. Berlin: Walter de Gruyter, 1995.

Carson, D. A. "Do the Prophets and the Law Quit Prophesying Before John? A Note on Matthew 11.13," JSNTSup 104 (1994) 179–94.

Childs, Brevard S. *Introduction to the Old Testament as Scripture.* Philadelphia: Fortress, 1979.

Chyutin, Michael. "The Redaction of the Qumranic and the Traditional Book of Psalms as a Calendar," *RevQ* 63 (1994) 367–95.

Christensen, Duane L. "Josephus and the Twenty-Two-Book Canon of Sacred Scripture," *JETS* 29 (1986) 37–46.

Collins, John J. "Before the Canon: Scriptures in Second Temple Judaism," in *Old Testament Interpretation: Past, Present, and Future: Essays in Honor of Gene M. Tucker,* James Luther Mays et al., eds. Nashville: Abingdon, 1995, 225–41.

Crawford, Sidnie White "Has Every Book of the Bible Been Found Among the Dead Sea Scrolls?" *BRev* 12 (1996) 28–33, 56.

Cross, Frank Moore. "The History of the Biblical Text in the Light of Discoveries in the Judaean Desert." *HTR* 57 (1964) 281–99.

Davies, Philip R. "Loose Canons: Reflections on the Formation of the Hebrew Bible," *Journal of the Hebrew Scriptures* 1 (1996–97) [http://www.ualberta.ca/arts/jhs/jhs.html].

———. *Scribes and Schools.* Louisville: Westminster/John Knox, 1998.

Dexinger, Ferdinand. "Limits of Tolerance in Judaism: The Samaritan Example," in E. P. Sanders, ed. *Jewish and Christian Self-Definition.* Vol. 2 Aspects of Judaism in the Graeco-Roman Period. Philadelphia: Fortress, 1981, 88–114, 327–38.

Di Lella, Alexander A. The Hebrew Text of Sirach: A Text-Critical and Historical Study. The Hague: Mouton, 1966.

Eberharter, A. *Der Kanon des Alten Testaments zur Zeit des Ben Sira auf Grund der Beziehungen des Sirachbuches zu den Scriften des Alten Teestaments dargestellt.* Münster: Aschendorff, 1911.

Ellis, E. Earle, *The Old Testament in Early Christianity: Canon and Interpretation in the Light of Modern Research.* Grand Rapids: Baker, 1991.

_____. "The Old Testament Canon in the Early Church," in *Mikra: Text, Translation, Reading and Interpretation of the Hebrew Bible in Ancient Judaism and Early Christianity* CRINT. M. J. Mulder and H. Sysling, eds. Minneapolis: Fortress, 1990, 653–90.

Eybers, I. H. "Some Light on the Canon of the Qumran Sect" *Die Ou Testamentiese Werkgemeenskap in Suid-Afrika.* Pretoria, 1962, 1–14.

Fabry, H.-J., "11QPs$^a$ und die Kanoniztät des Psalters," in E. Haag and F. L. Hossfeld, eds., *Freude an der Weisung des Herrn: Beiträge zur Theologie der Psalmen* (Festschrift Heinrich Gross; Stuttgart: Katholisches Bibelwerk, 1986), 45–53.

Flint, Peter W. *The Dead Sea Psalms Scrolls and the Book of Psalms.* STDJ 17. Leiden: Brill, 1997.

Fox, Douglas E. "Ben Sira on OT Canon Again: The Date of Daniel," *WTJ* 49 (1987) 335–50.

Freedman, David Noel. "Canon of the Bible," in G. Wigoder, et al., eds., *Illustrated Dictionary and Concordance of the Bible* New York: Macmillan, 1986, 211–216.

_____. "The Formation of the Canon of the Old Testament: The Selection and Identification of the Torah as the Supreme Authority of the Post-Exilic Community," in E. B. Firmage, et al., eds. *Religion and Law: Biblical-Judaic and Islamic Perspective* Winona Lake, IN: Eisenbrauns, 1990, 315–333.

_____. "The Symmetry of the Hebrew Bible," *ST* 46 (1992) 83–108.

_____. *The Unity of the Hebrew Bible.* Distinguished senior faculty lecture series. Ann Arbor: University of Michigan, 1991.

García Martínez, Florentino. *The Dead Sea Scrolls Translated: The Qumran Texts in English.* Second ed. Leiden: E. J. Brill, 1996.

Goodblatt, David "Audet's Hebrew-Aramaic List of the Books of the Old Testament Revisited," *JBL* 101 (1982) 75–84.

Goodman, Martin, "Sacred Scripture and 'Defiling the Hands'," *JTS* ns 41 (1990) 99–107.

Goshen-Gottstein, Moshe H. "The Psalms Scroll (11QPs$^a$): A Problem of Canon and Text," *Textus* 5 (1966), 22–33.

Harrington, Daniel, J. "Introduction to the Canon," in *The New Interpreter's Bible*. Leander E. Keck, ed. Vol. 1.7–21. Nashville: Abingdon, 1994.

Harris, R. Laird, "Was the Law and the Prophets Two-thirds of the Old Testament Canon?" *BETS* 9 (1966) 163–71.

Harrison R. K. *Introduction to the Old Testament*. Grand Rapids, MI: Eerdmans, 1969.

House, Paul R. "Canon of the Old Testament," in *Foundations for Biblical Interpretation*, David S. Dockery, et. al, eds. Nashville: Broadman and Holman, 1994, 134–55.

Howorth, H. H. "The Influence of St. Jerome on the Canon of the Western Church. I." *JTS* 10 (1908–9) 481–96.

_____ "The Influence of St. Jerome on the Canon of the Western Church. II." *JTS* 11 (1909–10) 321–47.

_____ "The Influence of St. Jerome on the Canon of the Western Church. III." *JTS* 13 (1911–12) 1–18.

Jeffrey, Arthur, "The Canon of the Old Testament," *IB*, ed. George Arthur Buttrick, 1.32–45 Nashville: Abingdon, 1952.

Kalin, E. R. "How Did the Canon Come to Us? A Response to the Leiman Hypothesis," *CurTM* 4 (1977) n. 1, 47–51.

Katz, Peter. "The Old Testament Canon in Palestine and Alexandria," *ZNW* 47 (1956) 191–217; 49 (1958) 223.

Kee, Howard Clark *The Cambridge Annotated Study Apocrypha. New Revised Standard Version*. Cambridge: Cambridge, 1994.

Koch, Klaus, "Is Daniel Also Among the Prophets?" *Int* 39 (1985) 117–30.

Koole, J. L. "Die Bibel des Ben Sira," *OTS* 14 (1965) 374–96.

Kraemer, David. "The Formation of Rabbinic Canon: Authority and Boundaries." *JBL* 110 (1991) 613–30.

Lacocque, André. "L'insertion du Cantique des Cantiques dans le Canon," *RHPR* 42 (1962) 38–44.

Leiman, Sid Z. *The Canonization of Hebrew Scripture: The Talmudic and Midrashic Evidence*. Transactions of the Connecticut Academy of Arts and Sciences 47. 2nd ed. New Haven: Connecticut Academy of Arts and Sciences, 1991.

_____. "Inspiration and Canonicity: Reflections on the Formation of the Biblical Canon," in *Jewish and Christian Self-Definition*. 2nd ed. E. P. Sanders, A. I. Baumgarten and Alan Mendelson, eds. Philadelphia: Fortress, 1981, vol. 2, 56–63.

Lévi. Israel. *The Hebrew Text of the Book of Ecclesiasticus.* Semitic Study Series 3. Leiden: Brill, 1904; reprinted 1951.

Lewis, Jack P. "What Do We Mean by Jabneh?" *JBR* 32 (1964) 125–32.

Lienhard, Joseph T. *The Bible, the Church, and Authority: The Canon of the Christian Bible in History and Theology.* Collegeville, MN: Liturgical, 1995.

Lightstone, Jack. M. "The Formation of the biblical canon in Judaism of late antiquity: Prolegomenon to a general reassessment," *SR* 8 (1979) n. 2, 135–42.

Maier, J. "Zur Frage des biblischen Kanons in Frühjudentum im Licht der Qumranfunde," in I. Baldermann, *et. al.* (eds.), *Zum Problem des biblischen Kanons* (JBTh, 3; Neukirchen-Vluyn: Neukirchener Verlag, 1988) 135–46.

McDonald, Lee Martin. *The Formation of the Christian Biblical Canon.* rev. and expanded ed. Peabody, MA: Hendrickson, 1995.

_____, "The Integrity of the Biblical Canon in Light of Its Historical Development," *BBR* 6 (1996) 95–132.

Metzger Bruce, ed. *The Oxford Annotated Apocrypha.* Expanded ed. New York: Oxford, 1977.

Meyer, R. "The Canon and the Apocrypha in Judaism," in G. Kittel, ed., *TDNT*, vol. 3, 978–87.

Middendorp T. *Die Stellung Jesu Ben Siras zwischen Judentum und Hellenismus.* Leiden: Brill, 1973.

Milik, J. T. "Les modéles araméens du livre d'Esther dan la grotte 4 de Qumrân" *RevQ* 15 (1991) 321–406.

Miller, John W. *Origins of the Bible: Rethinking Canon History.* New York: Paulist, 1994.

Neusner Jacob, *The Talmud: A Close Encounter.* Minneapolis: Fortress, 1991.

Newman, Robert C. "The Council of Jamnia and the Old Testament Canon," *WTJ* 38 (1975–76) 319–49.

Oikonomos, Elias, "The Significance of the Deuterocanonical Writing in the Orthodox Church," in *The Apocrypha in Ecumenical Perspective*, ed. Siegfried Meurer. UBS Monograph Series 6 (Reading, UK: United Bible Societies, 1992, 16–32.

Orlinsky, Harry M. "The Canonization of the Bible and the Exclusion of the Apocrypha," in *Essays in Biblical Culture and Bible Translation*, New York: KTAV, 1974, 257–86.

_____. "Some Terms in the Prologue to Ben Sira and the Hebrew Canon," *JBL* 110 (1991) 483–90.

Purvis, James D. *The Samaritan Pentateuch and the Origin of the Samaritan Sect.* Cambridge: Harvard, 1968.

Qimron, Elisha and John Strugnell. *Qumran Cave 4 V: Misqat Ma'ase HaTorah.* DJD 10. Oxford: Oxford, 1994.

_____."An Unpublished Halakhic Letter from Qumran," *Biblical Archaeology Today: Proceedings of the International Congress on Biblical Archaeology, Jerusalem, 1984* (Israel Exploration Society, 1985), 400–407.

Roberts, Bleddyn J., "The Old Testament Canon: A Suggestion," *BJRL* 46 (1963) 164–78.

Rüger, Hans Peter. "The Extent of the Old Testament Canon," in *Apocrypha in Ecumenical Perspective,* ed. Siegfried Meurer. UBS Monograph Series 6 (Reading, UK: United Bible Societies, 1992), 151–60.

_____. *Text und Textform in hebräischen Sirach.* (BZAW 112, 1970).

_____. "Der Umfang des alttestamentlichen Kanons in den verschiedenen kirchlichen Traditionen," in S. Meuer (ed.), *Die Apokryphenfrage im ökumenischen Horizont: Die Stellung der Spätschriften des Alten Testamens im biblischen Schrifttum und ihre Bedeutung in den kirchlichen Traditionen des Ostens und Westens* (Die Bibel in der Welt 22; Stuttgart: Deutsche Bibelgesellschaft, 1990), 137–45.

Ryle, Herbert Edward, *The Canon of the Old Testament: An Essay on the Gradual Growth and Formation of the Hebrew Canon of Scripture.* 2nd ed. London: Macmillan, 1892.

Sanders, James A. "Cave 11 Surprises and the Questions of Canon," *McCormick Review* 21 (1969) 288 = *New Directions in Biblical Archaeology* ed. D. N. Freedman and J. C. Greenfield. Garden City: Doubleday, 1969–71, 101–16.

_____. *The Dead Sea Psalms Scroll.* Ithaca, NY: Cornell, 1967.

_____. "Ps 151 in 11QPss," *ZAW* 75 (1963) 73–86.

_____. "The Qumran Psalms Scroll (11QPs[a]) Reviewed" in *On Language, Culture and Religion: In Honor of Eugene A Nida* The Hague: Mouton, 1974, 79–99.

_____. *Torah and Canon.* Philadelphia, 1972.

_____. "Two Non-canonical Psalms in 11QPs[a]," *ZAW* 76 (1964) 57–75.

_____. "Variorum in the Psalms Scroll (11QPs$^a$)" *HTR* 59 (1966) 86–87.

Sanderson Judith E. *An Exodus Scroll from Qumran: 4QPaleoExod$^m$ and the Samaritan Tradition.* HSS 30. Cambridge: Harvard, 1986.

Sarna, Nahum M. *Ancient Libraries and the Ordering of the Biblical Books.* Center for the Book Viewpoint 25. Washington: Library of Congress, 1989.

_____. "The Order of the Books," in Charles Berlin, ed., *Studies in Jewish Bibliography, History and Literature in Honor of I. Edward Kiev.* New York, 1971, 407–13.

_____. "St. Jerome and the Canon of Holy Scriptures," in F. X. Murphy, ed., *A Monument to Saint Jerome.* New York, 1952, 259–87.

Schechter, S. *Documents of Jewish Sectaries.* vol. 1. Cambridge: Cambridge, 1910; repr., New York: KTAV, 1970.

Schechter, S. and C. Taylor, *The Wisdom of Ben Sira: Portions of the Book of Ecclesiasticus from Hebrew Manuscripts in the Cairo Genizah Collection Presented to the University of Cambridge by the Editors.* Cambridge: Cambridge, 1899.

Schnabel, Eckhard J. *Law and Wisdom from Ben Sira to Paul.* Tübingen: Mohr, 1985.

Sheppard, Gerald T. "Canon" in *The Encyclopedia of Religion* ed. Mircea Eliade.; New York: Macmillian, 1987. v. 3, 62–69

Silberman, L. H. "The Making of the Old Testament Canon," in C. M. Laymon, ed., *The Interpreter's One-Volume Commentary on the Bible.* Nashville, 1971, 1209–15.

Silver, D. J. *The Story of Scripture: From Oral Tradition to the Written Word* New York: Basic Books, 1990.

Skehan, Patrick W. "A Liturgical Complex in 11QPs$^a$," *CBQ* 35 (1973) 202–5.

_____. "Qumran and Old Testament Criticism," in M. Delcor, ed. *Qumran: sa piété, sa théologie et son milieu* BETL; Gembloux: Duculot, 1978, 163–82.

Skehan, Patrick W. and Alexander A. Di Lela, *The Wisdom of Ben Sira.* AB 39. New York: Doubleday, 1987.

Smith, Morton, *Palestinian Parties and Politics That Shaped the Old Testament.* New York: Columbia University, 1971.

Steck, O. H., "Der Kanon des hebräischen Alten Testaments: Historische Materialien für eine ökumenische Perspektive," in J. Rohls and G. Wenz, eds., *Vernunft des Glaubens: Wissenschaftliche Theologie und kirchliche Lehre. Festschrift zum 60. Geburtstag von Wolfhart Pannenberg* (Göttingen: Vandenhoeck and Ruprecht, 1998), 231–52.

Stuart, Moses. *Critical History and Defence of the Old Testament Canon*. Andover, MA: Warren F. Draper, 1865.

Sundburg, Albert C., Jr. "Canon Muratori: A Fourth-Century List" *HTR* 66 (1973) 1–41.

_____,"The Old Testament: A Christian Canon," *CBQ* 30 (1968) 143–55.

_____. *The Old Testament of the Early Church*. Harvard Theological Studies 20. Cambridge: Harvard, 1964.

_____. "The Old Testament of the Early Church (A Study in Canon)" *HTR* 51 (1958) 204–26.

_____. "A Symposium on the Canon of Scripture," *CBQ* 28 (1966) 189–207.

Talmon, Shemaryahu "Pisqah Be'emsaʿ Pasuq and 11QPsᵃ," *Textus* 5 (1965) 11–21.

_____. "Was the Book of Esther Known at Qumran?" [Hebrew] *Eretz Israel* 25 (1996), 377–82.

Torrey, C. C. "The Hebrew of the Geniza Sirah" in Saul Liebermann, ed. *The Alexander Marx Jubilee Volume*. New York: Jewish Theological Seminary of America, 1950, 597.

Tucker, Gene M. "Prophetic Superscriptions and the Growth of a Canon" in G. W. Coats and B. O. Long, eds., *Canon and Authority: Essays in Old Testament Religion and Theology*, Philadelphia: Fortress, 1977, 56–70.

Turner, C. H. "Latin Lists of the Canonical Books," *JTS* 1 (1900), 554–60.

Ulrich, Eugene, "The Bible in the Making: The Scriptures at Qumran," in E. Ulrich and J. Vanderkam, eds., *The Community of the Renewed Covenant: The Notre Dame Symposium on the Dead Sea Scrolls* (Christianity and Judaism in Antiquity 10; Notre Dame: Notre Dame, 1994), 77–93.

_____. "The Canonical Process, Textual Criticism, and Latter Stages in the Composition of the Bible," in *"Sha'arei Talmon": Studies in the Bible, Qumran and the Ancient Near East Presented to Shemaryahu Talmon*, Winona Lake, IN: Eisenbrauns, 1992, 267–91

_____. "Pluriformity in the Biblical Text, Text Groups, and Questions of Canon," *The Madrid Qumran Congress: Proceedings of the International congress on the Dead Sea Scrolls Madrid 18–21 March, 1991,* Studies in the Texts from the Desert of Judea; ed. J. T. Barrera and L. V. Montana. Leiden: Brill, 1992, 1.23–41.

Vasholz, Robert I. *The Old Testament Canon in the Old Testament Church.* Ancient Near Eastern Texts and Studies 7. Lewiston, NY: Edwin Mellen, 1990.

VanderKam, James C. *The Dead Sea Scrolls Today.* Grand Rapids: Eerdmans, 1994.

Wacholder, Ben Zion, "David's Eschatological Psalter 11Q Psalms[a]," *HUCA* 59 (1988) 23–72.

_____. "The Letter from Judas Maccabee to Aristobulus: Is 2 1:10b–2:18 Authentic?" *HUCA* 49 (1978) 89–133.

Waltke, Bruce K. "How We Got the Old Testament," *Crux* 30 (1994) 12–19.

Wenham, Gordon J. "Daniel: The Basic Issues," *Themelios* 2 (1977) 49–52.

Wesselius, J. W. "Language and Style in Biblical Aramaic: Observations on the Unity of Daniel II-VI," *VT* 38 (1988) 194–209.

Wilson, Gerald H. "The Qumran Psalms Manuscripts and the Consecutive Arrangement of Psalms in the Hebrew Psalter," *CBQ* 45 (1983) 377–88.

_____. "The Qumran Psalms Scroll Reconsidered," *CBQ* 47 (1985) 624–42.

Wolfenson, L. B. "Implications of the Place of the Book of Ruth in Editions, Manuscripts, and Canon of the Old Testament," *HUCA* 1 (1924) 151–78.

Yamauchi, Edwin M. "Archaeological Backgrounds of the Exilic and Postexilic Era: Part I. the Archaeological Backgrounds of Daniel," *BSac* 137 (1980) 3–16.

_____. "Daniel and Contacts Between the Aegean and the Near East Before Alexander," *EvQ* 53 (1981) 37–47.

_____. "Hermeneutical Issues in the Book of Daniel," *JETS* 23 (1980), 13–21.

Ziegler, J. "Zwei Beiträge zu Sirach," *BZ* N.F. 8 (1964), 277–284.

# Index of Passages

## Church Fathers and Early Church Documents

## Midrash

# Index of Modern Authors

Andrew Steinmann holds a B.S. from the University of Cincinnati, an M. Div. from Concordia Theological Seminary (Ft. Wayne) and a Ph.D. in Near Eastern Studies from the University of Michigan. He has served as pastor of St. John Lutheran Church, Fraser, Michigan (1981–86); taught at Concordia College, Ann Arbor (1986–91); served as editor at God's Word to the Nations Bible Society (1991–94); served as staff pastor at Lutheran Home, Westlake, Ohio (1995–2000); and taught at Ashland University and Seminary (1996–2000). Since 2000 he has served as Associate Professor of Theology and Hebrew at Concordia University, River Forest, Illinois. Dr. Steinmann has published articles and essays in national and international journals including *Concordia Journal, Concordia Theological Quarterly, The Journal of Biblical Literature* and *Revue de Qumran* and several reference works. He is the author of seven books including *The Oracles of God: The Old Testament Canon* (Concordia, 1999), *Fundamental Biblical Aramaic* (Concordia, 2004 with Andrew Bartelt's *Fundamental Biblical Hebrew*), *Is God Listening?: Making Prayer a Part of Your Life* (Concordia, 2004) and *Proverbs* in the Concordia Commentary series (forthcoming, 2006). He is currently writing *Daniel* in the Concordia Commentary series and is contributing editor to the forthcoming textbook *Called to Be God's People: An Introduction to the Old Testament,* as well as a consultant for the new Lutheran Study Bible to be published by Concordia Publishing House. Dr. Steinmann and his wife, Rebecca, have two children, Christopher and Jennifer.

Andrew Steinmann
Associate Professor of Theology and Hebrew
Concordia University
River Forest, IL